THE INTERNATIONAL SYSTEM
SYSTEM
Theoretical Essays

BOOKS FROM
THE CENTER OF INTERNATIONAL STUDIES

Woodrow Wilson School of Public and International Affairs
Princeton University

Gabriel A. Almond, *The Appeals of Communism*

Gabriel A. Almond and James S. Coleman, editors, *The Politics of the Developing Areas*

Robert J. C. Butow, *Tojo and the Coming of the War*

Bernard C. Cohen, *The Political Process and Foreign Policy: The Making of the Japanese Peace Settlement*

Percy E. Corbett, *Law in Diplomacy*

W. W. Kaufmann, editor, *Military Policy and National Security*

Herman Kahn, *On Thermonuclear War*

Klaus Knorr, *The War Potential of Nations*

Klaus Knorr, editor, *NATO and American Security*

Klaus Knorr and Sidney Verba, editors, *The International System: Theoretical Essays*

Lucian W. Pye, *Guerrilla Communism in Malaya*

Rolf Sannwald and Jacques Stohler, *Economic Integration: Theoretical Assumptions and Consequences of European Unification.* Translated by Herman F. Karreman

Glenn H. Snyder, *Deterrence and Defense*

Sidney Verba, *Small Groups and Political Behavior: A Study of Leadership*

Charles De Visscher, *Theory and Reality in Public International Law.* Translated by P. E. Corbett

Myron Weiner, *Party Politics in India*

THE
INTERNATIONAL
SYSTEM

EDITED BY

KLAUS KNORR AND SIDNEY VERBA

PRINCETON, NEW JERSEY
PRINCETON UNIVERSITY PRESS
1961

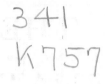

CONTENTS

THE INTERNATIONAL SYSTEM

SYSTEM

Theoretical Essays

INTRODUCTION

By KLAUS KNORR and SIDNEY VERBA

UNLIKE the theory of international trade and payments, theorizing on international relations or the international "system" is of fairly recent origin, has attracted relatively few scholars, and—in terms of achievement—is still in a rather underdeveloped stage. But there has in fact been important progress during the last twenty-five years, much of it along tentative, experimental, and not necessarily congruent lines. Nowadays there seems to be new interest in such theorizing and the Center of International Studies at Princeton University thought it useful to collect a reasonably representative sample of recent thinking and, toward this end, to call upon younger scholars in the field rather than on the established leaders, such as Harold Lasswell, Hans Morgenthau, Richard Snyder, Arnold Wolfers, and Quincy Wright.

The papers contained in this volume were first presented at a symposium on international relations theory that was sponsored by the Center of International Studies and held in Princeton in September 1960. Most of the authors attended it and the individual papers as well as the general subject of theory in international relations were discussed. In this discussion, the authors were joined by Harold Sprout, Harry Eckstein, and Andrew Janos of Princeton University and James Rosenau of Douglass College. The papers were then revised in light of the discussion.

In preparing their contributions, the various authors were given little guidance by the editors as to the direction the papers ought to take. The topic of our symposium was "international relations theory"; and when one thinks of the ambiguities of that topic and the multiplicity of interests of those who write on international relations, it is little wonder that the papers included in this volume differ in scope and method, and cover a wide range of topics. In fact, the volume is essentially that: a collection of essays comprising a wide range of approaches and considerations in connection with international theory. Any further unity in the volume, to provide the usual disclaimer, is purely coincidental.

Yet the question of the interconnections among these essays is an important one. The editors were vague in the directions they provided not because they believe that a disparity of directions is desirable *per se*, but because they were not confident enough of their knowledge of the *right* direction to impose any strict limitations upon the contributors. Nevertheless, in the long run, progress will be made in theories of the international system only if various approaches begin to converge and move in the same direction. Only in that way will our work, both theoretical and empirical, begin to be cumulative. In this respect, it is encouraging to note some convergences in these papers. While their themes reflect the diversity of interests of students of international relations, the convergences bode well for the future development of a unified field. Often the convergence is more a matter of raising similar questions than of finding similar answers, but this convergence in questions may be as important as a convergence in answers, if not more so.

One significant convergence involves the question of the general role of theory in international relations. The problem is raised in a number of papers, and in fact touched on in almost all. This sort of pre-theoretical consideration, or "theory of theories," as it is sometimes called, is an unfortunate necessity in the study of theories of international relations—unfortunate, for it leads at times to frustration and the belief that we should talk about international affairs and stop talking about *how* one ought to talk about international affairs; and a necessity, for there are many unanswered questions about how to theorize and why to theorize about international affairs. And the answers to these latter two questions will have significant effects on the type of theory we attempt to create. As the study of international relations becomes more mature as a science—and as a science it is young indeed—we may hope that these first questions will have been answered so that energies may be expended on the more obviously relevant second question of the specific theory of international affairs that we need. At the present moment these pre-theoretical problems require consideration.

What are some of these considerations? Most writers in the field of international relations would probably agree with Kurt Lewin that there is nothing as practical as a good theory; but agreement would proceed little beyond this. While theories are useful, they may be put to a variety of uses and different uses require different types of theory. On the one hand, one may want to use a theory for understanding and predicting concrete events in the realm of international relations. And, on the other, one may use it in order to clear up one's thinking about international affairs, to rise above the level of specific events to more general statements about the patterning of international relations. Both goals are important but they tend to be in conflict. The more one approaches the "engineering applications" of theory, to use Morton Kaplan's phrase, the more complicated the theory becomes, the more variables one needs to consider, and the more the theory has to be embedded in concrete historical reality. Consequently, the theory loses generality and suffers in its ability to perform its more analytic function—making clear the relations among isolated variables by abstracting them from reality. The more we attempt to apply theory, the more we lose the unique advantages of theory. And yet why else do we want theory, if we do not at some point want to apply it?

The dilemma is a real one, and several of the papers in this volume deal with it—in particular the papers by Burns, Kaplan, Quandt, Schelling, and Verba. They raise the question of what sorts of simplifying assumptions have been made in theories of international relations, what significant variables have been left out of the models of the international system, and what is the price of attempting to put them back in. In particular, several of the papers discuss the problems associated with the use of game theoretical models and with the assumption of rationality of the actors in international affairs. They represent, however, relevant comments upon the problems of using any sort of precise (mathematical or non-mathematical) model of the international system. In fact, the comments on the difficulties of theory-application and theory-verification are relevant to social-science theorizing in general, and not merely to theories in international relations.

It would be too much to suggest that the papers in this collection offer any clear way out of this predicament. If anything, they are more effective in making the predicament explicit than in resolving it, but, after all, undertaking the first task is a requisite for the accomplishment of the second. Nevertheless, several papers suggest approaches that lie somewhere between the precision of mathematical models and the confusion of historical reality. These approaches include the mixed-motive games of Schelling and the bargaining theory referred to by Burns.

The papers in this collection are, however, not merely on the theory of theories. If some of them deal with the process of model building, others deal with the content of the models. Again we find some similarity in the questions raised, but great diversity in the answers. If one wants to create a theory of international relations, what is the subject matter that one wants to explain? In a number of different ways this question as to the focus of attention of international relations theory is raised in this volume. What, if anything, is the "international system"? What are its characteristics? Who are the actors in that system? To what extent are international systems unique, or can they be conceptualized in terms similar to other systems? The paper by Singer deals most explicitly with the focus of attention of theories of international relations. As he points out, one may approach international relations on several levels; in particular he concentrates on the approach from the point of view of the total system and from the point of view of the nation-state. The two approaches, he suggests, though not mutually exclusive, represent different emphases and lead to different types of theories and explanations.

Of special relevance to the problem of levels is the question of what one ought to know about the nations that make up the international system. Is it fruitful to omit from models of the international system variables relating to the internal operations of the nations that form the system? Though information as to internal decision-making processes of nations is clearly relevant, especially as one gets closer to applied theories, the introduction of these characteristics greatly adds to the complexity of one's theory. How much it is useful to know about the actors in the international system is discussed in several papers, but of particular relevance are those by Riggs and Modelski. These papers, in attempting to develop conceptual models of the international system, suggest that international systems may be conceptualized in terms similar to national systems and that the operations of various international systems will differ according to the types of national systems of which they consist. A significant convergence between the two papers is their focus on the continuum between traditional and modern societies as the prime dimension for characterizing both nation-states and international systems. The further development of this scheme for the analysis of both international and national systems, and for the analysis of the interrelations between national and international systems, may do much to remove the gap between the study of international relations and comparative politics.

One way of resolving the dilemma between the precision and generality of abstract theory and the confusion and specificity of historical events is to attempt to theorize about more limited phenomena. Rather than attempting to theorize about international relations in general, one can focus on some specific aspect. Two papers in this collection do just that—McClelland writes of the acute international crisis as a phenomenon in international relations, and Hoffmann of international law as an aspect of international politics. The danger in concentrating on more specific aspects of international relations is that the field may be carved up into unconnected areas. In this respect, it is important to note that both McClelland and Hoffmann approach the specific topics they deal with as aspects of some more general approach to international relations. In the case of McClelland, the acute international crisis is analyzed in relation to his interest in general systems theory; and in the case of Hoffmann, the comparative study of international law is conceived of as one of the tasks of a broader historical sociology of international relations.

The road to a theory of international relations will be, as one of our authors has pointed out elsewhere, a long one. If ever the goal is reached, the rewards will be great but, in any case, the journey itself is exhilarating. This volume leaves us still far from the goal but, hopefully, somewhat farther along on the journey.

PROBLEMS OF THEORY BUILDING AND THEORY CONFIRMATION IN INTERNATIONAL POLITICS

By MORTON A. KAPLAN

THERE is a great demand for theories in international relations. The term "theory" has become so honorific that hypotheses, statements of fact, and intuitive guesses are often dressed up as theories. In part this longing for theory can be ascribed to a desire for the status of a "hard science" like physics, since the "hard sciences" are often viewed by laymen as the theoretical sciences par excellence. They have displayed their power in revealing the secrets of nature and, when applied to the affairs of men, have achieved notable practical successes like the construction of the atomic bomb.

On the whole this demand for theory is probably good. We cannot reason without generalization and, where matters are complex, the web of reasoning logically takes the form of a theory. Most historical investigations and case studies employ theories inexplicitly—often in the belief that the generalizations follow from the straightforward presentation of "purely factual" material. There is usually no recognition that interpretations of factual material can always be presented in a form isomorphic with theories from the sciences of economics, psychology, sociology, and so forth.

While it is doubtful that theories in social science, and in international politics in particular, can ever have the power of theories in physical science or be applied with the success achieved by physical scientists in making applications from their disciplines, the present sorry state of social science is no proof in itself that social science cannot attain such predictive power. Theoretical physical science lay fallow from the time of the Greeks until Galileo. The theory of international politics may indeed be awaiting its Galilean revolution. However, only an inquiry into the nature of the subject matter can inform us whether such expectations are justified on the basis of present knowledge.

According to some modern scientists, Galileo succeeded in revolutionizing physics as a theoretical science because he set himself a simpler problem than the Greek physicists set themselves. For instance, the Greeks tried to investigate the nature of perfect motion; only circles and straight lines fell within this category. Every other type of motion was treated as a deviation from perfect motion. Galileo set himself the simpler task of discovering where a body would be at time 2 if he knew its position, direction, and momentum at time 1.

Modern theoretical physical science has reared its present lofty edifice by setting itself problems that it has the tools or techniques to solve. When necessary, it has limited ruthlessly the scope of its inquiry. It has not attempted to predict the path a flipped chair will take, the paths of the individual particles of an exploded grenade, or the paths of the individual molecules of gas in a chamber. In the last case, there are laws dealing with the behavior of gases under given conditions of temperature and pressure, but these deal with the aggregate behavior of gases and not the behaviors of individual particles. The physicist does not make predictions with respect to matter in general but only with respect to the aspects of matter that physics deals with; and these, by definition, are the physical aspects of matter.

Every prediction of physics can be expressed as a consequent following upon certain antecedent conditions. Where the influence of extraneous considerations is minimal, as in matters of astrophysics, the distinction between the formal character of a physical prediction and a historical prediction can be neglected without causing any serious problems. The general behavior of astral bodies thus can be studied directly; physicists can measure the red shift of the sun's light in order to confirm relativity theory; and soon an atomic clock may be placed in a satellite to confirm certain relativity propositions concerning time. In the last case, however, we must rest our conclusion on a faith that, among other things, the scientists involved are not careless or dishonest, and that no malicious or fun-loving outer planetary race substitutes a different clock in the satellite. These may be extraordinarily reasonable assumptions—so reasonable that no sane man would doubt them; yet they reinforce our assertion that the prediction refers only to what will happen under specified antecedent conditions. The real world conditions may be different; but the physicist's prediction, except in engineering applications of physics, ignores this.

We have specified two factors that help the physical scientist to achieve the predictive power manifested by modern physics. He deals with a simple problem, or, put another way, with a problem in which only a small number of important variables are operative; and he carries on his studies and experiments in a laboratory that is closed to outer-world or historical forces.[1] Now it appears that the less these

[1] See the discussion in Morton A. Kaplan, *System and Process in International Politics*, New York, 1957, pp. xi ff. (referred to hereinafter as *System and Process*);

factors aid the physicist, the less developed theoretically is the particular phase of physical science to which he applies his talents. There seems to be a hierarchy of biology, chemistry, and physics within the physical sciences, with the degree of theoretical development ascending from one to the next; each science appears bound by the laws of the former as it adds new laws or propositions that distinguish its particular subject matter. On the other hand, each science gets less theoretical as we move from laboratory generalizations to engineering applications and to the complexities and uncertainties of the real world. The problem of engineering a theory of international politics to real world conditions is fundamental and itself requires to be understood at a theoretical level.

The small number of variables to which theories of international politics are restricted necessarily abstract from a far richer historical context. The theories therefore can be used for the derivation of consequences *only* under explicitly stated boundary or parameter conditions. For instance, the statements concerning alignment patterns of the "balance of power" model in *System and Process* apply only at the level of type of alignment, and do not specify the actual actors who participate in specific alignments. And they specify even this broad consequence only for stated values of the exogenous and endogenous variables. The first attempt to bring the models closer to the richness of history occurs in Chapter 3. In this chapter the models are varied for specified differences in the internal political and regulatory structure of nation-states. It is specifically recognized that the "structural features chosen to classify national actors are quite gross and, therefore, are not sufficient for any analysis aspiring to high predictive power" (p. 56). Even so, these gross features result in an enormous number of matrix boxes and cannot be used in general theoretical formulations, but only in formulations where the international systems aspects of the models are held constant as parameters. That is, as we come closer to reality— and this is still at a high level of abstraction—we lose generality. We begin to employ procedures closer to the step-by-step engineering applications of physical theory than to generalized theoretical statements of physical theory.

Even these gross characteristics of national actors are far removed from their historical complexity. "Any attempt to describe the actual

---

and in idem, "Toward a Theory of International Politics," *Journal of Conflict Resolution*, II (December 1958), pp. 335-47. The skepticism expressed in the present paper was stated clearly and repeatedly in *System and Process*, but apparently was not understood by some commentators.

actor systems would founder under the weight of the parameters which individualize these systems—*even when their structural characteristics are similar* [italics added]. Such things as capability factors, logistic factors, and information, including history of the past, are specific to the system . . ." (p. 54). When we include the important factors that are contingent from the standpoint of theory, such as personality factors (an effort is made in Chapter 6 of *System and Process* to relate such factors to the models in a generalized sense), economic and political conditions, technological developments, invention, and other intranational and transnational factors, the complexity becomes so great that serious efforts to discuss them all and relate them all to models systematically would founder under the detail. If we want to apply our models to concrete cases, we must choose just those factors and just those factor values that we have some reason to believe operate in the particular instance we wish to understand and explain. In the endeavor, as our analysis gains in richness of relevant detail, we face a continuing loss of generality and a growing vagueness and lack of specification concerning the weight that each factor contributes to the total event or situation. This is the price we must pay when we deal with actual history. The models are useful in making these applications, but "do not correspond with reality except at the indicated levels of abstraction" (p. 2). They can be applied only in a step-by-step process, holding certain factors constant while attempting to work out the effects of additional factors not included in the models.

To repeat, we require models to test the generalizations we must employ at the level of international systems. There is no alternative— no other method to state or to analyze these generalizations. Such models can include only a restricted number of variables. In using such models, we pay the price of abstracting out many of the factors affecting the concrete course of events. When we wish to employ the model for more detailed engineering—not to test the broad generalization but to relate it to the historic context in which events are embedded—we lose theoretic generality. We come closer to step-by-step engineering applications. The practical and not the theoretic tends to dominate. We gain in historic richness, in the adequacy of our explanations, and lose in terms of precise understanding of how the variables under analysis are related. Our predictions become cruder in the sense of being less clearly related to an analytic process of reasoning and deduction. We pay a price whether we use models or engage in "historic" investigations. Neither method is "wrong" or "right" in the abstract. Both perform important functions and both contribute to each other if properly understood.

Which is to be employed as the primary tool of application depends upon the objective the researcher prefers to achieve.[2]

If the preceding assertions are correct, they should give the social scientist pause, for they indicate that the factors inhibiting the development of a powerful, predictive, theoretical social science are fundamental and that it is not merely a matter of waiting for a Galilean breakthrough. This does not imply the absence of predictability. We are all familiar with predictions of suicide rates based upon the assumption that, within a society, the forces operating for suicide will not change greatly from year to year; with sufficiently large numbers involved, statistical predictions will have a reasonable degree of accuracy. Similar predictions are made in regard to rates of automobile accidents. Sampling and interview methods have been used with reasonable accuracy to predict voting behavior and consumers' responsiveness to new products. In cases of this kind, however, although the statistical theories involved may be complex and powerful, the applications are not matters of complex social theory. Complex theories have also been applied to the measurement of certain human or social capacities. Factor analysis and Guttman scales, for instance, have been employed in such tasks. Again, however, the theories appear more methodological than substantive.

Substantive social theories in disciplines other than international politics appear to be of a number of different kinds. In economics, input-output analyses and linear programming reduce problems more or less to matters of methodological engineering. Beginning with Adam Smith, the mainstream of economic theory consists of substantive social theory of a highly abstract nature. To treat it with extreme brevity, the characteristics of certain kinds of markets are delineated and, on the assumption of economic rationality or profit maximization, the conditions of market equilibrium are specified.

Actually, however, economic theory can be viewed from two different perspectives. It can be viewed as a prediction of what will happen when economic actors behave according to the specified parameters of the theory. It can also be viewed as a prescription for maximizing profits or minimizing losses. Thus the marginal cost curve may be viewed as predicting that output will increase until marginal cost and price are in equilibrium, or as prescribing that production be increased until marginal cost equals price. Nothing in classical economic theory will account for the behavior of the old Chinese merchant who, having only

[2] For a recent detailed discussion of this problem, see Joseph J. Schwab, "What Do Scientists Do?" *Behavioral Science*, v (January 1960), pp. 1-27.

three items of a particular type, wants $1 apiece or $7 for all three, on the ground that if he sells all of them, he will lose face when someone else asks for the item. Nor would classical economic theory account for situations where attempts to maximize profits by lowering selling price resulted not in competitive behavior but in economic retaliation, including the withholding of supplies, by an infuriated economic community.

The mainstream of economic theory does not deal with real businesses or industries, or real markets. It deals with representative firms and abstract markets. It deals with generalities like the interest rate or the flow of money. It deals with aggregates of happenings and not with individual transactions. It does not predict individual behavior but general behavior and even here, if we want to be precise, it is necessary to add that it predicts not what the behavior will be but what the consequences of different kinds of behavior will be under certain specified assumptions.

The economist studies different kinds of markets—for instance, competitive, oligopolistic, and monopolistic; perfect and imperfect. Luckily for him, the economy simultaneously presents him with close analogies of most kinds of markets. If economic developments transform a competitive market into an oligopolistic one, he can look elsewhere for another competitive market to study. His theories concerning transitional developments from one kind of market to another are weaker than his theories concerning the behavior of a specified type of market.

In a society in which social constraints on the profit motive are minimal and economic rationality, as defined by economics, is a significant, if not the sole, motivating factor in economic behavior, the economist's predictions are likely to be confirmed. It is true that the economy is more complex than any economic model, and that feedback factors are so involved and complex that the most highly abstract theories concerning rate of economic growth and the economic consequences of different kinds of monetary management are difficult to demonstrate satisfactorily. But it is less difficult to see that production does tend to increase, under properly specified conditions, until price equals marginal cost, and so forth. Money is a reasonably tangible and countable commodity. Calculations concerning costs and so forth are fairly easy to make. If most firms behave according to principles of economic rationality, those which fail to do so tend to disappear and can be ignored.

Let us repeat: economic theory consists of models that abstract from the real world certain selected variables, and concerns itself with their interrelationships. One of the variables is motivation and thus the theory has a normative element when viewed from one aspect. The theory is based upon monetary units. Thus the operations of arithmetic can be used and all participants can come to reasonably similar conclusions at least with respect to certain critical aspects of economic processes. In some societies, the key boundary conditions like motivation can be determined independently with reasonable accuracy; and empirical investigations, using the monetary yardstick, can thus investigate the corollary predictions of economic theory. Although the theory is not highly confirmable with respect to other aspects of economic reality, such as innovative gambles, the fact that the economy persists and that it includes many different kinds of markets provides economic theory with a continuing relevance. We will see, for reasons to be specified later, that such models are not as promising when applied to problems of international politics.

There is a second major type of social theory which has had some significant success—although, for reasons that will become clear, this type of theory has less relevance to the most important and broadest problems of international politics. This is the type utilized by G. P. Murdock in working with the materials of the Human Relations Area Files and by S. N. Eisenstadt, particularly in his recent and as yet unpublished study of the modern historical bureaucratic states. This type of theory is less abstract and is more closely linked to empirical materials than that associated with the mainstream of economic analysis. To simplify Eisenstadt's theory almost to the point of distortion, he attempts to show that rulers can carry out certain kinds of policies only when there is a certain level of resources available to them, that these resources can be only of a kind developed by various types of free rather than feudal strata in society, and that these resources can be utilized and these free strata encouraged to engage in their activities only when there is a particular kind of bureaucratic development in the society.

It is relatively easy to show the level of resources required for particular kinds of policies. To show that feudal elements cannot provide this level of resources, and indeed might interfere with the implementation of these policies, requires a combination of social theory and comparative empirical research. To show that bureaucratic development is a necessary requirement for the flourishing of these free resources requires the application of social theory. Comparative research can then investigate the empirical relationships between the continued existence of such free resources and the development and maintenance of the historical bureaucracies. It appears from Eisenstadt's research that a direct relationship exists. Work of this kind emphasizes an extremely close relationship between theoretical structure and empirical materials. But its success depends both upon the existence of sufficient comparative materials and upon the fact that the relationships involved take on the characteristics almost of a force of nature. Although cultural factors might stifle the free resources and consequently stifle the bureaucracy, or vice versa, it must not be within the limits of variability for a bureaucracy to persist in the absence of the free resources, or for the free resources to continue to exist in the absence of the bureaucracy. Human misjudgment or differences in cultural patterns and objectives must be quite indifferent. For reasons that will emerge below, this particular kind of method is not easily applicable to the most important problems of international politics.

It may do some violence to the varieties of systematic social theory to claim that the two methods just discussed exhaust the universe of possibilities. But in a broad sense they do. Different techniques of analysis may be employed and more or less elaborate and sophisticated theoretical structures built and certainly different substantive conclusions may be reached, but every type of systematic social theory that is substantive rather than methodological in nature can be cast in one form or the other.[3]

It is now our task to investigate the peculiarities that attend a theoretical investigation into the most important substantive problems of international politics, and the difficulties which this involves for both theory construction and theory confirmation. It appears to me that the main task of a theory of international politics is to investigate the institutional regularities that attend the course of international political life, just as political science in general investigates the institutional regularities of national political life. As political scientists, we are not interested in the solution of a particular cabinet crisis as an isolated problem. We are interested in such affairs for the light they shed on the

---

[3] I do not contend, of course, that these types of theory exhaust the kinds of analysis that might be made. Obviously, the historian who attempts to explain a concrete sequence of events or the genesis of a specific event proceeds in ways that differ in part from those analyzed. The student of voting behavior interested in prediction of voting trends usually adopts a different form of analysis, although this need not invariably be the case. Attempts at statistical correlation of historic events are also of a different order. A case in point is Teggart's *Rome and China*, although one might contend that he used his statistical information to build a theory of a strictly biographical-causal type. Similarly, attempts to relate international activities to form of government or to trade rivalry may be restricted to explanations that are based on correlations, or may extend to causal sequences and to theories of one of the two specified types. I would contend, however, that for the kinds of problems this paper attempts to deal with at the theoretical level—that is, problems involving systematic social theory—the two broad types of theory specified roughly exhaust the field.

generalities of such occurrences; and, if there are no generalizations to be made, there is no political science, although we may still have a journalistic interest in political affairs.

If we are interested in institutional regularities—and, as a consequence, in comparative differences[4]—in international politics, we must recognize certain peculiar features of the subject matter. Although political science is dedicated to the study of the state as the source of political authority, international politics deals with relations between or among these ultimate or "sovereign" bodies. Nations are built of hundreds or thousands of cross-cutting social roles manifesting themselves in behavior. There are labor unions, religious organizations, industries, and so forth. The web of relationships produces a host of organized pressures, some of which can be likened to forces of nature. The individual and his decisions become lost, "averaged out," in the flow of decisions. In the international system there is only a small number of major actors or nation-states. During the nineteenth century they could be counted on

---

[4] Regularities may be thought of in many ways. For instance, the fact that 2 is the first integer greater than 1 is a regularity of our ordinary number system. That winter follows fall is a regularity of weather in temperate climates. That the candidate with a majority of the votes takes office is a regularity of our political system. That a system of at least five essential actors goes along with the essential rules of the "balance of power" system is a regularity of my "balance of power" model. Attention to regularities directly implies attention to differences. For instance, in *System and Process* six comparative types of international systems are specified and differences postulated with respect to three different sets of variables: the essential rules, the endogenous variables of the system, and the parameters or exogenous variables. The search for regularities in *System and Process* was itself responsible for the construction of a comparative international typology for perhaps the first time in the discipline.

I do not know how to separate the search for regularities from the search for differences in political science. Nor can I understand the assertion that the search for regularities must operate "only at the level of wholes" (Stanley J. Hoffmann, ed., *Contemporary Theory in International Relations*, Englewood Cliffs, N.J., 1960, p. 42). Regularities in my theory always involve the values of variables of systems, not "wholes," just as differences do. Of course, there are irregular events and processes, and also random ones. Reality cannot be forced into preconstructed molds. But the existence of regularities (and thus of regular differences) is necessary for the development of theory. The predisposition to search for regularities is essential to finding them and is desirable, provided it does not involve a dogmatic rejection of evidence to the contrary.

There is, of course, the important problem of level or precision of analysis. For instance, two thermostatically constant and equivalent temperatures may on analysis be discovered to have different patterns of variance around the mean temperature. Of two superficially identical ovens, one may have a concealed timer that halts its operation automatically after some given period of time. Of two presidential systems of government, one system may at a particular time have a strong president and the other a weak president; one may operate according to an item-veto principle and the other not. Some differences at the more precise level of analysis may affect the system in a way relevant to our inquiry; others may affect it but only after a certain period of time; others may affect it in no relevant way. In *System and Process* such problems are considered as related to the "levels of abstraction" problem and are linked to coupled systems and to engineering problems.

one's fingers. At the present time, the United States and the Soviet Union are the most important; there is a small number of nations of intermediary significance; and the total number of nations approximates one hundred. In systems of this kind, individual decisions are not canceled out in the mass. In some cases they may have a decisive effect. A change in the number of nations, particularly a reduction in the number of important nations, may have considerable effect upon the stability of the entire system of organized political relationships. Unlike the situation frequently encountered in economics, where a change in a particular market affects only that market and not the whole economy, a change in a part of the international political system often has an effect on the whole system. That means dynamic aspects of the process at the margin are of considerable importance, and that the factors making for stability or instability, or changing the number of participating actors, are also of great importance.

The cross-cutting social roles within nations produce a great number of solidary relations within the national web of relations; in general the relations between individuals and groups, on one hand, and the nation, on the other, are solidary. The relations of nations toward one another or toward the international system do not tend to be solidary, although nations may have instrumental reasons for supporting other nations or for helping to maintain the normative forms of the international system. The competition is not only for a "share of the spoils" but in addition may involve the most ultimate considerations. Although in domestic politics the form of political organization is usually taken for granted except during transitional periods, the very existence of the nation and the nature of the interrelationships among nations may be at stake in the play of international politics. The fact that there is only a small number of significant nation-states makes for a subsystem-dominant system of relations in the international arena—that is, a set of relations that exist not as parametric "givens" for the actors but as conditions that can be affected by their actions. Thus there is a highly strategic aspect to the central core of international political activity.

There is another difference between national and international politics that is significant for the task of constructing and confirming theory. Within national political systems, political organization is formal and durable. In the international arena, political organization is informal— at least with respect to those kinds of political action that historically have been the most important, like the alliance. This applies in particular to the methods of negotiation, bargaining, and conflict that characterize the interalliance activity governing the international political system.

Moreover, although particular alliances come into and pass out of existence with frequency in systems like the "balance of power" international system, the kind of alliance characteristic of the system endures for a considerable period of time. The kind of alliance system that is manifested in different and changing alliances through time is less tangible than the formal political organization characterizing the modern nation-state. This requires explanation at a high level of abstraction.

In addition, the international system is not a primary sphere of action in the same sense that national political systems are. Although we probably cannot understand the differences among the Italian city-state system, the nineteenth-century "balance of power" system, and the present bipolar system without knowledge of the number of essential actors, their relative capabilities, military instrumentalities, their relationships with the environment, and their modes of political intercourse, important aspects of international activity stem from intranational considerations. Internal political pressures—whether cultural and historical as in the anti-Westernism of the new nations, or whether stemming from the need to divert domestic discontent, the need for markets, desires for national aggrandizement, population explosions, technological innovations, and so forth—may have major consequences for international political decisions. That is, the focus of the decision may be as much on internal political and economic needs as on external ones.

We can now state certain things about the kind of theory we should have to construct to handle the central theoretical problems of international politics and the kinds of difficulties we are likely to run into in attempting to confirm such theories. Having learned our lesson from physical science, we will attempt in our theory to deal with only a limited number of variables. The central variables will include the major kinds of actors participating in international politics, their capabilities, including military capability, their motivations, their goal orientations, and their style of strategic and political activity. Even these central variables indicate great complexity in the theory. We must leave out, except as boundary conditions, all other variables, including intranational causes of international activity, although these may later be built into engineering applications of the theory. But it is quite clear that the set of variables to be included in the theory never exists in isolation in nature, as do the variables that the physicist deals with. As in economics, the central variables must be built into models that can be viewed either as normative or empirical, depending upon the way in which they are used. If the motivations and goal orientations are taken for granted, then the models are predictive for given specifications of the boundary conditions. If the boundary conditions are specified and the goal orientations or motivations left open, then the models may be viewed as prescriptions for maximizing certain kinds of objectives. Unfortunately there are certain differences from the situation in economics, shortly to be considered, that make the enterprise somewhat difficult.

For reasons already made clear, the model must be predictive or prescriptive with respect to activity at a high level of generality—that is, the *kind* of activity, whether political or normative—and not with respect to individual items of activity. It specifies what kinds of coalition patterns and goal objectives and limitations go along with given kinds of nations, capability ranges, economic and political systems, military forces, and so forth. It specifies the consequences which changes in certain of the internal or boundary conditions are likely to cause, but does not predict what will happen in a specific case. It predicts what kind of coalition should occur, and how its objectives should be limited if certain interests of the member nations are to be protected, but does not predict which particular nations will be members of which coalition.

For instance, the model of the "balance of power" system developed in *System and Process* predicts the kinds of shifts in membership according to short-term interests that occurred during the Congress of Vienna, but is not specific enough to predict the members of any particular alliance. It predicts that the stability of other variables of the system, such as the number of essential national actors or the limitations of objectives, depends upon a series of shifting, short-term, interest-oriented alliances, but does not predict that such alliances will occur in any particular case. It only predicts that if some factors external to the set of essential variables of the system persistently interfere with the alliance-patterning, then other variables of the system will also change in value.

The model must be strategically oriented. The small number of actors and the subsystem-dominant nature of the system entail this. Strategic play involves attempts to fool and to gain the better of opponents. The n-player nature of the system entails coalition problems. Game constraints on coalitions are weak. If the styles of play and strategies of the nations playing in the international political game are to converge to equilibrium, the analysis must be able to indicate the dynamic process which leads to this conclusion.

This has been done heuristically by the present writer. But in terms of a precise analysis sufficient to demonstrate the conclusion, the results so far are discouraging. No game model yet exists from which the conclu-

sion can be derived. To prove that the equilibrium strategy is optimal—
and thus rationally would be chosen by the players—by programming
the game on a computer has so far been too complex to be practicable.
All possible strategies and counterstrategies for all possible distributions
of the spoils would have to be anticipated by the computer in making its
decisions, or it would have to play through all the possibilities. As an
alternative, Burns, Quandt, and Kaplan have constructed a table-stakes
game of a simplified nature employing a remarkably complex computer,
the human brain, in order to test some of the statements of the heuristic
model.[5] We operate on the assumption that the human mind will
eliminate the least likely strategies and divisions of the spoils, and that a
series of plays by human players against one another will then perform
the remaining eliminations necessary to discover the equilibrium strategies. The table-stakes game, however, is only a substitute for more
desirable game or computer solutions and has, in any event, not yet been
employed systematically.

Thus the problem of insuring the consistency and formal adequacy of
the model is still unsolved. In addition, there is the danger that there are
no optimal equilibrium strategies, in which case the whole theoretical
enterprise would become murky—since the range of responses might be
too great to handle—unless we discovered that there were in fact
equilibrium strategies and styles of play employed by nations even
though these did not follow from a consistent formal theory of strategy.
That is, players might engage in non-optimal equilibrating strategies for
cultural reasons, or there might be a formal solution that permitted a
particular player at some stage of the play to secure dominance because
of unavoidable and unpredictable momentary advantages. But as long as
he did not have the advantage of the formal theory and did not know
this, he might decide to employ the equilibrating strategy. And as long
as disequilibrating strategies were not employed at these decisive points
of time, the system would continue to function. There is another possibility: the disequilibrating strategy could be employed successfully by
one of the players only at one of the aforementioned fortuitous stages of
play. If a player in fact used the disequilibrating strategy appropriately,
and if the opponents employed clearly optimal responses and could not
prevent predominance by this player, we would in fact have a confirmation of the theory. If, however, there were no such thing as an optimal
style of play, or if there were always a better line of play against any

[5] Morton A. Kaplan, Arthur L. Burns, and Richard E. Quandt, "Theoretical Analysis
of the 'Balance of Power,'" *Behavioral Science*, v (July 1960), pp. 241-52. See also the
article by T. C. Schelling in the present symposium.

particular set of equilibrium strategies, then the explanation of any empirical equilibrium would have to be found either in false conceptions of optimal play which were not challenged by deviant players, or in certain kinds of cultural inhibitions on styles of play. If our theory told us these should or should not produce equilibrium under specified conditions, we could then get some confirmations. Or, given a particular style of play as general, we might be able to make predictions concerning the consequences of individual deviance from the style, and confirm them.

Suppose that we are temporarily satisfied with the heuristic model, or that someday we possess a precise model which gives us greater confidence in the internal consistency of our theory. There still remain enormous problems with respect to the empirical confirmation of the theory. Here the differences from the situation facing the economic theorist assume first-order importance. There is not an easily calculable unit like money involved. If the concept of gross national product is rather fuzzy, the concept of national capabilities is even fuzzier. Nor is there a good measuring rod like that of profit to indicate the viability of the nation. Although there are considerations of capital strength such that a very big company might undersell its competitor uneconomically in order to insure its hold on the market, international political rivalry is much more direct than economic rivalry, since it involves not merely competition for a market but occasional forcible seizures of desired objectives. In the rare case that such things occur in the economy, they are not treated by economic theory. Motivation and rationality are reasonably evident when an entrepreneur increases production until marginal cost equals price. They are not so clear when a nation acts in terms of the precepts of the model of a system—for example, the "balance of power" system.[6] It is difficult to decide whether a particular action occurred because of strategically rational considerations or because of a particular ideological pattern of beliefs or because of internal political inhibitions. And even where a constraining pattern of beliefs can be demonstrated, it may be difficult to decide whether it accounts for the empirical pattern of activity or is merely a rationalization of activity decided upon for more strategic reasons.

[6] For example, in the prisoners' dilemma, if the prisoners acted irrationally and remained silent instead of talking because they misunderstood the strategic situation, they would in fact obtain a jointly more desirable result than in the case of a rational decision and might be led to believe that they *had* acted rationally. See Morton A. Kaplan, *Some Problems in the Strategic Analysis of International Politics*, Research Monograph No. 2, Center of International Studies, Princeton University, January 12, 1959; and *System and Process*, ch. 10.

There are many free variables in the type of model we have advocated both with respect to the variables internal to the model and with respect to those at the boundary. It may be especially difficult to determine which of the variables produced a particular result. When internal political factors, capabilities, military factors, strategic estimates, the credibility of opponents' offers and threats, and so forth vary simultaneously, there is the danger that almost any explanation can be fitted to the determinable facts, even though careful empirical investigation may eliminate with reasonable probability some of these possibilities.

Another important problem of empirical analysis concerns the vagueness of the criteria of the variables employed in the theory. The fuzziness of the concept of capability has been mentioned, as has the possibility of differing estimates of the factual situation. In addition, however, concrete actions like initiating a war, seizing booty or war objectives, entering into alliances, etc., have to be interpreted in terms of the more abstract variables of the theory. When is an objective limited? Clearly there may be vast gray areas here. When is a coalition designed to halt an actor with supranational objectives rather than merely to prevent military defeat? And does this difference have any importance as long as the same countercoalition is to be predicted in any case? What is an action to increase capabilities, and how do we distinguish between effective and ineffective action? England increased its capabilities during the Baldwin period although these actions were clearly inadequate, and engaged in at least some anti-German activities under Chamberlain although these, too, were clearly inadequate. We can obviously make reasonable judgments on these matters, but the determination is not specified by criteria presently employed in the theory. As a consequence, there is the danger that the theory can be fudged to explain almost any set of facts.

Unlike the economist, the student of international politics cannot examine simultaneously operating firms and markets of different kinds, and make detailed comparative or statistical analyses in order to determine which factors probably produce which result. He is not even in as good a position as the student of comparative politics. His only comparisons are comparisons in time, and in this case not one but many factors are varying simultaneously. For this reason analogies are quite perilous.

For the reasons analyzed previously, we must give up the hope that a theory of international politics can have either the explanatory or the predictive power of a "hard" science. Nonetheless we cannot study international politics theoretically without consideration of the constraints imposed by purely international factors on the international action process. The generalizations of historians and statesmen about the "balance of power" or the protection of national interests focus on such considerations. There are no tools other than the scientific tools to be applied, and their weakness in the particular case warrants skeptical caution rather than outright rejection.

It is in the nature of sophisticated and explicit theories that their careful statement reveals their weakness. The still greater weaknesses of ordinary common-sense generalizations are hidden by the implicit and inexplicit nature of the argument. If it is the case that generalizations of a scientific nature about the systematic properties of the international system cannot be avoided in significant analyses of international events, it is necessary to make theories concerning such events as explicit as possible. Although we may then recognize that our analyses are of a heuristic order—that is, that they permit us to order our experiences in a convincing but not highly demonstrable manner—they can still perform valuable functions. In addition, we may then be able to specify research designs that buttress the reasonable probability of our theoretical statements. For instance, the table-stakes game on which Burns, Quandt, and Kaplan are working is one such possibility, for it at least may give insight into the ways in which human beings in particular cultural settings succeed or fail in strategic undertakings that may not simulate international politics but resemble it with respect to certain key variables.

In such games, we may vary the number of players, the rate of economic development, relative and absolute military capabilities; we may instruct some players to use specified styles of play, some players to use deceit, and so forth; we may by varying the rewards put higher or lower premiums on "risky" moves or on attempts to gain hegemony, and try to establish the conditions under which this motivates players to pursue radically different styles of play. We can attempt to factor out as much as possible the cultural element in choice. We at least have in such methods a tool for the analogical testing of generalizations that are in fact made with respect to international politics and that are of the greatest importance in formulating theoretical systems or in determining practical policy decisions. In addition this is probably the only tool that will permit us systematically to investigate unstable systems as well as more stable systems. We are, however, presently inhibited from making ambitious generalizations concerning unstable systems by the paucity of our knowledge.

The statesman faced with a choice between limiting his gains in order to preserve his future alliance potential or grabbing as much as he can at the moment ought rationally to be interested in which course better enhances his ability to maintain the independence of his country or to gain hegemony, etc., and whether and to what extent the answer is dependent upon cultural as distinguished from purely strategic factors. Is a revolutionary dictator such a threat to a "balance of power" system that other nations would be wise to gang up on him immediately and inflict extra punishment on the nation he represents, or is his ability to disrupt the system dependent largely on the spread of a revolutionary ideology that immobilizes the normal responses of the other members of the system? Would a system of "power-mad" dictatorships rationally be forced to adopt the rules of a "balance of power" system?

To what extent are the answers to questions such as these dependent upon the number of nations involved, their relative and absolute military capabilities, etc.? These are not obscure theoretical or practical questions. Even though answers to them framed in general terms do not fully determine answers to specific applications, because of boundary influences considered in engineering applications, they cut to the heart of questions concerning national activity and the advisability of common attempts to change the modes of international organization. If, for instance, the "balance of power" system is inherently unstable, there are more reasons for scholars and statesmen to consider alternative modes of international organization, and the plausible strategies to achieve them, than exist where the system is inherently stable. Strategic analysis thus raises explicitly questions essential both to policy and to theoretical understanding of international politics, even if it is not the key to all relevant questions. It is a tool that permits for the first time the explicit specification of certain key variables in the international political process and also permits for the first time the testing of hypotheses concerning these variables, even if only indirectly or by analogy. It is a tool for the development of more and more sophisticated tests and for the application of the elementary canons of scientific discourse to the analysis of the strategic aspects of international politics. The difficulties involved in formal strategic analysis—which we have discussed—are inherent in the nature of the subject matter. Less formal or non-strategic modes of analysis evade the problems involved in using strategic theory by evading the problems involved in the subject matter of international politics.[7]

[7] I do not disagree so much with the qualifications concerning game theory as it now stands that Burns makes elsewhere in this symposium as with his tendency to throw the baby out with the bath. For efforts to modify game theory to increase its relevance to international politics, see Thomas C. Schelling, *The Strategy of Conflict*, Cambridge,

In addition to gaming techniques for investigating the adequacy of statements derived from models of theories of international systems, we may turn to historical materials. We may examine cases that puzzle historians or for which historians do not have a convincing and sophisticated explanation, and see whether our theories seem to account for the state of affairs. The number of free variables involved may exclude dogmatism, but if, upon analysis, the theory provides a deeper and intellectually more satisfying explanation than the normal historical explanation, this is a mark in its favor. We can explore whether the theory is congruent with certain kinds of normative conduct and incongruent with others, as Katzenbach and Kaplan have been doing.[8] If the theory seems to specify the differences that actually do occur in the normative structure of international law during different historic periods, then this converging explanation gives us added reason to prefer the theory to alternative explanations.

Despite the weakness of comparative method with respect to problems of international politics, we might investigate differences in international behavior during different historic periods. For instance, we might study the ancient Greek system, the Italian city-state system, and the eighteenth- and nineteenth-century "balance of power" system— all of which have certain "balance of power" features in common. If some of these historic systems are stable and others not—for instance, a "roll-up" may occur—and if empirical study isolates the difference that seems to account for this, we can then hunt for additional examples where this specific difference seems to be the important one, and see whether the same difference in behavior occurs. We can also build the difference into our table-stakes game and see whether the same sort of different behavior is produced in the course of it. If so, we have a converging explanation. If not, we may experiment and see whether we can produce the behavior in the game in some other fashion, and then turn back to our historical studies to see whether enlightenment comes from this particular explanation rather than from the one we originally hit upon. Possibly some aspects of international theory are not dependent on strategic analysis and can have the solidity of theories like Eisenstadt's.

In any event, our explanations or theories can never have the authority of theory in physics, or its explanatory or predictive power. The impor-

---

Mass., 1960; Kaplan, *System and Process*, ch. 11; and idem, *Some Problems in the Strategic Analysis of International Politics*.

[8] See Morton A. Kaplan and Nicholas de B. Katzenbach, *The Political Foundations of International Law*, New York, 1961.

PROSPECTS FOR A GENERAL THEORY
OF INTERNATIONAL RELATIONS

By ARTHUR LEE BURNS

HOW far may we hope to go in theorizing about international affairs? That question is at the center of this article, which consists of several more or less eclectic stabs at the problem.

I shall be writing as though some theory of power politics were the only possible candidate for being *the* theory of international relations. Let that be regarded as an act of methodological faith—certainly I can think of no scientific demonstration of it, and I would rather leave the philosophy of the matter for another occasion. There are a number of stock objections against any general theory of international relations oriented towards power politics, and these I shall try to rebut, chiefly by extending and correcting my own previous efforts in the genre. I shall then introduce objections of a rather more abstract sort, and, again from my own previous work, I shall try to show that the difficulties which these latter present are indeed formidable. But I hope it will be understood that neither kind of objection need be relevant to theories of international relations other than those built around the concepts of force, power, and security.

"International relations are relations between Powers" is the near-truism from which a theory of power politics can begin. It may then develop in various directions: we are not straitened to the paranoid version, that Powers are related only by the conflict of their interests. Indeed, the adoption of drastic measures like unconditional surrender and total warfare is needed if international affairs are to be reduced to a zero-sum or "ruin" game. To quote George Modelski, the subject is usually "more mellow."

Critics of the power approach have condemned it as generating a "single-factor" theory.[1] If it does, then so does the classic approach to economics. But the power approach is directed less to the motives than to the means of international relationship—that is, it assumes only that armed might is the nexus between Powers, and not necessarily that it is their most preferred good. Even so, the nexus of real-life international transactions is far more often a token for force of arms than armed force itself (thus also the cash nexus in orthodox economics).

[1] E.g., Lord Lindsay of Birker, *Scientific Method and International Affairs* (Roy Milne Lecture, 1956), Canberra, Australian Institute of International Affairs, 1957, *passim*.

Nor can the power approach offer any theoretical objection against the peacemaker's aspirations—to compose all conflicts of national interest, and to reduce all forces-in-being to the level of police forces. (Below that level, there sets in the paradox of pacifism as a national policy— viz., that the total-pacifist government requires armed police to put down any recalcitrant minority which might of its own accord offer armed resistance against the foreign invader.) Thus, disarmament is a perfectly proper item on the agenda of power-political studies.

The later sections of this paper will point up certain grave difficulties in the way of developing a truly general theory from the power approach. But first I shall try to show how catholic and hospitable an approach it can be; in particular, how it can incorporate "other factors," to use that misleading expression.

I

My essay of 1956, *From Balance to Deterrence*,[2] was an attempt to derive a rigorous theory of pure power politics, as exemplified in two successive international orders or systems: (1) the balance-of-power system that arose in Renaissance Europe and by the time of the First World War had involved half of the globe; and (2) the system of reciprocal deterrence which seems to have come into force during the last decade. In that essay I abstracted all those geographic constraints and facilities that go to shape the actual world's political map. In the initial versions of the "Game of Power" which Kaplan, Quandt, and I made up as a device for developing theoretical hypotheses about international relations, and for detecting the mathematical properties that some of them are supposed to possess, geography was likewise disregarded: every player is, as it were, equidistant from all other players.[3] (A brief description of the game is appended to this paper.)

Now, for a game intended to reveal, by the Monte Carlo method, whether there is any arithmetical foundation for the balance-of-power hypothesis (viz., that a world of several Powers is more apt to stabilize than is a bi-polar world), that rule of "equidistance" was necessary. We wished to test the *unaided* strength of the hypothesis, so we activated against it as many conditions and motivations as we could. We punished weakness and poverty of resources; we rewarded hegemony

---

[2] Australian National University, Social Science Monograph No. 9, December 1956; revised for publication as "From Balance to Deterrence: A Theoretical Analysis," in *World Politics*, ix (July 1957), pp. 494-529 (citations hereinafter refer to revised version).

[3] Morton A. Kaplan, Arthur L. Burns, and Richard E. Quandt, "Theoretical Analysis of the 'Balance of Power,'" *Behavioral Science*, v (July 1960), pp. 240-52.

and elimination of other players; we used Driggs's simulation of the Lanchester Square law exchange-rate for battles[4] so as to make elimination possible; and in later versions we increased possible "spoils of victory" so that warfare might pay better. But we did not wish to have "geography" facilitating the task of the would-be-balancers. We did not want at that stage to favor some particular player's defense in such a way that he could safely intervene to prevent any one player or coalition from dominating the rest, as Great Britain from her island sanctuary is supposed to have trimmed the Continental balance of power.

The latter supposition—that geographic differences are stabilizers—will be turned, however, into an hypothesis testable in our game, once we have discovered how much there is to be said for the former, purely arithmetical, hypothesis. For example, we could thus far put some geography into the game, by (1) designating, instead of one, *two* types of military force not substitutable for each other; (2) setting apart one (or more) player so that, in order to attack him with Type A forces, any other player or players would have had first to have eliminated his Type B forces; and (3), to modify his advantages a little, subjecting his resources to some modest tax whenever his Type A forces should engage those of other players. This variation of the game might test the purely arithmetical component of the idea that when navies exist, island Powers tend to be balancers. A similar and complementary distinction could be made between types of resources;[5] and procedures for building up credits and for "trading" could be added to the game, so that the islanded player would be favored as to one type of trading and handicapped as to other types, while the rest of the players were variously handicapped and favored with respect to each other, as Powers on a continent are supposed to be.

Next, to attempt a more difficult, dynamic problem: During a seminar in 1958, Professor W. C. Fox took issue with the seventh of my Principles in "From Balance to Deterrence": "Any system embodying the balance of power has some intrinsic tendency to diminish the number of its constituent Powers or blocs, and no intrinsic tendency to increase that number."[6] Professor Fox pointed out that the classical instance of balance of power—the European system of the eighteenth and nineteenth centuries—had by 1914 increased the number of nations involved in it; and this, not only from such extrinsic causes (which,

---

[4] I. Driggs, "A Monte Carlo Model of Lanchester's Square Law," *Operations Research*, IV (April 1956), pp. 148-51.

[5] We already distinguish between nuclear and non-nuclear, long-range and short-range forces. See Kaplan, Burns, and Quandt, *op.cit.*, Rules 5-10.

[6] See Burns, *op.cit.*, p. 508.

indeed, I had specifically excepted from my Principle Seven[7]) as industrial revolution and other forms of economic growth, but also and more
importantly from intrinsic causes: the inclination of Powers within
the system to reach out and take new areas as colonies, or to acquire
new allies from outside the system. Principle Seven would therefore be
valid, if at all, only when the ring was held—when no further reaching
out was possible.

Clearly enough, the plausible explanations of the European system's
expansion fall within the compass of a power approach; my previous
theorizing overlooked both the facts of expansion and their explanations. It is more difficult, but not impossible, to extend our Game of
Power so as to allow for something like the expansionist effect: either
by having the game played on a board, somewhat like n-person chess;
or—theoretically a more elegant alternative—by the introduction of
certain constricting and enabling rules which would be equivalent to
geographic conditioning of national potentials.

On the first alternative, we would need to alter the gaming procedure
as follows. At the start of the game, each player would be allocated an
area on the board (instead of some of the general-purpose pieces allocated under the present rules). His capacity to earn "income" should be
related to the size of this area, and, if necessary, to some ratio for its
productivity, which in turn could be related to arbitrarily differentiated
natural products. Several of these areas ("national territories") could
border upon each other; these, we would expect to form an "international" system. There might be several such systems on the board,
as well perhaps as certain isolated players, separated from each other
either by unoccupiable areas ("sea") or by areas as yet unoccupied.
Corresponding to the Type A and Type B forces mentioned above,
there could be two types of vehicle for non-military communication, to
enable the trading of differentiated products (even under our game's
present rules, there is nothing to forbid borrowing and lending of
resources). A schedule of costs for taking over unoccupied territory
could be imposed. Lastly, one could build in procedures for recalling
to the game, at the instance of some semi-random device, players previously eliminated by conquest, whose former territories were being held
by militarily weakened conquerors; and for similarly introducing quite
new players to represent new nations established through colonial
revolt.

To dispense altogether with a board or playing area, we would need
to substitute, for (e.g.) borders and variations of territorial possession,

[7] *Ibid.*

a set of constraining and enabling rules. For example, with colors as players, the geographical restriction preventing Blue from occupying the White area might be that a system made up of Green, Yellow, Red, and Black lay between them. This could be represented *non*-spatially by *asymmetric* rules—viz., that White could be controlled only by some members of the intervening system (say, Red or Black); and similarly that Red and Black could not directly attack Blue. (The geometry of a chessboard is similarly reproducible by a set of non-spatial rules.) Our Game of Power, under its present rules, allows each player a "frontier" with each other player—i.e., it enforces completely symmetric geographic relations. This is one of the several reasons why we have been unwilling to call the game a simulation of international relations.

The imposition of arbitrary and asymmetric rules, however, changes the game's role: from being a device for exploring the structure of models and theories in general, it becomes a particular simulation (or model, in the extended sense) of a particular constellation of variously related Powers. This change is a logically significant one. If we may now regard the Game of Power-with-geographic-detail as a *family of games* whose potential members are as numerous as the alternative possible arrangements of the "world" permitted by the game's variable features—i.e., though not an infinite number, an indescribably large one. Each member of the family would be a competitive game in its own right, and for it there should be, *in principle*, a game-theoretical solution. These solutions would of course differ among themselves, in accordance with differences between the various games' geographies. Again in principle, a catalogue of all the games and of their solutions could be analyzed to bring out any significant higher-order correlations in the pattern of varying relationships between solutions and their geographic conditions. Those variations could be given mathematical expression, and this would yield a truly general theory of the geographic family of games.

But the geographic are not the only conditions which produce asymmetries among the ingredient Powers of an international system. Ideologies, economic and political institutions, size of populations, balance among agriculture, industry, and commerce, levels of technology, religious affiliations—all, obviously enough, have some bearing upon the conduct of power politics. Most of them bear upon each other also, and in complicated ways. Nevertheless there seems to be nothing *in principle* to prevent our incorporating into the geographic family of games a representation of the whole complex of constraints and facilitations imposed by the non-geographic, after the fashion outlined above for geographic constraints and facilitations. This would yield a second family of games, even larger than the merely geographic family. Many members of this second family, furthermore, would be dynamic games— i.e., during the playing of them, there would tend to be changes in all sorts of fundamental ratios (e.g., in the exchange-rate for forces in battle), because of prior changes in size of population, in technology, and in the balance of the economies.[8] If, as another concession to realistic representation, some of the technological changes were arranged so as to be unpredictable[9] by players of the game, the theoretical possibility of their discovering optimal strategies (at least by the canons of ortho-dox game theory) would be removed—and with it, of course, the possibility of any game-theoretic solution for the game (see further below). Otherwise, we can assume that each game in the family is *in principle* soluble and that there might be, therefore, a truly general mathematical theory of this "multi-factor" family of games. That, of course, could not be immediately claimed as a general theory of inter-national relations, since there is at least a *prima facie* case that no game, however realistic, can represent anything as momentous as real-life international affairs, even in principle.

Unfortunately, it is also impossible in practice to formulate a theory of the multi-factor game. Our simple, unmodified Game of Power itself involves an order of numbers quite beyond the range of practical computation, and therefore a game-theoretical solution. (That is why, in order to answer our elementary question about the relations between numbers of players and degree of stability, we would have to resort to Monte Carlo methods.) *A fortiori*, a theory of the multi-factor game is practically impossible.

In the next section, further arguments from other bases are offered to show that game theory and its "neighbors" cannot be applied posi-tively and directly to international relations.

II

So far, I have been contending (a) that if we can quantify the power approach, then in principle we can also subsume within it many other factors commonly believed to contradict the hypothesis that the course

---

[8] Rules 5-10 already allow for "induced" changes in the weapons exchange-rate.

[9] The unpredictability here referred to does not mean "knowing that there is a probability P that technology will change in such and such a way"; nor "knowing that there is a probability P of there being a probability P that technology will change in such and such a way"; nor any subsequent item in such a series. See C. L. Hamblin, "The Modal 'Probably,'" *Mind*, lxviii (April 1959), pp. 234-40; and Arthur L. Burns, "Inter-national Consequences of Expecting Surprise," *World Politics*, x (July 1958), pp. 512-36.

of international affairs is a partly competitive, partly cooperative contest for national power and security;[10] (b) that to subsume these other factors is further to complicate the power approach; (c) that even without other factors—even with such a small range of quantities as our original Game of Power employed—the order of numbers involved makes a game-theoretical solution to the contest for power impossible in practice; and therefore (d) that game theory, which is *prima facie* the only candidate for a general theory to formalize the power approach to international politics, cannot as a matter of fact succeed in its candidature.

I shall now turn to certain prior questions. First: are international affairs essentially a contest? Are they necessarily competitive, even in small degree? If competition is only an accidental (though frequent) feature, game theory can be used as no more than the theory of that feature of international affairs, and we shall need to look elsewhere for a general theory of the subject as a whole—i.e., we shall have shown the power approach to be a partial view mistakenly universalized.

Historically, the power approach is well supported. I cannot think of any time in which the interests of at least two Powers were not held to be in conflict. Only a philosophic analysis, however, can distinguish between essence and recurrent accident. We need therefore to argue more or less as follows: one mark of statehood—one of the criteria by which indubitable Powers decide whether a given group of people constitutes or does not constitute a Power—is evident ability to govern and to maintain order. But that argues at least the ability to maintain an armed force capable, if necessary, both of quelling any subordinate armed force within the group, and of making some show of repelling attack upon the frontiers of the group's living-space. Significant national forces of almost any type can be used for attack as well as for defense. Therefore, where two or more state-controlled armed forces exist, the possibility remains of conflict between them. And where a state exists, the possibility remains that it will maintain armed forces. Thus, armed conflict is a permanent possibility in anything definable as an international system.

Obviously, national interests usually come into conflict from non-military causes. Strictly, conflicts of economic interest on a world-wide scale are mostly between *economies*, but in many historical periods, each economy has been more or less coextensive with a particular state or block of states. Militant ideologies and religions from time to time are taken over by or take over states and alliances. Though, as argued

10 See Burns, "From Balance to Deterrence," pp. 495ff.

in the previous section, it is possible and not unreasonable to incorporate these other sources of conflict as added conditions within the prior situation of competition for power and security between states, a profound methodological difficulty arises when we ask ourselves how each particular national leader or decision-maker reconciles in his own mind the competing claims of his state as a Power, of its economy as a welfare-producing system, and of the ideological movement (if any) as associated with it.[11]

This difficulty is acute for any game-theoretical treatment of international politics. Even if we have convinced ourselves that international affairs are a contest, we have still to identify the contestants and, in technical terms, to show that each one has a consistent schedule of preferences (to apply game theory in any of its currently developed forms, a further necessary condition is that all such schedules should be expressible in the cardinal utilities of von Neumann and Morgenstern). But if, as is the case, international contests are actually played out by real persons who make their decisions in terms of preferences which cannot be assumed to be ordered as though these persons or committees of persons *were* the Powers they severally represent ("L'état, c'est moi"), then game theory cannot be assumed to apply directly to the real world. At best, we can construct a model in which semi-mythical entities— "the United States," "the USSR," "Western Germany"—do duty for real states with the quotes removed, we having imputed to each a schedule of preferences derived from its supposed power-political interests as a contestant in the international "game."

Why can't we derive the preferences of a state's actual leaders and spokesmen in a similar way—i.e., by recognizing that the men are the true contestants in the game of power politics, and by examining their actions for clues as to how each orders the two or three fundamental interests relevant to his task as a member of government? The short answer is that by the time one had "sufficiently" examined the actions, the situation one wanted to predict with the help of game theory would have passed. Even more it is important to notice that no overarching postulates of rationality are available[12] from which one can derive the "proper, rational" ordering of any particular leader's fundamental interests, in the fashion that one imputes to a semi-mythical state a consistent ordering of preferences derivable solely from the objective of national security or national power.

[11] See A. L. Burns, "International Theory and Historical Explanation," *History and Theory* (The Hague), 1, No. 1 (December 1960), pp. 55-74.
[12] *Ibid.*

Furthermore, it would be a bold assumption that each leader's actual schedule of preferences is "rational"—i.e., transitive—at any given moment, or that it undergoes no rearrangement during the contest for which we want a game-theoretical resolution. (I shall try later to show that the possibility of this sort of rearrangement adds to the process of international negotiation a dimension which is actually contradictory to the postulates of current bargaining theory.) But we cannot regard the leader as a "rational" contestant unless we make that bold assumption.

Even so, national policy is rarely made or implemented by a single leader only: usually, it issues from a committee. The policy-forming debate of a committee can of course be treated as a "game" in the technical sense, each person or group that has a distinct schedule of consistent and rationally ordered preferences being deemed a distinct contestant whose objective is to have the committee adopt a schedule as much as possible like his own. The game is then supposed to proceed by the contestants' trading items from their several schedules. Now, it has been acknowledged since the days of Condorcet that the resultant joint policy may very well be itself intransitive—e.g., each of the three Chiefs of Staff, to use Herman Kahn's imaginary example, may have a completely transitive schedule of preferences, but jointly they might prefer rockets to bombers, bombers to submarines, and submarines to rockets. There are logical procedures for guarding against joint intransitivity, but it would be surprising if any government ever used any device more recondite than the obvious course of electing one man to make the decisions. (The British cabinet system, with its adjunct of a constitutional opposition, works in somewhat the same direction.) But in general, national policies are as apt to be intransitive as transitive.

The policy of an *alliance* is therefore quite likely to emerge as a tangle of compounded intransitivities, a horror to the game theorist and a fascinating problem for the analytic historian. Is it intellectually treasonable to wonder whether such technical irrationalities are *always* subversive of sound policy? I shall suggest in another section that formal consistency of preferences may be purchasable only by arbitrary disregard of the possibility of novelty. But first I must continue the case against orthodox game theory.

The conception of a *mixed strategy* may never have direct application in international politics, though in the military sub-games of that grand contest it frequently does. But the possibility of a mixed strategy is certainly bound up with orthodox game theory. In particular, the *expected value* of a game has to be derived by multiplying every payoff by its probability and adding them up.[13] Among the outcomes of current international situations for which the game theorist would have to determine payoffs, there may well be annihilation of one of the contestants (either annihilation of all or most of a state's population, or at least destruction beyond the point of recovery as an independent nation-state). Some leaders may regard this not only as the worst of possible outcomes, but also as infinitely or quasi-infinitely evil. Other leaders may instead regard some moral failure (willingness to surrender rather than be annihilated; *or* willingness to annihilate the enemy rather than surrender to him) as *the* infinite evil. In either case, an expected value for the game cannot exist, for mathematical reasons.[14] Therefore orthodox game theory cannot apply where such infinite or near-infinite values are in question.

This is a pity, since other game-theoretical concepts—those of *dominance* and the *saddlepoint*—seem peculiarly apt and illuminating as characterizations of such states of affairs as mutual deterrence before a sudden and unilateral access of first-strike capability. Perhaps we shall be driven to concede that, in fields to which the theory that generates them does not apply, the use of these technical terms can be only analogical. But there may be another basis for their direct use: a new version of game theory may be derivable from weakened postulates. In particular, we may be able to dispense with cardinality, both of utilities and of probabilities, and instead operate with cardinal series.

Along such lines, two papers by C. L. Hamblin[15] develop the idea of a calculus of *plausibility*, derived from a weakened version of the usual postulates for probability-calculus. Hamblin's proposal would not of course resolve by itself most of the difficulties of game theory mentioned in the present section, but it would avoid the last that I shall be mentioning.

This consists in the frequent impossibility of listing *all* the alternative outcomes of an international contest. In orthodox game theory, an outcome is simply the "meet" or conjunction of two (or, for the *n*-person game, *n*) strategies. As each contestant is supposed to have complete lists of his own and his opponent's alternative strategies, the completion of a list of outcomes presents no problem. But part of the substance of international politics is to know that one does not know all the alterna-

[13] Herman Kahn and Irwin Mann, *Game Theory*, P-1166, The RAND Corporation, July 30, 1957, p. 5.
[14] See A. L. Burns, "NATO and Nuclear Sharing," in Klaus Knorr, ed., *NATO and American Security*, Princeton, N.J., 1959, p. 153, n. 3.
[15] See Hamblin, "The Modal 'Probably,'" *op.cit.*, and "Surprises, Innovations, and Probabilities," May 1958 (manuscript).

tives. A simple example: in 1945 no one could have been expected to foresee even the possibility that seven years later there would be two Chinas, one of them on the island of Taiwan. This means that if we were to try to interpret international relations as a series of games, in which success in one game is rewarded by right of entry into the next (so that the expected value of Game 1 is derived at least in part from the expected value of Game 2, and so on, but with sufficiently increasing discount on the future to prevent an infinite regress), then we should have to admit that if Game 1 were supposed to end at 1949, no expected value could be found for it, since no one could be sure of so elementary a fact about Game 2 as the number of "contestants" in it by 1952.

Hamblin's calculus of plausibility makes it formally possible to complete the list of an opponent's alternative strategies by allowing some degree of plausibility to the residual alternative—i.e., the possibility that one's opponent will use a strategy that one has not thought of at all.[16] Given symmetry of conditions, one should also include in the list of one's own alternatives the possibility of *creating* a new strategy. If to the latter one also attributes some particular degree of plausibility—i.e., "It is just (*or*, fully) plausible that I shall think up some new strategy"—then the formally exhaustive list of outcomes which one can derive may also be allocated plausibilities by derivation; and amongst the outcomes there will be the conjoined event: that both one's opponent and oneself create and employ new strategies.

It may seem that the last-mentioned type of outcome could not be given a value (even an ordinal value) and therefore that our heterodox version of game theory has lost both its usefulness and its last vestige of resemblance to an orthodox game-theory matrix. But valuation would become impossibly difficult only to the extent that, while the residual outcome (*both* contestants creating new strategies) was highly plausible, all other outcomes were less plausible than that.[17] Otherwise, one might assign, for example, a middling value to the residual outcome, on the ground that neither oneself nor one's opponent has the resources or the talents to pull off a really decisive innovation.

The sort of reformed theory of games here outlined[18] would of course lack many of the properties of the orthodox variety. In particular, one would expect far more of undetermined than of soluble games. I am

[16] See Burns, "International Consequences . . . ," *passim.*
[17] See Hamblin, "Surprises, Innovations, and Probabilities."
[18] See D. L. Brooks, "Choice of Pay-offs for Military Operations of the Future," *Operations Research*, XIII (March-April 1960), pp. 159-68, where a similar *ordinal* procedure is outlined.

not really in desperate earnest about actually applying it. But the notion of a game theory reformed by weakening of postulates may help drive home the point that orthodox game theory cannot be applied to international affairs. On the other hand, we may hope to salvage some of those precise technical terms that have in fact illuminated the international and military scenes for some students,[19] so that, by using them cogently but without the bogus quantitative exactitude of orthodox game theory when artificially applied, we might begin to construct a new, if less ambitious, theoretical structure for the power approach.

III

In "From Balance to Deterrence," after asserting that international conflicts were to be interpreted as "that class of infinite essential n-person non-zero-sum games in which the payoff consists for the most part of staying indefinitely in the game,"[20] I proceeded, by way of several more or less definitional principles, to elaborate a *statics* of the balance of power, and later, of the balance of terror.[21] In the middle and at the end of the article, I tried to develop a *dynamics* out of the statics—i.e., to show how international systems of several sorts changed into other varieties.

To begin from statics seemed the only possible course, since I was trying to develop an international theory after the fashion of economic theory. It also seemed natural to assume that the statics, as prior elements in the theory, would be more cogent, less speculative, than the dynamics.

I now consider the latter assumption a mistake. Because of the above objections to applying game theory, it now seems to me very difficult indeed to construct a useful model for the regular workings of a particular international system: each Power enjoys quite a variety of alternatives, and the sort of considerations which I had thought conclusive for one alternative look less so when one reminds oneself of some of the others.[22] And, turning from theory to history, it would not be easy, working only from a description of the European system after the Peace of Westphalia (1648), to predict its subsequent history until the Peace of Utrecht (1713).

---

[19] See Kahn and Mann, *op.cit.*, pp. 1-2.   [20] *Op.cit.*, p. 495.

[21] *Ibid.*, pp. 509ff. I did the same kind of thing in *Power Politics and the Growing Nuclear Club* (Policy Memorandum No. 20, Center of International Studies, Princeton University, June 8, 1959), which, like "From Balance to Deterrence," takes too little account of the sort of particular constraints and facilitations discussed in the opening sections of the present paper.

[22] Kaplan and I hope that some hints for an improved statics might emerge from Monte Carlo exploitation of our Game of Power.

One can, I think, have a little more confidence in the dynamics. From introspection, I would say that what one does is to review a number of alternative imaginary histories of some system's[23] regular workings, and to find that a surprising proportion of them seem to end in the same kind of *systemic* change. To take a hint from the last section's proposals for a reformed game theory: if, on consideration, the outcomes of a number of alternative imaginary histories appear equiplausible but more plausible than any other alternative imagined, and if in turn a number of them seem to amount to the same general kind of change from one type of international system to another, the hypothesis suggests itself that the system in question, because of its structure, has a tendency to change itself along those lines. The next step should be to reconstruct another imaginary history as nearly equiplausible as can be, but deliberately designed to escape the tendency if possible—i.e., a serious effort to disprove the hypothesis may, if it fails to do so, lend the hypothesis very strong support.

A priori, all this seems highly improbable. If statics offers so many different alternatives, is it likely that many of them will exhibit the same long-run trend? And even if that does happen with abstract and imaginary models of the international system, will the resultant hypotheses have any explanatory or predictive power in the real world?

To approach the latter doubt first: historians of international affairs can usually produce convincing explanatory narratives of particular international systems[24]—one sees at each stage how some particular Power arose, why it was resisted, and so on. But because of the discursive, concrete form of good historical explanation, it is often easy for both historian and reader to lose sight of the longer-run processes, and not to notice that a narrative which explains satisfactorily, step by step, may not have accounted for some more or less surprising trend in the whole process. One of the uses of the type of dynamic theory I have been talking about is to call attention to those longer-run directions in actual historic processes which are *not* in accord with what one would expect from general and theoretic considerations, and which therefore call out for special and particular historical explanation. The theoretical framework, then, helps one assess the *a priori* plausibility, or initial likelihood, of a long-run process.

In returning to the objection that convergence of static possibilities

---

[23] Here I was thinking in the first instance of an abstract model—say, of the balance of power. But it is not impossible to do something like this with a historical instance (see following note).

[24] For an illustration, and another version of the present argument, see Burns, "International Theory and Historical Explanation."

upon a dynamic outcome is improbable, we shall have to go back over the ground covered in some of the earlier sections. I remarked in passing that the conception of a *mixed strategy* is unlikely to have a place in international politics—i.e., statesmen do not usually allow the choice among particular alternatives before them to be selected by a roulette wheel.[25] This means, as we saw, that the criteria of *expected value* are not on the whole what determines their choices. Power-political preferences, in other words, can no doubt be ordered, but not ordered by cardinal numbers. Power-political choices are, more often than not, once-for-all (though it may well be the other way around as far as concerns professional diplomats in a protracted sequence of negotiations). Whereas orthodox game theory thus enforces an actuarial approach to any kind of conflict, our reformed version suggests a different political style: the choosing of an international strategy that seems, of all the alternatives, least apt to be upset by other contestants' abilities to produce surprise innovations. This is not identical with the *minimax* solution of orthodox game theory, because of the difficulty in world politics of evaluating possibilities of creative strategy on either or both sides. In such circumstances—which, to repeat, are those of real life, where it is an important datum that no one can name all the things that *could* happen—the possibilities of disaster, and of falling into unmaneuverable positions or situations of no return, must appear to impose their shape quite forbiddingly upon the contest. (Here we are all in T. C. Schelling's debt for his emphasis on *salience*—when for the best of reasons one knows one can't determine what would be the best to choose, it is usually rational to choose the most clearly marked course. Cf. the Marxist-Leninist objections to "adventurism.") But this is to say that considerations of *dominance* are peculiarly persuasive in international situations.[26] Some examples may help.

It is now a commonplace that the new weapons of the last two decades have incidentally changed the nature of the international system. Similar changes were induced during former eras. To current changes, other undesigned and uncontrollable features (e.g., swift mass communication, economic disparity, and disparate rates of growth) have added their considerable weight. The effects of all such elements make themselves evident despite a great turmoil of luck, misjudgment, and very fine-run conflicts. Orthodox game theory is most applicable to the

[25] But I have heard T. C. Schelling liken certain political "warnings" to a threat of mutual Russian roulette.

[26] In "On the Rationality Postulates Underlying the Theory of Cooperative Games," *Journal of Conflict Resolution*, v (June 1961), pp. 179-96, John C. Harsanyi criticizes Schelling's work along such lines.

type of study in which salience can be set aside as an irrelevant alternative,[27] where the findings of statics are often immediate and definite, while dynamics remains a tendentious and sometimes obscure extension of statics.

The clearest example of world politics' harshly simple anatomy may be the comparative permanence, between wars, of the major Powers—a fact almost wholly explicable by the old-fashioned considerations of comparative national potential. Even in terms of the new weapons, we notice that their effective possession is in fact confined to four of the most powerful industrial states.

We may now state a provisional answer to the first question in this paper. A truly general theory of international relations based upon the power approach and "aspiring to the condition of economics" is not to be had; many of the facts of economic affairs (e.g., system-dominance, to use Kaplan's expression[28]) have no counterpart in world politics. On the other hand, there is plenty of room for theorizing—and even for the construction of theoretical models—about dynamic or systemic change. In particular, theorizing is called for at the point where economic theories of growth (presently, the frontier-breaking part of economics) pass over into factual analyses of national potential. But though in most respects the forces working at this level of international relations are massive and simple, we can have no use for a determinist theory, since real uncertainty, innovation, and the possibility of strategic creativeness are data in the situation itself.

IV

In conclusion, let us see whether anything can be learned about the scope for theorizing in world politics if we turn from the most general aspects of the subject to one particular topic included in it and perhaps peculiar to it—negotiation. We shall consider three approaches to the question, all to some degree theoretical, but one more formally so than the others.

Bargaining theory is for the most part an extension of orthodox game theory. Its broad methodology is the same; its postulates include or are strengthened formulations of those from which game theory was derived. A recent study by J. C. Harsanyi illustrates the method.[29] His purpose in extending by four postulates[30] the original two "weak postu-

[27] *Ibid.*

[28] Morton A. Kaplan, *System and Process in International Politics*, New York, 1957, pp. 17-18.

[29] Harsanyi, *op.cit.*   [30] *Ibid.*, pp. 183-84.

lates of rationality"—*individual utility maximization* and *mutually expected rationality*[31]—is to provide an otherwise unavailable determinate solution to the bargaining problem. I now want to ask whether we can consider as pertinent to international "bargaining" (i.e., to negotiation) Harsanyi's six "strong postulates of rationality." As he has renumbered them, these are (1) *individual utility maximization*; (2) *efficiency*— "*A*. Out of the set of all decision rules consistent with postulates 1, 3, 4, 5, and 6, the players will select a pair (R_1, R_2) of most efficient decision rules. *B*. However, if there is an alternative pair (R_1', R_2') even more efficient than (R_1, R_2), then the players will adopt (R_1', R_2') instead of (R_1, R_2) so long as R_1' and R_2' are consistent with postulates 3, 4, 5, and 6, even if they are *not* consistent with postulate 1"; (3) *acceptance of higher payoffs* (this means that any player will accept from the other better terms than he himself has offered the other); (4) *symmetry* (as between the mathematical forms of the players' decision rules); (5) *restriction of variables*; and (6) *mutually expected rationality*.[32] I shall not here consider the logical properties of the set of postulates as a set,[33] but rather the connotation of one of them— Postulate 5—as that applies to "open" negotiation.

The bargaining theorist restricts his use of the concept "rationality" to situations which are, of necessity, closed. As Harsanyi acutely points out, his Postulate 5 performs just that function—and rightly so, if the bargaining situation to be resolved *is* a closed situation. But, as I argued in the previous section, international situations are not closed in this sense—for, since one may have to allow something for the other party's (and one's own) propensity to create and to innovate, one cannot be sure, at the beginning of a bargaining situation, what are and what are not the "irrelevant variables extraneous to the criteria of rational behavior."[34]

But if international negotiations (in contradistinction to some cases of economic bargaining) are essentially an open process, what is the status of a negotiator's schedule of preferences at the beginning and the end (however we define those *termini*) of a negotiation? As in orthodox game theory, the postulates of orthodox bargaining (e.g.,

---

[31] *Ibid.*, p. 179.   [32] *Ibid.*, pp. 183-84.

[33] Note, however, that Harsanyi's postulates form a partially *self-referring set*: (2A) refers to (1), (3), (4), (5), and (6); (2B) refers to (2A), and to (3), (4), (5), and (6), while permitting an exception to (1). Such sets cannot be guaranteed free from the *paradoxes of self-reference*. Agreed, it may be possible so to restate and reorder Harsanyi's as to remove the self-reference. But intuitively it would seem that the process of reciprocal imputation, which is of the essence of bargaining and strategic situations, somehow has self-reference built in.

[34] *Ibid.*, p. 185.

Harsanyi's Postulates 1, 3, 5, and 6) require that the preference schedules must remain constant, except in the case where a sub-game is
played which includes among its payoffs (i.e., end-points) the acquisi-
tion of power to alter some other person's schedule of preferences. In
other words, bargaining theory presupposes that it can never be rational
during a negotiation to change one's own ordering of preferences (or
to seek to change that of an opponent) in respect of the substance under
negotiation. But I suggest that in negotiation (as distinct from "horse-
trading") there is always recognized to be the possibility of such a
change.[35] I shall now put forward, as a second kind of approach to the
analysis of negotiation, the outline of a negotiating model built upon
this possibility of a change of preferences. It will be in many respects
akin to the "reformed game theory" proposed in the previous section.

The abortive negotiations on disarmament in 1960, for example,
proceeded by the putting forward of *sets of proposals*. These sets are
unlike the offer of a price in a bargaining negotiation, since the
ingredient proposals are *not* indefinitely substitutable units. Each set
is rather a part-picture of a possible world—part of what the logicians
call a "state-description." I shall refer to them as "possible worlds." Each
negotiating party, even before the other(s) has published his (their)
proposals, must have at least two "possible worlds" before him—
the present world, and the world of his first set of proposals. Unless the
latter is not a genuine offer but instead a negotiating feint, it must be
rational for him to prefer the latter to the former. When the other
negotiating party makes public *his* set of proposals, the first party will
have to decide whether or no he prefers the other party's proposals to
the present world. (If the unlikely occurs, and he finds that he actually
prefers the other's to his own proposals, he must then envisage a fourth
possible world—i.e., another set of proposals even more to his liking
than the first proposal of the other party, because the revelation to him
of the fact that the other party's preferences are eminently in line with
his own should suggest to him that in such favorable circumstances he
might do even better for himself.[36]) If he *wholly* prefers the present
world to the other's proposed world, he may reasonably indicate that
the negotiations seem hopeless. But he may be able to derive from the

[35] I owe this idea to an as yet unpublished paper by Lord Lindsay of Birker, American
University, Washington, D.C.

[36] J. C. Harsanyi, in "Bargaining in Ignorance of the Opponent's Utility Function"
(Cowles Foundation Discussion Paper No. 46, New Haven, Conn., Cowles Commission
for Research in Economics, December 11, 1957), concludes from this kind of situation,
among others, that it is always irrational to enter into bargaining when all parties are
ignorant of each other's utility function.

other's proposals a reduced set which, by *leaving out* some particular objectionable item, appears to him as a possible world preferable to the present one. Logically, this possibility implies that a finite number of other possible worlds can be telescoped out of the other's proposals by each negotiator. Of *this* set of derived possible worlds, he may wish to offer to the other party the one most preferred by himself. He may also assume that the other already has, *implicitly*, some orderable preference or another for each item in the derived set.

There will be, however, an alternative way of proceeding open to each negotiator, once the other, by publishing a proposal or by criticizing another's proposal, has given some indication of his preferences: each may try to create a *novel* or partly novel "possible world" in the hope that it will prove more desirable to both (or all) the negotiating parties than does the present one at least. Now since *ex hypothese* the other party has not yet conceived of this possible world, even implicitly, the publishing of it as a proposal must alter his schedule of preferences, either by the simple addition of a new item to the schedule, or also by a subsequent reordering of the original items as well. The model here sketched presupposes that it can be rational to alter one's preferences in the light of new information. The orthodox postulates of rationality (e.g., Harsanyi's Postulate 5) imply that the addition of a wholly new item to an already consistent schedule of preferences must not be allowed to alter the order (or even the cardinal degree of utility) of the items comprising the original set.

I doubt whether this condition can be met in every case, or whether, if it were, we would regard the sort of person who always met it as rational in any ordinary sense. Indeed, we often take as a mark of insanity the kind of inflexible consistency *not* open to drastic amendment by truly novel information. But such a commitment to openness can have awkward implications: while one is in process of reordering one's preferences to allow a proper place to some newly recognized possibility (a process more like art than like logical inference), the chances are that one's schedule will be quite intransitive. That is, we have to buy long-run rationality—"right reason"—at the price of short-run irrationality. I can see no way around this difficulty.

There is a third approach to negotiation recently expounded by Joseph Nogee.[37] I may put rather more into my exposition of it than Nogee would wish to be responsible for. The chief premise is that in some types of negotiation (e.g., for disarmament), agreement is very

[37] See Joseph Nogee, "The Diplomacy of Disarmament," *International Conciliation*, No. 526, January 1960.

nearly the last thing that any party wants to reach. Only less do they all dislike the prospect of appearing to have broken off negotiations, or to have taken up such a recalcitrant position as would "force" the other party to break off negotiations. Therefore a frequently preferred strategy is to offer a set of proposals "calculated to have wide popular appeal" but containing a "joker"—i.e., "at least one feature that the other side could not possibly accept, thus forcing a rejection" of the whole claim.[38]

This kind of negotiation, it is clear, does not approximate either to a bargaining situation, or to the model that I have just sketched. Rather, it resembles an ordinary contest, in which the payoffs are gains and losses of prestige, and the possible strategies are "quasi-proposals," complete with "joker." This kind of contest may well be open to game-theoretical analysis, even of the orthodox variety. It is, however, a game parasitic upon the phenomena of genuine negotiation. Therefore the theory of it, though very likely valid and sufficient in its own universe of discourse, cannot purport to be the one and only Theory of Negotiations (Nogee does not suggest that it is). The model that I have suggested, however, could be developed to include Nogee's suggestion.

Thus, a quasi-proposal is "quasi" only because of the joker that is believed certain to preclude its acceptance. But if we neglect this element of belief (itself a fact inferred from the course of many disarmament negotiations), we have a negotiating situation in which (1) each party offers the other a possible world which he himself prefers to the present one, but which the other does not; (2) each envisages a (common) fourth alternative—a world like the present world, except that in it negotiations have been broken off; and each prefers the present world to that fourth one, but the fourth one to the world first proposed by the other; and (3) each may then try to think out a second set of proposals which, while appearing to the other less preferable than the breaking-off of negotiations, also appears more preferable than the other negotiator's first offer. This variant of the game must, it would seem, be broken off by one party or another, sooner or later. (If, however, there is anything in the later-expounded parts of my model, each party must recognize that there remains the bare possibility of his wanting to accept some quite novel proposal himself.) Indeed, the game described by Nogee could hardly continue if that were not so.

Let us now consider briefly the 1960 disarmament negotiations. At first glance it is clear that all of our three more-or-less rival theories of negotiation will need to be complicated a great deal in order to take care of the fact that while the USSR can design its own proposals and

[38] *Ibid.*, p. 282.

therefore modify them quite freely, Western proposals are themselves the products of negotiation amongst allies, and must therefore be put forward in a much more uncompromising fashion. Further, Soviet proposals are not necessarily addressed to the West as a unitary "negotiator,"[39] and must therefore telescope into a number of alternative outcomes agreeable to the Soviet Union in varying degrees.

The proposals of June 2, 1960, represent the Russians' last major move before their final walk-out. The course of negotiation in the following three weeks fits in only too well with Nogee's hypothesis. Though their new proposals discarded a joker which the West had been indicating as such for some considerable time, it retained another in the form of a timing of conventional disarmament which, as the West maintained, would have jeopardized the security of Europe.

On the other hand, the Soviet representatives seem to have gauged correctly the likelihood that at this time the United States would certainly prefer the breaking-off of negotiations, even at great cost in prestige, above any far-reaching measure of disarmament. The US proposal forestalled by Russia's walk-out also threw away a number of jokers, but retained at least one, the Controlling Principle No. 5: "The treaties shall remain in force indefinitely subject to the inherent right of a party to withdraw and be relieved of obligations thereunder if the provisions of the treaty, including those providing for the timely installation and effective operation of the control system, are not being fulfilled and observed." One striking feature of the last stages of this particular "game" was the close approximation between the two parties' final sets of quasi-proposals.

Nogee's informal "theory of quasi-negotiation" thus receives further support—i.e., the disarmament negotiations of 1960, like their predecessors for many years, can be interpreted as a contest for prestige. If gains and losses of prestige were measurable (in fact, they are not) the negotiating contest would begin to look like a zero-sum game, in which each contestant's objectives were (1) to increase his own prestige before a world-political audience by offering proposals that would look reasonable and conciliatory, and (2) to reduce his opponent's prestige by forcing him to reject such reasonable proposals or to break off negotiations. Even so, however, the contest would not be strictly amenable to orthodox game-theoretical treatment, if only because neither the columns nor the rows of the matrix would be finite in number or definite in quality. These indefinitenesses are irremediable in

---

[39] E.g., the Soviet delegation's conciliatory attitude toward the French in respect to their proposal for control of vehicles used for delivering nuclear weapons.

the real world. Furthermore, by being open to creative innovation the negotiating contest is apt to induce violations of at least one basic postulate of "rationality"—viz., that each contestant's preferences remain transitive.

For the latter reason, if for no other, interpretative insights such as Nogee's cannot be formalized into a rigorous General Theory of Negotiations. I do think, however, that they can be subsumed under still more general interpretations—one of many of those being my scheme of "possible worlds" that rival each other in the process of negotiation. But even that scheme cannot be called a General Theory of Negotiations; it is merely a sketch of an approach more hospitable than is orthodox bargaining theory to the possibilities of novelty and inventiveness, and to the brute fact of real, non-statistical uncertainty in human affairs. Moreover, it resembles a philosophy rather than a science; for it takes cognizance of a second order of rationality, to which we come when revaluing our former preferences in the face of some new possibility to which we cannot remain indifferent. Agreed, only transitive preferences are rational; but closed and impregnable rationality would be less than human.

Our conclusion, then, is that a truly general and rigorous theory of power politics is unobtainable. But piecemeal theoretical insights are possible; and those that we have owe much to hints and suggestions derived from both the rigorous and the informal varieties of game theory and bargaining theory.

Appendix

A BRIEF DESCRIPTION OF THE GAME OF POWER*

The players are "nations" competing around a table for pieces (chips or dice). Each has a board on which are marked the frontiers he shares with every other competitor and also a homeland area. Pieces represent units of resources; or they can be set aside as reserved forces which, when deployed on "frontiers" against other nations, become "sources of firepower." Undeployed resources—i.e., those neither deployed on frontiers nor in the reserve of forces—earn proportionate income, but in proportions that may vary by chance from round to round.

Players take turns to move. A move can be passed; or it can be used to deploy, reserve, or withdraw forces, or to "make war" with forces already deployed. If at war, opposed pieces on a given frontier exchange at a rate

* Extracted from Kaplan, Burns, and Quandt, *op.cit.*, pp. 249-50.

determined by throwing the deployed dice until one side's pieces deployed on that frontier are eliminated. The regular sequence of moves is suspended by warfare, until the initial conflict or battle is finished, and each contestant has had an opportunity to redeploy and to make war. Players know that the game either will be played to a finish or will conclude after a specific number of rounds, with a payoff (in either case) that will depend on the number of pieces then possessed.

"Alliance" consists of two or more nations' reciprocal withdrawing of forces from a common frontier or frontiers. "Pressure" consists of a nation's increasing the forces it deploys against another. Degree of pressure is an increasing function of predominance at specific frontiers because of the Lanchester-type exchange-rate in war.

The object of the game is to have as many pieces as possible at the end of the game. If a player finishes with a smaller total of pieces, deployed and not deployed, than some number decided beforehand by the players, he shall be deemed to have scored zero, and such pieces as he has shall be put into the kitty, which shall then be distributed among those who have at least as many as they started with, in proportion (to the nearest whole number) to the totals they finished with. (A good and theoretically significant game may be obtained by relating the minimum payoff to the number of moves played; e.g., a player gets nothing if he finishes with fewer than the number he started with, plus one for every two rounds played.)

The players shall jointly determine beforehand the time, or the number of rounds, by which the game is to finish. When more than two are playing, the game will be more exciting if it continues for a number of rounds greater than the number of pieces initially in the kitty divided by the number of players. The fewer the players, and the earlier the round in a game, the shorter the time a round will take. A more realistic variant could be obtained by agreeing to play until *either* all but one are eliminated, *or* a unanimous agreement to stop is reached—bribery being permitted if it brings about agreement. Players might pay severally for their initial pieces, and jointly for the initial kitty.

EXPERIMENTAL GAMES
AND BARGAINING THEORY

By T. C. SCHELLING

GAMES have been used in the study of international politics; if they were not so demanding of time and energy, they would probably be used more. A Berlin crisis, or a busy day in the life of the United Nations, lends itself to this procedure. Participants usually represent "countries" and they may be encouraged to play the "role" of the country, acting as they believe the country would act, or they may be encouraged to behave in the game as they believe the country ought to behave in its own interest. The game may be organized for research, the participants being scholars and policy analysts; or it may be organized as training, to give students vicarious experience in the complexities of international politics.

And *complexities* are precisely what the game usually generates. Games organized for the benefit of students are invariably reported as having opened their eyes, in an unprecedented way, to the varieties of choice that can confront nations, to the varieties of interpretation that can be put on a country's behavior, to the great cloak of detail that surrounds even the simplest international crisis, and to the limitations on formal theory as a guide to international conduct in the real world. These complexities motivate, too, the games organized to examine a problem rather than to raise the sophistication of a student; part of the rationale of game organization is that no straightforward analytical process will generate a "solution" to the problem, predict an outcome, or produce a comprehensive map of the alternative routes, processes, and outcomes that are latent in the problem.

Games do generate these complexities and, by most reports, do it in a fruitful and stimulating way. If an understanding of international politics requires familiarity with both theory and practice, busy games seem to provide an important touch of practice. But though they may be peculiarly suitable for bringing out the rich complexity of international processes, games are not limited in principle to that end of the scale. Frequent references to chess remind us that more austere games may be useful in the study of bilateral or multilateral conflict. The more abstract and stylized game can certainly not pretend to provide vicarious experience in the practice of international politics, but it may have a role in the theory.

A game may be useful in revealing the *structure* of conflicts rather than the details. A game may be useful in the articulation of a theoretical model if it is designed for that purpose, just as games richer in detail may help to fit theory into its institutional context. The purposes do not necessarily compete with each other, nor do the games. It is worthwhile to examine international politics in all its complexity, and worthwhile to examine the underlying structure by the use of an abstract model. Similarly, games may be helpful at either end of the spectrum, or in between.

The methodology will be different, though. One kind of game may be used to elucidate a theoretical model, the other to show its limitations. One may be used to bring out the order, the rationality, and the coherence of the international structure; the other to illustrate the disorder, the irrationality, and the incoherence. Depending on the purpose and what is to be emphasized, one not only designs the game differently but defines the purpose differently. One can question whether an experimental game serves an essential purpose, or even any useful purpose, toward the end of the spectrum that can be encompassed by a theoretical model. Toward the other end, where theory meets its limitations, some need to generate a "sample" of vicarious experience may seem to be compelling; but the haphazard quality of game playing, while helpful in supplementing theoretical models, might seem to be precisely what one wants to eliminate in examining the theory itself.

The question is a sound one, but it does admit an answer. Even the most austere and economical theoretical model is unlikely to be fully determinate. It will be too complex to yield to any straightforward comprehensive analysis. It is not usually a mathematical problem to be "solved," but a model that generates a variety of potential behavior even within the framework of a few variables and constraints. Furthermore, among the processes that it leaves indeterminate will be some that inherently involve the interaction of two or more decision centers.

For this reason there is likely to be, even within the simplified model, some scope for "free activity," for bargaining, for the reaching of understandings and misunderstandings, for accommodation and co-operation, and for conjectures about each other's decision processes, value systems, and information. The theoretical model is thus usually not a comprehensive specification of how the participants behave, but rather a specification of the framework within which they pursue certain objectives according to certain criteria. What the model leads to in terms of *behavior* of the participants is usually beyond the reach of straight-forward analysis.

Even if it is not, the game itself may be a fruitful way of developing a working acquaintance with a theoretical structure. Just designing the game, checking it for internal consistency and for whether it contains the essentials of the desired theoretical model, can be a useful exercise and sometimes a check on the consistency of the concepts in the model. The game furthermore provides an extensive definition of the terms of the theory, and may facilitate communication and comparison. One can point to phenomena that the game generates, and not be limited to abstract characterizations of what he has in mind.

But the game can go one step farther. A theoretical model often has the characteristic that it is not formally or mathematically determinate of behavior even for fully rational participants who understand the game. The reason is that, among the phenomena of international politics that a theory wants to elucidate, are the processes of understanding and misunderstanding. The theory may therefore want to leave scope for misunderstandings, as well as understandings; and a game designed to correspond to the theory will want to provide for behavior that can lead to understandings and misunderstandings. And there is no straight-forward way, no formal analytical way, for ordinary "rational" analysis to anticipate the outcome. The reason is simple: it takes two to make a misunderstanding.

Consider an example. A theoretical model permits certain kinds of communication; correspondingly, a theoretically oriented game permits the transmittal of messages. How can we discover the various ways in which a message may be misinterpreted? Keep in mind that the mis-interpretations that the sender of a message can perceive and anticipate, he can guard against; the ones that matter most are those he cannot perceive in advance. The question then becomes, how do we identify the possible interpretations of a message that did not occur to the person who sent it? Putting it more crudely, and more generally, how can an analyst draw up a list of the things that would never occur to him? If the essence of the game is that there are two or more separate partici-pants, two or more centers of consciousness and of decision, we can generate understandings and misunderstandings. Thus the "game" formulation of the theory is a meaningful one; it can contain some-thing essential to the theory. And to study it in relation to the theory— in a sufficiently abstract model to permit theoretical handling, and the isolation of critical variables—an austere, abstract, stylized, theoretical game may have a use.

I. A Game for the Study of Theory

This paper is about such a game, in a research project just being initiated. It is an experimental study of the bargaining process involved in limited war and other conflicts, a process in which bargaining is by maneuver as much as by words, in which communication is poor, legal enforcement is unavailable, and the participants make irreversible moves while they bargain, are uncertain about each other's values, and have some power to inflict gratuitous damage on each other. The research will utilize variants of an experimental game.

The game in its present form bears no particular resemblance to war. It does use a map, but so do a lot of children's games. It may remind one of the game that goes under the name of "Salvo" or "Battleship," in which each player places his ships on a set of squares and takes turns firing at the other's ships whose whereabouts he can learn only when the other reports a hit. But there is a difference between the game proposed here and the familiar two-person parlor games.

The difference is that two-person parlor games are always "zero-sum" games—games of pure conflict in which one's gain is the other's loss. Mutual gain and mutual loss are out of the question; and bargains, threats, and co-operation—even grudging co-operation—cannot occur if both players understand the game and play to win. In the game proposed here that is not so. Some outcomes are better for both players than others and the player is to be motivated to get the highest *absolute* score for himself, not to impose a low score on an opponent, and *not* to concern himself with his *relative* score.

The fundamental idea is that war—whether a "fighting" war or a process of strategic maneuver—is not a zero-sum game. It requires at least some co-operation or accommodation between the two sides. It is a "bargaining situation," in which the conflict and the interdependence are inseparable. While secrecy may play a role, it is usually necessary to reveal preferences to reach efficient trades and compromises, to make threats credible, and to demonstrate inability to comply with proposals and threats. It is important to impress on the opponent (partner) some truth about one's own mode of behavior. Communicating one's intentions and what one expects of the other is important to successful play, and is necessarily a preoccupation of the players. The players are both partners and adversaries, as concerned to avoid severe mutual damage as to gain at the expense of each other.

This kind of situation does not arise in the traditional parlor games.[1]

---

[1] The reason probably is that non-zero-sum games are no fun unless actual rewards are provided—i.e., unless the partners (competitors, rivals) can jointly beat the "house."

This is why a game like chess has only a limited relevance as a "war game." If one wants to study an actual parlor-type game—an abstract, formalized game—to get insight into the strategy of limited war or the strategy of threats, reprisals, deterrence, and bargaining, there are no ready-made games available. It has been necessary to invent a game.

The game used in this research has been designed to require co-ordination of strategies and to make co-ordination difficult. It has been designed to make it difficult to identify an obviously "fair" or symmetrical outcome. It has been designed to require no significant technical skill that has to be acquired through repeated plays. The skill involved is intended to be more akin to bargaining skills, strategic ingenuity, skill in coercing an opponent, rather than skill in the mechanics of the game itself.

The game differs from traditional war games in two respects. First, virtually all war games have been either explicitly or implicitly "zero-sum" games. They have involved no scope for collaboration between the adversaries; any motivation toward "winning" has been toward winning over the opponent, outdoing the opponent, winning relative to the opponent (except to the extent that, as in tennis, one may be interested in displaying style as well as in winning). Second, this game is not designed to look much like war; it is designed for minimum technical complexity. It is designed for research rather than training. (It does appear, though, to have some important value in the communication of ideas.) It is designed to have a simple enough structure, and few enough variables and parameters, to permit measurement, classification, manipulation, and analysis, in accordance with a theoretical framework. It is also designed to be economical in the interest of repeated plays, and to be capable of reproduction without access to unique materials.

It should be emphasized that in this game players are supposed to play to win. While in some variants there will be a scenario and other details suggestive of some "real" situation, it is not intended that subjects play any such version of it in a "role-playing" sense. The players are not to imitate decision-makers in some real situation that the game is trying to mimic. For the purpose of this game, in contrast to certain very different-looking and less stylized war games and, especially, "political games," one is playing to maximize his score and not for any other purpose.[2]

This poses a problem. Players have to interest themselves in their absolute scores, not just in how well they beat an adversary. While

[2] See note 7 at the end of the paper for references to other experimental games.

competitive spirit is precisely what one wants in studying a zero-sum game, like most parlor games, and can usually be relied on to make people value precisely the kind of score they are supposed to be maximizing, it cannot be relied on to make people interested in their *absolute* scores in a two-person game. Money rewards are therefore used, both to appeal to profit motives and to dramatize the payoff structure of the game and to attach symbolic value to it.

II. A Description of the Game and Its State of Development

A game has been developed. It involves a board and a set of chips or counters. The board is in the form of a map; the map in present use is simply an outline map of the United States, the 48 states being the units into which the map is divided.[3] Each of the two players has a supply of chips; at each play they place chips on the states and remove them, subject to certain limitations. When the game is over, the players' scores depend on the states they possess and the chips they have lost, and any other "damage" they have suffered. The states have different values; their values, furthermore, differ for the two players, and while each player knows the values to himself of the different states, he has little knowledge of his opponent's value system. Each does have full knowledge of the other's past moves. Chips are lost by the process of "fighting" for states; other damage can be suffered because each player has, among the moves available to him, one that is purely punitive in nature. The game is terminated when both players agree to stop. No communication is allowed between the two players.

The game is essentially one of "bargaining by maneuver," of signaling intentions, proposals, threats, refusals, and information about one's preferences through maneuver rather than through words.

The game is completely defined by a set of instructions and the map. The most recent version of the instructions is appended to this paper.

The game in its present form usually runs for a few hours. It takes about an hour of preliminary instruction to get a player conversant with the technical features of the game and to emphasize the idea that he is playing for an absolute and not a relative score; early in the game a player becomes aware of the possibility of signaling and its importance, and begins the process of working out a "language" with his opponent (partner) and of developing a few notions about strategy. For most of those who have played it, the game has proved to be engrossing and stimulating.

With moderate adaptation of the rules it can be made a three-person

---

[3] A 1958 map of 48 states is used.

or four-person game. With no change in the rules, it can be played by teams rather than persons.

The physical requirements of the game are modest—a good-sized table to hold two maps measuring about 20 x 30 inches, with a barrier between to keep the players from seeing each other's maps and each other's faces, together with a monitor who can see both maps at the same time. Alternatively the players can be on opposite sides of a room; without too much nuisance they could communicate by telephone. For team play, where privacy of conversation would be required, two rooms or booths would be needed, but telephone communication (two monitors with an open telephone line between) would permit some flexibility in location.

There are several features of the game that can be varied. The *values of the states* can be varied, particularly the correlation between the two players' value systems, i.e., the degree of potential conflict in the exercise of their preferences. The *information* that each has about the other's value system can be varied. The *communication system* can be varied, through the addition of symmetrical or asymmetrical arrangements for direct communication, either free or restricted to certain types of statements or proposals. The *map* can be varied, both to change the geometrical configuration and to change the political and other connotations that may influence the bargaining process. A *scenario* can be provided that may have an important power of suggestion; players may or may not be given information about the outcome of previous plays of the same game—knowledge which may constrain or facilitate the bargaining process. The *number of counters* can be varied; in particular, the number of chips available to the two players could differ. The *tempo* of the game can be affected by varying the number of chips played at each turn, and by requiring that the area claimed by a player's chips be enlarged only incrementally. The *role of reprisal* or *punitive action* can be varied, either in the costs of inflicting damage or by limits on the number or frequency of punitive moves. And new moves and new resources can be added to the game.

Further refinement of the game will take mainly the form of adapting these structural features and parameters. Variation will also, however, be part of the experiment itself, to study the effect on the mode of play and on the outcome, and on the players' interaction with each other.

Further development of the game will require a compromise, between (a) enriching the game's complexity, the variety of moves available, the suggestive details, the communication structure, etc., to generate interesting phenomena, and (b) keeping the game simple enough to be not only economical but susceptible of analysis in relation to a theoretical model.

III. Theory and Methodology

The basic notion underlying the use of an experimental game in an empirical study of the "bargaining process" is that formal theory—game theory, for example—is inadequate by itself, and necessarily so, in the study of bargaining games. Games of this sort necessarily contain an element of indeterminacy; the constraints imposed by the quantitative structure of the game are insufficient to determine a solution, even for "rational," internally consistent, strategies of behavior by the participants. In any game of this sort there is some need for the concerting of action, for reaching understandings, for communicating and inferring intentions, for arriving at consistent expectations of each other, and for the development of norms, traditions, or other constraints analogous to the limits in limited war. How the participants can interact to teach a shared expectation, how they can invent means of signaling their intentions, what kinds of rules and traditions they can perceive and recognize jointly cannot be arrived at by *a priori* reasoning, even by ideally rational players. There is an essential element of empirical study involved.

This is not, it should be emphasized, simply a matter of players' behaving in practice in a manner different from what a theory of rational behavior would suggest. Rather it is that players are capable, at least in some circumstances, of doing a good deal better than a purely formal theory of rational behavior could account for. How it is that they can do better is a question that, though amenable to theoretical analysis, ultimately requires empirical confirmation.

The possible relevance of experimental work seems demonstrated by some experiments with questionnaires that can be considered "one-move" non-zero-sum games.[4] The research initiated with this new game can be viewed as an attempt to do for bargaining extended over time what the questionnaire did for one-shot games.

An important question is whether the conclusions reached, or the phenomena observed, can be generalized to cover actual conflict situations, actual bargaining processes, of which limited war may be the most vivid example. Here it should first be said that a game of this sort is not intended to reproduce all the significant characteristics of a real conflict; it is not intended to epitomize real, live conflict or to constitute a "well-balanced" model in which all elements receive proper emphasis.

---

[4] Reported in T. C. Schelling, "Bargaining, Communication, and Limited War," *Journal of Conflict Resolution*, 1 (March 1957), pp. 19-36; reprinted in Schelling, *The Strategy of Conflict*, Cambridge, Mass., 1960.

It is intended rather to single out aspects of the problem that provide a coherent subject for analysis and are susceptible of experimental simulation in the laboratory. A game of this sort focuses mainly on the perceptual and cognitive processes of the participants, rather than on emotional behavior or individual value systems. (So far as possible the player's value system is provided him by the game itself; and while emotional involvement is undoubtedly present, even if we try to keep it out, it is on a different scale from the duress, tension, preoccupation, and panic that might occur in a real, live conflict situation.)

The game furthermore is limited in its relevance to the behavior of individuals (or perhaps very small groups) and to those aspects of organizational behavior, bureaucratic behavior, group political behavior, and other collective decision processes that most depend on, or are limited by, the capabilities and characteristics of individuals, or at least in which the capabilities and characteristics of individual decision processes can be isolated in analysis.

What makes a game of this sort, limited as it is, attractive as a means of coming to grips with some aspects of limited war and similar conflicts is that we are poor in alternative ways of studying the phenomena empirically. We are generally limited to intensive studies of a few particular cases. The knowledge we can get from experimenting with a game may not be comprehensive or terribly reliable, but, compared with what we have or can get in any other way, it looks good.

There is another reason for supposing that even a quite artificial game can produce results of real significance. A great many propositions about limited war, industrial disputes, etc., are phrased in such general terms, and based on reasoning or evidence of such simplicity and generality, that they would have to apply to a situation as simple and artificial as the kind of game described above. In other words, even if we are skeptical about the propositions that can be proved by the evidence of a game of this sort, a good deal of the existing theory, or lore, is susceptible of being disproved.

Consider, for example, propositions about the advantage or disadvantage of communication between adversaries in limited war, or propositions about the tendency for certain bargaining processes to display outcomes that have some property of "equality" or "symmetry." Many of these seem to be based on very general observation and introspection, expressed in phrases like "It stands to reason that . . ." or "No one would ever. . . ." A game of the sort described *can* demonstrate, with respect to a proposition, that its truth does not follow from any simple universal observation or intuitive hunch. The proposition may, of course, still be true; but if the reasoning and the evidence can be discredited, it must be abandoned unless new grounds for it can be found.

Take specifically the following question: if in a game like the one described here, which involves a great deal of ignorance on the part of each player about the other's value system, or even in one that involves (as the specific form of the game described above does not) ignorance about some of the moves available to the other player or the moves he has already made, a proposal is made to improve the players' knowledge about each other's value systems, moves available, positions reached, etc., what do we anticipate about the advantages and disadvantages to the two players? A proposition frequently expressed is "It stands to reason that the player to whom we give the greater knowledge about his opponent receives the advantage." Of course, in a game of this sort, both players can be advantaged or disadvantaged simultaneously, it being a non-zero-sum game; this pointed out, the proposition may be rephrased to the effect that the greater gain, or the relative advantage, is bound to go (other things being equal) to the one who gets the greater information. This proposition is based on faulty reasoning, but it seems compatible with intelligence and sophistication. If it is false, as is conjectured here, its falsity can be demonstrated by a game as simple and artificial as the one proposed. Those who hold to a proposition of this sort are likely to hold it on the basis of very general considerations—considerations so general as to be contradicted if the proposition proved to be strikingly false in regard to a simple little game that, simple as it is, is as complex as the theoretical model that was implicitly in mind when the proposition was voiced.

This example illustrates another aspect of the methodology involved in a game like this one. When a game simple enough to be analyzable produces a result contrary to expectation, it is likely to produce it for reasons that become apparent once the phenomenon is observed, particularly when it is observed in relation to the structure of the game or to alternative structures of the game. Thus a conclusion that is reached is not necessarily supported solely by statistical evidence from repeated play of a game whose relevance to the world is in question. Rather the conclusion, once it has been suggested by the experimental results, can often be rationalized in theoretical terms. The game is thus a tangible representation of a theoretical model, a model whose moving parts can be better understood if they can be articulated experimentally.

This point can be expressed in another way. Experimental games can be used to discover, and demonstrate, important *possibilities* that might have been missed without it. The significance and relevance of these possibilities may still depend on reasoning and on evidence obtained elsewhere; but the existence of the possibilities, and some notion of how they relate to the structure of the game, can be discovered by the artificial game. This would, for example, be true of the proposition that the advantage may well go not to the player who enjoys the increased knowledge and information but to the other player, and that it may even be an absolute disadvantage to one of the players to obtain new information if he cannot conceal the fact that he has it. (This point about information is not being emphasized here as the main one to be investigated, but as a readily comprehensible illustration of an hypothesis to which the experimental game would be relevant.)

On the whole, it is expected that conclusions reached by this kind of experimental research will not depend much on refined statistical analysis. We shall be looking for rather striking results. Since the intent is to relate the observed phenomena to some theory that closely parallels the game itself, as well as to demonstrate the potential significance (rather than the actual significance in a particular context) of the variables to be manipulated and observed, a main effort will be to learn how to manipulate the parameters and structural features of the game in order deliberately to generate particular results and phenomena. The intent is not, therefore, to pursue to the end a prearranged schedule for varying the parameters, and subsequently to analyze the results statistically. Instead there will be fairly continual feedback between the results observed and the further design of the experiments. The results of the questionnaire experiments referred to above illustrate, on a simple scale, this methodology.

There is a secondary purpose of this experimentation that relates to the development of theory. It has to do with the value of the sheer construction of the game and analysis of its structure and manipulation of its parameters. To build a game of this sort, and especially to build into the game particular features that one wishes to represent, requires that one define his concepts operationally. A game of this sort imposes discipline on theoretical model-building; it can be a test of whether concepts and propositions are meaningful, and a means of demonstrating so when they are. In the actual construction of the game, and in discussion of the game's features with persons who have played it or observed it played, it has frequently been the case that certain plausible concepts had to be abandoned when an effort to identify them (or to incorporate them) in the game revealed that they were meaningless or innocuous, or that they rested on inessential distinctions.

Closely related is the use of the game as a means of theoretical communication. If one wishes to define carefully, and to illustrate, a particular distinction or proposition about the strategy of conflict, the game often provides a tangible and unambiguous representation of the concepts involved—a way of pointing to what one means and avoiding reliance on ambiguous verbal description.

Two examples may help. One has to do with the notion of equality or symmetry in the outcome of a game. As mentioned above, the policy-oriented literature on limited war frequently uses words like "equality" and "symmetry" and "reciprocity" in describing the kinds of rules and limits or outcomes that may be acceptable to the parties involved; the theoretical literature on bargaining and game strategy does the same.[5] And with an exceedingly unambiguous model or "game" in mind, with perfect information about value systems and the moves and strategies available, concepts like "equality" and "symmetry" can at least be meaningfully defined. Suppose, however, that one enriches the game, even to the limited extent of the game described—or suppose that one goes farther still to add contextual detail which, though inessential to the logical structure of the game, contains some power of suggestion, or moral, casuistic, or legalistic significance, or which entails some precedent, tradition, or analogy. Then such concepts as "equality" and "symmetry"—in the strategies employed, in the rules and constraints that the players generate and observe, or in the outcome of the game—are embarrassed by the sheer lack of an obviously meaningful definition. The empirical contents of the original proposition therefore disappear. One cannot define "equality" in terms of the acceptability of an outcome or a rule to both players, and simultaneously preserve any empirical content in the proposition that rules or outcomes will be acceptable only if they meet the condition of "equality."

The second example concerns the structure of conflict that is built into the game. It is interesting to argue whether the game described, or a variant of it, captures the spirit of the conflict involved in war, race relations, industrial disputes, interagency disputes, bureaucratic rivalry, or competition in traffic for the right of way. If one doubts whether a particular game embodies the essentials of a particular dispute, it is

[5] Closely related is the idea that both sides must accept the "same" limits—a proposition that not only may prove false in actual play but can prove meaningless within the structure of the game unless the game itself is designed with a symmetrical move structure and scoring system. See, for example, James E. King, Jr., "Nuclear Plenty and Limited War," *Foreign Affairs*, xxxv (January 1957), pp. 238-56. For the symmetry notion in bargaining theory, see, for example, John Harsanyi, "Approaches to the Bargaining Problem Before and After the Theory of Games," *Econometrica*, xxiv (April 1956), pp. 144-57; R. Duncan Luce and Howard Raiffa, *Games and Decisions*, New York, 1957, pp. 114ff.; and T. C. Schelling, "For the Abandonment of Symmetry in Game Theory," *Review of Economics and Statistics*, xli (August 1959), pp. 213-44.

interesting to see whether the game can be made to represent that dispute by varying the scoring system, the information structure, or the timing and nature of the moves; if it cannot, it is interesting then to see whether radical changes in, or additions to, the moves and scoring system can reproduce the essentials of the dispute in question. In the trial plays held so far, it has frequently been the case that during *post mortem* a player denied the analogy between the game and the kind of conflict involved in international disputes; a revision in the scoring system was attempted to reflect someone's notion of what was essential to an international dispute. It is interesting that in many cases the revision that would satisfy a particular analyst could be demonstrated to be a non-essential change—a change only in certain parameters, and not in the structure of the game. In other cases it became clear that certain types of dispute were inherently incapable of being represented. But clarity and agreement could be reached much more quickly on these theoretical points by working with the actual game than if no tangible model had been present.

IV. Research to Be Undertaken

A general discussion of questions worth investigating with a game of this sort has already been published.[6] The present section will repeat some of those ideas, supplement them, and relate them to research procedure.

There are three main elements to describe. The first is the game, the rules and constraints under which it will be played, the background against which it will be played, the particular players who will play it, and so forth. The second concerns what will be observed—the outcome of the game, the behavior of the players, the records kept by the players, particular situations that develop in the course of play, and so forth. Third are the questions or hypotheses that guide the inquiry, toward which the manipulation of the game and the observation of game phenomena are oriented. To illustrate: one can have the game played with different rules of communication; one can observe the outcome in terms, say, of the two players' scores; and one can generalize about the value of communication or its absence to the participants in a bargaining process.

(1) THE GAME TO BE PLAYED

Under the first heading—the way the game will be played or used— the following arrangements are contemplated. First, a standard version

[6] Cf. Schelling, *The Strategy of Conflict*, pp. 259-63.

of the game will be used with a large number of players to study the relation of outcomes to modes of play, of outcomes to the players' interpretations of their own and each other's modes of play, and whether there tends to be continuity or discontinuity in the frequency distribution of outcomes. For this purpose, of course, a theoretical framework for the classification and analysis of outcomes, strategies or modes of play, and players' interpretations must be developed. This can be done only in the course of the project itself, since it requires actual play.

Second, certain features or parameters of the game will be varied. The communication structure has already been mentioned; the information structure (information of each player about the other's value system, etc.) will be varied; the suggestive details of the game will be varied— the scenario, the actual map, the precedents that can be created and brought to bear, the language describing the game and its purpose, hints about symmetry, hints about signaling, etc.; the quantitative features of the game will be varied—the extent of potential conflict generated by the scoring system, the potency of the "reprisal" moves available, the ratio of resources available to the two sides, etc.

Third, the arrangement of plays of the game will include schedules of repeated play within self-contained groups, play between members of different groups that have already experienced extended intra-group play, play that pairs experienced with experienced players, inexperienced with inexperienced, and experienced with inexperienced; play that involves teams; play that is under the influence of a "mediator" who can make certain kinds of proposals to the players; play with three or more players in which coalition behavior becomes possible; and possibly some play with the strategy prescribed for one of the players.

(2) PHENOMENA TO BE OBSERVED

A meaningful scheme for recording the outcomes of games must be devised. For a standard version of the game, this can be done in terms of individual net scores and gross scores (gross scores showing gross gains and gross losses). For comparing the outcomes of different variants of the game, a means has to be devised to "normalize" the scores; this is not an easy matter because there is no straightforward way, for example, of measuring what a player has got relative to what he should have been expected to get in the course of play. (Since one purpose of varying the game itself is to discover what difference doing so makes in the outcome, we cannot rely on *a priori* expectations about "reasonable" scores relative to which the actual scores might be normalized.)

A scheme for classifying the players' interpretations of what they are about also has to be set up initially in connection with actual play—that is, to some extent by trial and error. It must furthermore recognize that the players' perception of the game, and their mode of play, can undoubtedly be affected by the instructions they are given, the questionnaires they are asked to maintain, and the notes they are asked to take on their own strategies or on their partners' play. (How quickly a player becomes alert to the possibilities of signaling in the game is undoubtedly affected by whether he has been instructed to look for signals and to record his own. His actual perception of signals and choice of methods of signaling will likely be affected if particular types of signals that he is to look for are specified in the instructions.) In general, the player's self-consciousness is likely to be stimulated by any explicit analytical framework in which he is asked to record his intentions at each move, the intentions he imputes to his partner, and the understandings he thinks the two of them have reached. Nevertheless records of this sort will be an essential part of the research, since an important purpose is to study the development of understandings and misunderstandings, the process of inventing language for communicating proposals, the identification of critical "turning points" in the course of a game, the relation of each player's expectations to the suggestive details built into the game, the correctness of players' conjectures about missing information, and each player's basic conception of strategy, such as the claims he insists on and the risks he is willing to take. How many of these attributes of the course of the game, as perceived by a player, can be defined operationally and put into a log or questionnaire without disrupting the game too much remains to be seen; it also remains to be seen by trial and error which among these records produce data that promise to be interesting.

The analytical categories for observing and recording modes of play will also have to be worked out in actual observation of play. "Co-operative" vs. "unco-operative," "bold" vs. "cautious," "aggressive" vs. "fair and reasonable," "self-oriented" vs. "partner-oriented," and other distinctions may or may not prove useful in practice and are undoubtedly inadequate. It remains to be seen, too, whether a player, his partner, and the observer share similar perceptions about the mode of play, and the intentions behind it. The alertness of a player to his partner's proposals, his reliance on collaborating in search of a language, his interest in exploring his opponent's value system, his conception of the proper use of stubbornness or punishment, his refusal to communicate, or his pretense at not understanding his partner, as well as various more "topological" aspects of the moves he makes, may prove to be meaningful categories for analysis.

(3) LINES OF INQUIRY

A particular phenomenon to be investigated is the development of language, rules, and traditions in an inbred group of players. Repeated two-person play on a random or round-robin basis among, say, four to six players should provide an interesting opportunity for studying the invention of language through the medium of moves of the game, and the development of rules and limits of conflict that are governed by sheer force of tradition and expectation. The extent to which these processes can be retarded or stimulated by adding suggestive materials to the game; how the invention of signals interacts with any actual overt communication that is permitted; how rapidly signals or rules are converged on in the course of repeated play; the correlation among the signals and rules that develop in different inbred groups; and the question of what happens when pairs are drawn from two different inbred groups—all these will be part of the study. (Here it will be particularly difficult to get players to express themselves in response to interviews and questionnaires without contaminating the process itself.)

A specific feature of the game to be investigated is the determinants of "instability." By "instability" is meant here the tendency of a game to generate mutually destructive behavior and low scores. The trial plays of the present variant suggest that it may be difficult, at least for certain kinds of players, to get them out of a cautious and co-operative frame of mind and to create something analogous to "war" or observable conflict. Experiment suggests that more conflict can be generated by rearranging the values of states on the map. It seems worth conjecturing that the "reprisal" move contained within the game, or a change in the moves that gives a strong advantage to the player who breaks an agreement (engages in "surprise attack," for example), may create instability. There is also evidence that the tempo of the game, as measured by the number of moves that can be made at each turn, or the pace at which pieces can be advanced over the board, affects stability. And there is reason to conjecture (plus a bit of suggestive evidence from the trial plays) that the distribution of outcomes may be quite discontinuous with respect to continuous variation of certain parameters—i.e., that a strikingly bimodal distribution of scores (mainly due to the degree of "destruction" of value) occurs with respect to variation in one of these features.

There is no fixed schedule of plays and variations to be pursued. There is rather an array of important and fascinating questions that the game may help to pursue or may not. As indicated earlier, the general intention is to identify the most striking results, to pursue those questions to which the most interesting answers seem to be emerging, and to manipulate the game to generate interesting phenomena, particularly those that contradict offhand expectation. The initial experimentation will therefore have to be exploratory. In any case, a good deal of trial and error will be involved in working out the analytical framework. In other words, the object is not to test a set of available hypotheses, so much as to generate hypotheses through exploratory experimentation, to manipulate the game and its environment in an effort to bring the suggested hypotheses into clearer relief, and to rationalize the results in terms of a theoretical model that can be identified within the structure of the game.[7]

[7] A recent, fairly comprehensive description and discussion of less formalized "political games" that involve a good deal of free activity is in Herbert Goldhamer and Hans Speier, "Some Observations on Political Gaming," *World Politics*, xii (October 1959), pp. 71-83. A much more tightly formalized game structure has been used by Harold Guetzkow (and described in papers presented to conferences at Northwestern University in April 1959 and West Point in June 1959). An extensive history of war gaming, especially in the nineteenth century and up to World War II (but with some discussion of more recent games), is in John P. Young, *A Survey of Historical Developments in War Games*, Washington, D.C., Operations Research Office, Johns Hopkins University, March 1959; another rather comprehensive discussion is in Clayton J. Thomas and Walter L. Deemer, "The Role of Operational Gaming in Operations Research," *Operations Research*, v (February 1957), pp. 1-27.

A discussion of what war gaming can and cannot do is in Robert D. Specht, *War Games*, The RAND Corporation, Paper P-1041, 1957. For a discussion of whether experimental games have, in principle, research validity in the sense of producing empirical evidence, see Herman Kahn and Irwin Mann, *War Gaming*, The RAND Corporation, Paper P-1167. (The present proposal, and the questionnaire experiments reported in the earlier article, are at variance with the view expressed by Kahn and Mann.)

Some formalized one-move and two-move games, in some cases iterated through a series of plays, are reported in Morton Deutsch, "Trust and Suspicion," *Journal of Conflict Resolution*, ii (December 1958), pp. 265-79; in Merrill M. Flood, "Some Experimental Games," *Management Science*, v (October 1958), pp. 5-26; in Bernhardt Lieberman, "Human Behavior in a Strictly Determined 3 x 3 Matrix Game," *Behavioral Science*, v (October 1960), pp. 317-22; in J. Sayer Minas, Alvin Scodel, Philburn Ratoosh, and Milton Lipetz, "Some Descriptive Aspects of Two-Person Non-Zero-Sum Games," *Journal of Conflict Resolution*, iii (June 1959), pp. 114-19; and in Richard H. Willis and Myron L. Joseph, "Bargaining Behavior," *ibid.*, pp. 102-13.

Business games, which have come into vogue as training devices and as research tools, are usually nearer (in formalization) to the present game than the political games described by Goldhamer and Speier, are a degree more formal than the Guetzkow games, and are more like the older, highly stylized war games of the nineteenth century than like the war gaming presently practiced. For a buying-and-selling game that was designed for and extensively used in research, see Sidney Siegel and Lawrence E. Fouraker, *Bargaining and Group Decision Making*, New York, 1960.

The game that comes closest in spirit to the one described in the present paper is probably the "balance of power" game described in Morton A. Kaplan, Arthur Lee

Appendix

INSTRUCTIONS FOR THE GAME

Taking part in this study presents you with the opportunity of earning from a minimum of three dollars to a maximum of seven to ten dollars. This game is not like chess, checkers, or monopoly, where what one player gains his opponent loses. In this game it is often the case that certain outcomes will be better for *both players* than other outcomes. Some manner of play may maximize the amount each player can earn. But, at the same time, in the game there will probably be values (states worth money) which both you and the other player will want. Thus, the situation is one in which there is some element of conflict; but also some element of "common interest" or "common gain" is present. *The purpose of playing the game is not to defeat the other player but to earn as much money as possible.*

The game is not necessarily "fair" in the sense that if the players arrive at what appears to be an equal division of the states, they will each earn an equal amount of money. The number of colored states may be quite different for each player, and the arrangement of the colored states on their maps may tend to produce unequal earnings. It is also possible that an apparently unequal division of the states may yield earnings that are approximately equal.

The game involves a map, a set of chips, a scoring system, and a set of rules about moves. The players move in turn: at each turn a player can place a number of chips on the map and remove a number. At the end of the game a player's earnings depend on the configuration of his chips on the map, and on the "losses" he has suffered in the course of play.

The Map

The map is an ordinary outline map of the 48 states of the continental United States. The 48 states are the units into which the map is divided.

Player's Earnings

A player's earnings depend on the values of the states he possesses at the end of the game, plus the chips he possesses, minus the "damage" done to him.

State Values and Their Possession: The Integral Area

The values of many of the states differ for the two players. Each player knows the values of all the states to himself but not their values to the other player.

Each player has a number of colored states (red or blue) which have a

---

Burns, and Richard E. Quandt, "Theoretical Analysis of the 'Balance of Power,'" *Behavioral Science*, v (July 1960), pp. 240-52. While it is oriented toward different bargaining phenomena than the present game, its rationale and methodology are much the same, especially in the authors' interest in using it both as a "game" and as a "theoretical model."

premium value; they are worth 50¢. The remaining states are white and are worth 5¢ each. These values are what the states are worth to the players if he *possesses* them at the end of the game.

The colored states are chosen by a random process and so there is no way of determining, at the very beginning of the game, the colored states of the other player. It is possible that one or more states may be colored red *and* blue.

The play of the game uses two maps separated by a barrier. Each player has before him a map, with his own state value-system fully observable to him, but he is not able to see the other player's state values. Each player makes his own moves and also reproduces the other player's moves on his map. Thus all moves are visible to both players, but each other's state values are not.

A state is *possessed* by a player, *at the end of the game,* if it is part of an *integral area* that he occupies.

A player's *integral area* consists of a set of states which are *occupied solely* by his chips, or bounded by states which are occupied solely by his chips. The area must contain the player's home base and must not also contain his opponent's home base. The states in it must be geographically connected to each other and must form a distinct area. Each state within the area need not be occupied by the player's chips but a boundary must exist. This boundary must consist of states occupied solely by the player's chips, except that the border of the United States may be used to form the bounds of the integral area. States within the bounds of an integral area need not be occupied to be possessed.

Another way of defining an integral area is to say that it is an area (set of states), including the player's home base, which the second player cannot enter from his own home base without moving through a state (placing chips on it) which the first player occupies solely, or by going outside the border of the United States.

At the end of the game, if both players have chips on a state, neither can possess the state, nor are the chips lost. The state values possessed by a player at the end of the game consist of the sum of the values of the states contained in the area he possesses, including the boundary states, according to his own schedule of state values as indicated on his own map. The state values on the second player's map do not affect the first player's score.

During the course of play the first two integral areas formed by each player will be announced.

Home base, a specified state for each player, is marked on both maps and is known to both players. A player always occupies or possesses his home base, whether or not he places any chips on it. A player can never possess or occupy the second player's home base.

Chips and Their Use

Red, blue, black, and white chips will be used in the game. One player, known as "Red," makes his moves with red and black chips; the other, known as "Blue," makes his moves with blue and white chips.

A chip placed on a state can do one of the following things: it can *occupy solely, occupy jointly, challenge,* or *fight.*

When a player places one, or more, of his red (or blue) chips on a state he occupies it. He *occupies* it *solely* if the second player does not place (or has not already placed) his blue (or red) chips on the state. A state is *occupied jointly* if both red and blue chips are placed on it and it is not at *challenge*.

When a player places one of his black (or white) challenge chips on a state, that state is then at *challenge*. Challenges can be made whether or not the second player has chips on the same state, and even if there is no red or blue chip on a state. A player may make as many challenges as he wishes and withdraw as many as he wishes on each play, but only the player who made a particular challenge may withdraw it. Only one challenge chip may be on a state at any time.

If one player has chips on a state and the second places chips on the same state and challenges, the first must *withdraw* or *fight*. He withdraws by removing his chips from that state at his next turn. He fights by indicating so at his next turn, and both players' chips are removed from the state in equal numbers so that only the excess number of chips (if any) that one player had remains on the state. The chips so removed are *lost*. (At the end of the game lost chips do not contribute to a player's earnings.)

If a player responds to a challenge in a particular state by "fighting" for it, and places more chips on it than the other player has there, so that upon removal of equal numbers he has some remaining, his remaining chips are automatically at challenge at the next turn. (The fight, in effect, is still on.) The player who first challenged may add chips at his turn, removing equal numbers again, and so on until, *for one turn, one player adds no chips to the disputed state.* At that point "fighting is over" on that state; the remaining chips, once one player has played a turn without continuing the fight, are at challenge unless the challenge chip is removed.

If a player places chips on a state that has no chips of the other player, and challenges, the other player cannot subsequently place chips of his own on the state without automatically fighting, i.e., without removing equal numbers of chips for both players so that only the excess of chips of one player remains. (One may fight with a greater number of chips, thus having chips on the state after removal; one may fight with an equal number of chips, so that all chips are removed from the state; or one may fight with a lesser number of chips, so that the challenger retains some chips on the state.)

It can happen during the course of a dispute for a state that neither or only one player has colored chips (red or blue) on a state. In these cases neither player solely occupies the state unless the other player has had an opportunity to make a move (i.e., place one of his red or blue chips on the state) and has not placed chips on the disputed state.

Once a player has formed an integral area, the second player cannot place a chip within the boundary of that area. To place a chip within the boundary, he must first "break" the boundary of the integral area by placing one or more of his red (or blue) chips on a boundary state (or states, if this is necessary). (This may or may not result in fighting, depending on whether the boundary states are at challenge.)

Cutting off

At any time during the game that one player possesses an integral area, any chips of the second player within the area bounded may be (but need not be) removed by the first. If they are removed, they are *lost* to their owner.

Chips lost in this fashion are referred to as "cut off." Note that a chip may become cut off, if the player cutting it off completes a boundary by placing chips on unclaimed states, or if he accepts a challenge and fights, the fight ending with his possession of the state. If he has to challenge or fight in order to achieve sole occupancy of a state forming the boundary, the second player may, at his turn, remove the chips that are in danger of being cut off. (The number that may be removed is subject to the over-all limit on number removable at a turn, mentioned below.) In addition, the integral area is not completed until the fight for the state is completed, i.e., until the player who gives up the state has had an opportunity to place one or more chips on the state and has declined the opportunity.

If, after the game is terminated, a player's chips are within the other player's integral area, these chips are not cut off. They are removed from the board and returned to their owner.

Home-Base Damage

A chip may be used to inflict damage on the other player. This is done by placing it on his home base. If that is done, the chip is removed and lost to the player whose chip it is, but the player whose home base was so affected loses an amount of money equivalent to the value of five chips (25¢). A chip on a home base has only this result and does not "claim" anything.

Play

The play of the game consists of a series of moves. A move consists of removing and placing one or more chips on one or more states. Who makes the first move is decided by flipping a coin. At each turn, *a player may remove any number up to five of his own chips from states they were on and may place any number up to five of his chips on states.* He need not move any chips; this is done by indicating a "pass." (Chips removed, except when lost by fighting or cut off, are available to be placed again on the map, and may be so used at the same turn, subject to the limit of five in the total number that may be placed on states at a turn.)

A player may make as many challenges as he wishes at a turn, and withdraw as many challenges as he wishes.

There is no limit to how many chips a player may place, at a turn, on the other's home base (except, of course, that no more than five may be removed from states for that purpose at a turn in the event none are otherwise available).

Each player has 50 red and 50 blue chips. (Red's blue chips are used to reproduce Blue's moves on Red's map, and vice versa.)

The game is terminated when one player (a) makes no move and (b) makes an offer to terminate, and the other player accepts the offer, making no move. If the offer is not accepted, the player making the offer may not then move until his next turn.

At termination, if any state contains chips of both players (and is not at challenge), the chips are removed from these states and returned to each player. Neither player occupies or possesses the state.

The amount each player earns depends on the chips he has remaining (either on states or not on states), the values of the states he possesses, and the damage he has suffered. A player's earnings are not dependent on the other player's earnings. (It is *absolute earnings*, not relative earnings, that matter.)

No communication between players is permitted. Each player writes his move on a card and makes the move on his own map. The Experimenter then executes the move on the second player's map. He removes all chips that are lost through fighting or cutoff.

Some Arbitrary Geographical Rules

Where four states meet in a corner, in the southwest, a diagonal pair does not close a boundary (i.e., New Mexico, Utah, and Idaho do not form a boundary around the West Coast; New Mexico, Colorado, Utah, and Idaho do).

Upper and Lower Michigan, plus Lake Michigan, are considered a single state; thus Illinois and Indiana both border on Michigan and do not border on Canada. Ohio borders on Canada; so does Pennsylvania.

ON THE USE OF GAME MODELS
IN THEORIES OF
INTERNATIONAL RELATIONS*

By RICHARD E. QUANDT

I. Introduction

AMONG all the social sciences, the art of model building is perhaps best developed in economics. Models or theories are conceptualizations of and abstractions from reality; they rely intrinsically on "if-then" statements and should lead to testable propositions if they are to be of any use at all.

It would be difficult to give a brief description of all the important characteristics of economic models, for there are numerous types, designed to describe or explain completely different aspects of economic reality. Most of them contain as essential ingredients some statements about the technical environment (e.g., marginal cost curves rise after a certain point) and some statements about human motivation (e.g., the entrepreneur desires to maximize profits; the consumer maximizes utility). The models themselves can have either descriptive or normative use. The Keynesian model or theory "explains" the factors that cause the level of national income to be what it is and allows one to deduce the direction of change in national income resulting from changes in the parameters. The usefulness of such a descriptive model is determined by whether or not its conclusions are testable propositions. Normative models, most frequently encountered in economics in welfare economics and in operations research, also utilize statements about environment and motivations but do not pretend to predict; in fact they merely prescribe. The test of the usefulness of such normative models is whether or not their prescriptions are at least in principle implementable.

It is possible that the future will regard as a major breakthrough the fact that international relations are now considered to be within the domain of games of strategy. It is indicative of this new mode of thinking that at a recent conference on arms control an entire session was devoted to techniques of bargaining and negotiation—that is, to game-theoretic approaches to international affairs.[1]

* I am indebted to Mr. John Williamson for some critical comments.
[1] Princeton University Conference on Arms Control and Limitation, October 1960.

II. A Typology of Game Models in International Relations

Game theory, as is well known, involves not one model but several. The model of zero-sum two-person games is the mathematically best-developed one, but has been criticized as not being applicable to much of reality because it assumes that the participants' interests are directly antithetical.[2] Such strictly competitive games in fact assume that what A loses, B wins, and what A wins, B loses; moreover, they assume that this zero-sum property of the payoffs holds when they are expressed in utility terms. But even if one assumed away the difficulties that arise when payoffs have to be measured in utility terms, at least two fundamental objections to using the model in realistic contexts remain. First, the behavior required of the participants for the solution of a zero-sum two-person game may neither occur frequently in practice nor be desirable as a norm.[3] Secondly, the typical case of conflict in international relations may not satisfy the zero-sum property at all. Games in which the opponents or participants do not have strictly competitive interests have been felicitously named "mixed motive" games by Schelling. Much of game-theoretic thinking about international affairs is about mixed-motive or non-zero-sum games. How much these models will contribute either to understanding the actual process of international affairs or to arranging our own affairs in optimal fashion remains to be seen.

It is obvious that as an initial step we must admit that international affairs in general and many of its subcategories such as bargaining and negotiation in particular are subject to systematic analysis. Without such an admission no model-building is possible. But a paradox remains with respect to the objectives of model-building in this field. One could design models for the purpose of understanding, predicting, and regulating international affairs concretely. Or, one could build models for the purpose of clearing one's thoughts in some broad sense and discovering the essence of games which is inherent in the structure of the rules of a game without depending in any obvious way on the particulars of the situation.[4] These latter goals can be safely admitted and often are; the former are probably secretly aspired to.

[2] T. C. Schelling, "The Strategy of Conflict: Prospectus for a Reorientation of Game Theory," *Journal of Conflict Resolution*, ii (September 1958), pp. 203-64.

[3] D. Ellsberg, "Theory of the Reluctant Duelist," *American Economic Review*, xlvi (December 1956), pp. 909-23.

[4] Obviously, the rules of a game cannot be divorced from reality content, even if they are as general as those of some games designed to be played. Cf. T. Schelling's paper in the present symposium; and M. A. Kaplan, A. L. Burns, and R. E. Quandt, "Theoretical Analysis of the 'Balance of Power,'" *Behavioral Science*, v (July 1960), pp. 240-52.

The use of a model for illuminating reality has immediate value, arising from the fact that we design a model for the purpose of inferring relationships within reality from relationships within the model. In other words, models derive their usefulness from their isomorphism to reality. It also follows that the difficulty of designing reasonable models depends upon the difficulty of identifying relevant relationships.

The second objective, that of discovering the nature of a game which is independent (in some sense) of particular details, leads to meta-models, such as some gaming models. It was conjectured, for example, in "Theoretical Analysis of the 'Balance of Power,'" the article by Kaplan, Burns, and Quandt cited above, that in a certain class of partly competitive and partly co-operative games, which may for brevity be referred to as balance-of-power games, there is a certain optimal number of participants if stability is to be preserved in the system. The conjecture basically concerns a class of games and not the balance-of-power system as it existed in the eighteenth century. It is suggested that the conjecture be analyzed by means of a game that is designed for "playing out" hypotheses about games, and whose rules form in effect the backbone of a model of a model.

These two types of model, then, can be referred to as the isomorphic model and the metamodel.[5]

III. Some Difficulties of Game Models in International Relations

In assessing the knowledge of international relations that can be and has been gained through various game models, some grave difficulties must be pointed out. It is not suggested, of course, that these difficulties are so overwhelming that the entire approach should be abandoned. But the utilization of game models is not likely to become increasingly fruitful unless some of these problems are solved.

Consider as a first example the mixed-motive isomorphic games of the Schelling type. They involve elements such as communication (of various degrees), promise, threat, and more or less explicit or tacit bargaining which often have clearly defined counterparts in reality.[6]

---

[5] It is not claimed that the distinction between isomorphic models and metamodels is obvious in concrete cases, or that these categories are mutually exclusive. Nor is it intended to suggest that "gaming" approaches and the more orthodox game-theory approaches have much resemblance to each other beyond the fact that both deal with the nature of strategies and strategic responses.

[6] T. C. Schelling, "Bargaining, Communication, and Limited War," *Journal of Conflict Resolution*, 1 (March 1957), pp. 19-36; idem, "The Strategy of Conflict," *op.cit.*; and idem, *The Strategy of Conflict*, Cambridge, Mass., 1960.

A considerable number of important conclusions have emerged from the study of these models. A highly incomplete list must suffice for illustrative purposes: (1) In the absence of perfect communication, it is often possible to achieve common interests through tacit bargaining if the participants can identify the unique element in a situation. An implicit normative corollary would be as follows: if you wish to reach a tacit agreement, look for the unique aspects of the situation. (2) It may be to some player's advantage to destroy channels of communication. (3) Unilateral declarations and promises, while inherently unenforceable in the absence of an outside third power, may be essential ingredients of a tacit bargaining process. (4) It may be desirable under certain circumstances to relinquish the initiative.

These and the numerous other conclusions and sometimes genuinely surprising insights that emerge from Schelling's analysis lend importance to the models, but primarily in their capacity as metamodels. The fundamental difficulty in drawing conclusions from the models concerning reality is our almost complete ignorance of the existence of an isomorphism in some of the vital aspects of the problem. Let us hasten to add that this is not a criticism of the Schelling models. It is rather a warning against considering them to be isomorphic.

First, bargaining models presuppose that both parties have an interest in coming to an agreement of some kind. It is not obvious, for example, that this is true in the case of arms control negotiations between the United States and the Soviet Union. It is, of course, readily admitted that what we ought to mean by arms control—whether limitation or augmentation of certain types of weapon systems, etc.—must be the subject of analysis.[7] Nevertheless, it is conceivable that it is not in the interests of the USSR to come to any agreement concerning arms control.[8] Perhaps an even more plausible alternative is that, although arms limitation is, in some objective sense, in the interests of the Soviet Union, Soviet ideology prohibits the recognition of this interest. Under these circumstances it is likely to be futile to engage in tacit bargaining. It may, of course, be possible to utter appropriate promises and/or threats to convince the opponent that it is, contrary to his initial expectations, in his interest to reach an agreement. But even this does not avoid the basic difficulty, which is lack of information.

[7] T. C. Schelling, "Reciprocal Measures for Arms Stabilization," *Daedalus*, Vol. 89 (Fall 1960), pp. 892-915.

[8] Suppose that the USSR is both superior to the United States in military technology and convinced that the United States will not be an aggressor. Any agreement which diminished the military disparity of the two countries might then be contrary to Soviet interests, since it would increase the relative ability of the United States to retaliate. Obviously, any agreement which increased the disparity would be against United States interests.

Specifically, we are not certain about (1) the ultimate objectives of the opponent (subversion, conquest, coexistence, internal development, etc., and combinations of these); (2) immediate objectives (to reach or not to reach an agreement on arms control); (3) the particular payoffs accruing to the opponent for each strategy combination; (4) the opponent's evaluation of the payoffs accruing to us *and* to him.[9] Now it goes without saying that any concrete application of game theory models requires some knowledge of ends and of payoffs to the opponents. A great deal of useful analysis is possible in some social sciences such as economics without an exact numerical specification of parameters. The assumptions that a supply curve is positively sloped and a demand curve negatively sloped allow meaningful, albeit perhaps limited, analysis of a market. In applications of game theory we cannot even obtain qualitative conclusions without specifying payoffs numerically. Consider as an illustration the game situation expressed by the payoff matrix[10] where i and ii are strategies of A, I and II strategies of B, and where

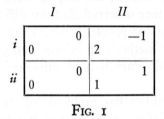

FIG. 1

the numbers in the boxes corresponding to each strategy pair represent payoffs to A and B respectively. It has been argued correctly that a promise by A to undertake strategy ii "brings its own reward" by inducing B to choose II. But imagine that A's evaluation of B's payoffs is faulty. Specifically, consider the two alternatives shown in Fig. 2 as representing reality.

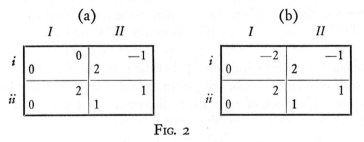

FIG. 2

[9] And, in addition, we are uncertain about the opponent's evaluation of our evaluation of our own and his payoffs, etc. How far this process can or should be carried is hard to say, but its relevance was seen, in a different context, some twenty-five years ago by J. M. Keynes (cf. *The General Theory of Employment, Interest and Money*, New York, 1936).

[10] Cf. Schelling, "The Strategy of Conflict," p. 229, Fig. 5.

In case (a), strategy *II* is dominated by strategy *I* and a promise by A is irrelevant since B will always choose *I*. In case (b), A's promise of *ii* has harmed him, since B will choose *I*; if anything, A should promise *i*. We cannot even be certain that a particular situation is or is not a mixed-motive game.

None of this is intended to imply that anything at all is "wrong" with Schelling's models or any other model in this general class. All that is meant is that models of this kind are quite far removed from the realities of international relations, that in fact these models are metamodels.

IV. Metamodels and Reality: Where Is the Missing Link?

It may be objected that none of this proves the impossibility of applying game-theoretic models to international relations nor does it prove that there is very little in the way of theoretical constructs that is useful. It may be further observed that the difficulties all boil down to problems of information; problems which can be solved at least in principle by (a) better methods of information-gathering in the real world and (b) internal generation of information through gaming approaches.

Each of these possibilities has problems of its own. Consider the internal generation of information through gaming experiments. It is plausible that games can be devised whose rules are reasonable replicas of the constraints in some real-life situations. Such games can be played with real participants or the play can be simulated by a computer. In either case, there are hypotheses that can be tested and there are pieces of information that can be extracted from such an approach.

Consider, for instance, the stability conjecture in balance-of-power games mentioned earlier. Assume that some operational definition of stability is at hand (e.g., "Stability is measured by the number of rounds or plays in the game which take place before the first player to be eliminated is in fact eliminated"). Let the game be played many times for each of a large number of parameter value combinations. Imagine that for a given set of values for all parameters (such as payoffs to winning wars, etc.) except the number of participants, the stability of the game appeared to be independent of the concrete identity of the players. It is then plausible to argue that statistical evidence concerning the relationship between the number of participants and the degree of stability is meaningful in a theoretical sense.

There are of course numerous other ways in which information can be extracted from artificial games. An ingenious game devised by Schelling[11] seeks not so much statistical regularities as striking deviations from intuitively expected results. In addition to the problem of stability, the game is designed to investigate some subtle problems of information and communication and particularly the possibilities of devising methods of communication in cases where full communication is precluded by the rules of the game. But whether we insist on statistical evidence from the game or on the revelation by the game of some striking modes of behavior, the game simply remains a model of some game-theoretic model. The closest it can possibly come to reality is by presenting us with alternatives that we would not normally have thought of.[12] Such games may therefore enlarge the theorist's set of alternatives but not the policy-maker's. To be more specific: no amount of experimentation with artificial games—whether by human participants or by computer simulation—can lead to any of the following types of conclusion: (a) that in a particular real-world situation a particular event is likely to occur; (b) that in order to achieve a particular result in a concrete situation, one type of action is likely to be more successful than another. The reasons for such an agnostic position are simple: (a) in the general case, the motivations of opponents are unknown; (b) even if they were known and participants in an artificial game could be instructed to act in accordance with them, the players would not be facing the concrete payoffs which accompany real-life strategy alternatives. Two illustrations will suffice.

(1) It may well turn out that a gaming model which attempts to reproduce the essential features of today's world is considerably more unstable than reality in the sense that it induces mutually destructive behavior more frequently. It is further possible that alterations in the parameter "ability to wage war"—considered as a proximate cause of armed conflict—will have opposite effects on stability in the model and in the real world: in a game in which no real penalties are exacted, an increase in military potential may soon overcome considerations of risk, whereas in reality such an increase in military potential may reinforce the perception of risk.

(2) It has been suggested in various contexts that it may be to the advantage of a power to reduce its ability to receive communications (but maintain its ability to send messages). A gaming approach may indeed tend to verify such hypotheses. But it is not implausible that in

[11] See Schelling's paper in this symposium.
[12] This point is also stressed by Schelling in *ibid*.

realistic situations an opposite force may be active: a power may benefit in the long run by being unable to put itself publicly in a position from which it may eventually have to retreat.

Gaming models and other metamodels are thus left with basically two uses: (1) to test particular hypotheses about *models*, and (2) to enlarge the catalogues of possible outcomes and strategies. It is not possible, in general, to proceed from metamodel to reality.

It may be improbable but not impossible that the converse is easier— i.e., that it may be feasible to restructure the real political environment in accordance with the structure of a metamodel. A similar procedure is implicit in welfare economics: it is recommended (with qualifications) that conditions of perfect competition be established *because* perfect competition leads to a Pareto optimal allocation of resources. In the present case it might be desirable in reality to agree on certain rules of the game in order to reproduce the features of some manageable metamodel. There are, however, two major difficulties. First, getting agreement on the rules of the game may be as difficult as getting agreement on what arbitration scheme to use in settling a dispute. The participants, knowing the outcomes of various arbitration schemes such as the Nash solution or the Shapley solution,[13] would each desire the issue to be settled under the arbitration scheme most favorable to him, thus creating the issue of how to arbitrate the choice of arbitration schemes. Secondly, even if this problem were solved, the absence of any external enforcement agency makes it doubtful that the rules of the game would be adhered to. There is, of course, a method of forcing continued compliance with the rules—namely, by installing a Doomsday Machine.[14] If it is unacceptable to make response to violations in rules automatic and unspeakably massive, this final attempt to find potential links between reality and metamodels fails, too. These are then relegated to the role of purely mathematical or logical models, and cannot be handmaidens of theories of international relations.

[13] R. D. Luce and H. Raiffa, *Games and Decisions*, New York, 1957, ch. 6.
[14] H. Kahn, "The Arms Race and Some of Its Hazards," *Daedalus*, Vol. 89 (Fall 1960), pp. 744-80.

THE LEVEL-OF-ANALYSIS PROBLEM
IN INTERNATIONAL RELATIONS

By J. DAVID SINGER

IN any area of scholarly inquiry, there are always several ways in which the phenomena under study may be sorted and arranged for purposes of systemic analysis. Whether in the physical or social sciences, the observer may choose to focus upon the parts or upon the whole, upon the components or upon the system. He may, for example, choose between the flowers or the garden, the rocks or the quarry, the trees or the forest, the houses or the neighborhood, the cars or the traffic jam, the delinquents or the gang, the legislators or the legislative, and so on.[1] Whether he selects the micro- or macro-level of analysis is ostensibly a mere matter of methodological or conceptual convenience. Yet the choice often turns out to be quite difficult, and may well become a central issue within the discipline concerned. The complexity and significance of these level-of-analysis decisions are readily suggested by the long-standing controversies between social psychology and sociology, personality-oriented and culture-oriented anthropology, or micro- and macro-economics, to mention but a few. In the vernacular of general systems theory, the observer is always confronted with a system, its sub-systems, and their respective environments, and while he may choose as his system any cluster of phenomena from the most minute organism to the universe itself, such choice cannot be merely a function of whim or caprice, habit or familiarity.[2] The responsible scholar must be prepared to evaluate the relative utility—conceptual and methodological—of the various alternatives open to him, and to appraise the manifold implications of the level of analysis finally selected. So it is with international relations.

But whereas the pros and cons of the various possible levels of analysis have been debated exhaustively in many of the social sciences, the issue has scarcely been raised among students of our emerging

[1] As Kurt Lewin observed in his classic contribution to the social sciences: "The first prerequisite of a successful observation in any science is a definite understanding about what size of unit one is going to observe at a given time." *Field Theory in Social Science*, New York, 1951, p. 157.

[2] For a useful introductory statement on the definitional and taxonomic problems in a general systems approach, see the papers by Ludwig von Bertalanffy, "General System Theory," and Kenneth Boulding, "General System Theory: The Skeleton of Science," in Society for the Advancement of General Systems Theory, *General Systems*, Ann Arbor, Mich., 1956, I, part I.

discipline.[3] Such tranquillity may be seen by some as a reassuring indication that the issue is not germane to our field, and by others as evidence that it has already been resolved, but this writer perceives the quietude with a measure of concern. He is quite persuaded of its relevance and certain that it has yet to be resolved. Rather, it is contended that the issue has been ignored by scholars still steeped in the intuitive and artistic tradition of the humanities or enmeshed in the web of "practical" policy. We have, in our texts and elsewhere, roamed up and down the ladder of organizational complexity with remarkable abandon, focusing upon the total system, international organizations, regions, coalitions, extra-national associations, nations, domestic pressure groups, social classes, elites, and individuals as the needs of the moment required. And though most of us have tended to settle upon the nation as our most comfortable resting place, we have retained our propensity for vertical drift, failing to appreciate the value of a stable point of focus.[4] Whether this lack of concern is a function of the relative infancy of the discipline or the nature of the intellectual traditions from whence it springs, it nevertheless remains a significant variable in the general sluggishness which characterizes the development of theory in the study of relations among nations. It is the purpose of this paper to raise the issue, articulate the alternatives, and examine the theoretical implications and consequences of two of the more widely employed levels of analysis: the international system and the national sub-systems.

I. The Requirements of an Analytical Model

Prior to an examination of the theoretical implications of the level of analysis or orientation employed in our model, it might be worthwhile to discuss the uses to which any such model might be put, and the requirements which such uses might expect of it.

Obviously, we would demand that it offer a highly accurate *description* of the phenomena under consideration. Therefore the scheme must present as complete and undistorted a picture of these phenomena as is possible; it must correlate with objective reality and coincide with our empirical referents to the highest possible degree. Yet we know that

---

[3] An important pioneering attempt to deal with some of the implications of one's level of analysis, however, is Kenneth N. Waltz, *Man, the State, and War*, New York, 1959. But Waltz restricts himself to a consideration of these implications as they impinge on the question of the causes of war. See also this writer's review of Waltz, "International Conflict: Three Levels of Analysis," *World Politics*, XII (April 1960), pp. 453-61.

[4] Even during the debate between "realism" and "idealism" the analytical implications of the various levels of analysis received only the scantiest attention; rather the emphasis seems to have been at the two extremes of pragmatic policy and speculative metaphysics.

such accurate representation of a complex and wide-ranging body of phenomena is extremely difficult. Perhaps a useful illustration may be borrowed from cartography; the oblate spheroid which the planet earth most closely represents is not transferable to the two-dimensional surface of a map without *some* distortion. Thus, the Mercator projection exaggerates distance and distorts direction at an increasing rate as we move north or south *from* the equator, while the polar gnomonic projection suffers from these same debilities as we move *toward* the equator. Neither offers therefore a wholly accurate presentation, yet each is true enough to reality to be quite useful for certain specific purposes. The same sort of tolerance is necessary in evaluating any analytical model for the study of international relations; if we must sacrifice total representational accuracy, the problem is to decide where distortion is least dysfunctional and where such accuracy is absolutely essential.

These decisions are, in turn, a function of the second requirement of any such model—a capacity to *explain* the relationships among the phenomena under investigation. Here our concern is not so much with accuracy of description as with validity of explanation. Our model must have such analytical capabilities as to treat the causal relationships in a fashion which is not only valid and thorough, but parsimonious; this latter requirement is often overlooked, yet its implications for research strategy are not inconsequential.[5] It should be asserted here that the primary purpose of theory is to explain, and when descriptive and explanatory requirements are in conflict, the latter ought to be given priority, even at the cost of some representational inaccuracy.

Finally, we may legitimately demand that any analytical model offer the promise of reliable *prediction*. In mentioning this requirement last, there is no implication that it is the most demanding or difficult of the three. Despite the popular belief to the contrary, prediction demands less of one's model than does explanation or even description. For example, any informed layman can predict that pressure on the

---

[5] For example, one critic of the decision-making model formulated by Richard C. Snyder, H. W. Bruck, and Burton Sapin, in *Decision-Making as an Approach to the Study of International Politics* (Princeton, N.J., 1954), points out that no single researcher could deal with all the variables in that model and expect to complete more than a very few comparative studies in his lifetime. See Herbert McClosky, "Concerning Strategies for a Science of International Politics," *World Politics*, VIII (January 1956), pp. 281-95. In defense, however, one might call attention to the relative ease with which many of Snyder's categories could be collapsed into more inclusive ones, as was apparently done in the subsequent case study (see note 11 below). Perhaps a more telling criticism of the monograph is McClosky's comment that "Until a greater measure of theory is introduced into the proposal and the relations among variables are specified more concretely, it is likely to remain little more than a setting-out of categories and, like any taxonomy, fairly limited in its utility" (p. 291).

accelerator of a slowly moving car will increase its speed; that more or less of the moon will be visible tonight than last night; or that the normal human will flinch when confronted with an impending blow. These *predictions* do not require a particularly elegant or sophisticated model of the universe, but their *explanation* demands far more than most of us carry around in our minds. Likewise, we can predict with impressive reliability that any nation will respond to military attack in kind, but a description and understanding of the processes and factors leading to such a response are considerably more elusive, despite the gross simplicity of the acts themselves.

Having articulated rather briefly the requirements of an adequate analytical model, we might turn now to a consideration of the ways in which one's choice of analytical focus impinges upon such a model and affects its descriptive, explanatory, and predictive adequacy.

II. The International System as Level of Analysis

Beginning with the systemic level of analysis, we find in the total international system a partially familiar and highly promising point of focus. First of all, it is the most comprehensive of the levels available, encompassing the totality of interactions which take place within the system and its environment. By focusing on the system, we are enabled to study the patterns of interaction which the system reveals, and to generalize about such phenomena as the creation and dissolution of coalitions, the frequency and duration of specific power configurations, modifications in its stability, its responsiveness to changes in formal political institutions, and the norms and folklore which it manifests as a societal system. In other words, the systemic level of analysis, and only this level, permits us to examine international relations in the whole, with a comprehensiveness that is of necessity lost when our focus is shifted to a lower, and more partial, level. For descriptive purposes, then, it offers both advantages and disadvantages; the former flow from its comprehensiveness, and the latter from the necessary dearth of detail.

As to explanatory capability, the system-oriented model poses some genuine difficulties. In the first place, it tends to lead the observer into a position which exaggerates the impact of the system upon the national actors and, conversely, discounts the impact of the actors on the system. This is, of course, by no means inevitable; one could conceivably look upon the system as a rather passive environment in which dynamic states act out their relationships rather than as a socio-political entity with a dynamic of its own. But there is a natural tendency to endow that upon which we focus our attention with somewhat greater potential than it might normally be expected to have. Thus, we tend to move, in a system-oriented model, away from notions implying much national autonomy and independence of choice and toward a more deterministic orientation.

Secondly, this particular level of analysis almost inevitably requires that we postulate a high degree of uniformity in the foreign policy operational codes of our national actors. By definition, we allow little room for divergence in the behavior of our parts when we focus upon the whole. It is no coincidence that our most prominent theoretician—and one of the very few text writers focusing upon the international system—should "assume that [all] statesmen think and act in terms of interest defined as power."[6] If this single-minded behavior be interpreted literally and narrowly, we have a simplistic image comparable to economic man or sexual man, and if it be defined broadly, we are no better off than the psychologist whose human model pursues "self-realization" or "maximization of gain"; all such gross models suffer from the same fatal weakness as the utilitarian's "pleasure-pain" principle. Just as individuals differ widely in what they deem to be pleasure and pain, or gain and loss, nations may differ widely in what they consider to be the national interest, and we end up having to break down and refine the larger category. Moreover, Professor Morgenthau finds himself compelled to go still further and disavow the relevance of both motives and ideological preferences in national behavior, and these represent two of the more useful dimensions in differentiating among the several nations in our international system. By eschewing any empirical concern with the domestic and internal variations within the separate nations, the system-oriented approach tends to produce a sort of "black box" or "billiard ball" concept of the national actors.[7] By discounting—or denying—the differences among nations, or by

---

[6] Hans J. Morgenthau, *Politics Among Nations*, 3rd ed., New York, 1960, pp. 5-7. Obviously, his model does not preclude the use of power as a dimension for the differentiation of nations.

[7] The "black box" figure comes from some of the simpler versions of S-R psychology, in which the observer more or less ignores what goes on within the individual and concentrates upon the correlation between stimulus and response; these are viewed as empirically verifiable, whereas cognition, perception, and other mental processes have to be imputed to the individual with a heavy reliance on these assumed "intervening variables." The "billiard ball" figure seems to carry the same sort of connotation, and is best employed by Arnold Wolfers in "The Actors in International Politics" in William T. R. Fox, ed., *Theoretical Aspects of International Relations*, Notre Dame, Ind., 1959, pp. 83-106. See also, in this context, Richard C. Snyder, "International Relations Theory—Continued," *World Politics*, XIII (January 1961), pp. 300-12; and J. David Singer, "Theorizing About Theory in International Politics," *Journal of Conflict Resolution*, IV (December 1960), pp. 431-42. Both are review articles dealing with the Fox anthology.

positing the near-impossibility of observing many of these differences at work within them,[8] one concludes with a highly homogenized image of our nations in the international system. And though this may be an inadequate foundation upon which to base any *causal* statements, it offers a reasonably adequate basis for *correlative* statements. More specifically, it permits us to observe and measure correlations between certain forces or stimuli which seem to impinge upon the nation and the behavior patterns which are the apparent consequence of these stimuli. But one must stress the limitations implied in the word "apparent"; what is thought to be the consequence of a given stimulus may only be a coincidence or artifact, and until one investigates the major elements in the causal link—no matter how persuasive the deductive logic—one may speak only of correlation, not of consequence.

Moreover, by avoiding the multitudinous pitfalls of intra-nation observation, one emerges with a singularly manageable model, requiring as it does little of the methodological sophistication or onerous empiricism called for when one probes beneath the behavioral externalities of the actor. Finally, as has already been suggested in the introduction, the systemic orientation should prove to be reasonably satisfactory as a basis for prediction, even if such prediction is to extend beyond the characteristics of the system and attempt anticipatory statements regarding the actors themselves; this assumes, of course, that the actors are characterized and their behavior predicted in relatively gross and general terms.

These, then, are some of the more significant implications of a model which focuses upon the international system as a whole. Let us turn now to the more familiar of our two orientations, the national state itself.

III. The National State as Level of Analysis

The other level of analysis to be considered in this paper is the national state—our primary actor in international relations. This is clearly the traditional focus among Western students, and is the one which dominates almost all of the texts employed in English-speaking colleges and universities.

Its most obvious advantage is that it permits significant differentiation among our actors in the international system. Because it does not require the attribution of great similarity to the national actors, it encour-

---

[8] Morgenthau observes, for example, that it is "futile" to search for motives because they are "the most illusive of psychological data, distorted as they are, frequently beyond recognition, by the interests and emotions of actor and observer alike" (*op.cit.*, p. 6).

ages the observer to examine them in greater detail. The favorable results of such intensive analysis cannot be overlooked, as it is only when the actors are studied in some depth that we are able to make really valid generalizations of a comparative nature. And though the systemic model does not necessarily preclude comparison and contrast among the national sub-systems, it usually eventuates in rather gross comparisons based on relatively crude dimensions and characteristics. On the other hand, there is no assurance that the nation-oriented approach will produce a sophisticated model for the comparative study of foreign policy; with perhaps the exception of the Haas and Whiting study,[9] none of our major texts makes a serious and successful effort to describe and explain national behavior in terms of most of the significant variables by which such behavior might be comparatively analyzed. But this would seem to be a function, not of the level of analysis employed, but of our general unfamiliarity with the other social sciences (in which comparison is a major preoccupation) and of the retarded state of comparative government and politics, a field in which most international relations specialists are likely to have had some experience.

But just as the nation-as-actor focus permits us to avoid the inaccurate homogenization which often flows from the systemic focus, it also may lead us into the opposite type of distortion—a marked exaggeration of the differences among our sub-systemic actors. While it is evident that neither of these extremes is conducive to the development of a sophisticated comparison of foreign policies, and such comparison requires a balanced preoccupation with both similarity and difference, the danger seems to be greatest when we succumb to the tendency to overdifferentiate; comparison and contrast can proceed only from observed uniformities.[10]

One of the additional liabilities which flow in turn from the pressure to overdifferentiate is that of Ptolemaic parochialism. Thus, in overemphasizing the differences among the many national states, the observer is prone to attribute many of what he conceives to be virtues to his own nation and the vices to others, especially the adversaries of the moment. That this ethnocentrism is by no means an idle fear is borne out by perusal of the major international relations texts published

[9] Ernst B. Haas and Allen S. Whiting, *Dynamics of International Relations*, New York, 1956.

[10] A frequent by-product of this tendency to overdifferentiate is what Waltz calls the "second-image fallacy," in which one explains the peaceful or bellicose nature of a nation's foreign policy exclusively in terms of its domestic economic, political, or social characteristics (*op.cit.*, chs. 4 and 5).

in the United States since 1945. Not only is the world often perceived through the prism of the American national interest, but an inordinate degree of attention (if not spleen) is directed toward the Soviet Union; it would hardly be amiss to observe that most of these might qualify equally well as studies in American foreign policy. The scientific inadequacies of this sort of "we-they" orientation hardly require elaboration, yet they remain a potent danger in any utilization of the national actor model.

Another significant implication of the sub-systemic orientation is that it is only within its particular framework that we can expect any useful application of the decision-making approach.[11] Not all of us, of course, will find its inapplicability a major loss; considering the criticism which has been leveled at the decision-making approach, and the failure of most of us to attempt its application, one might conclude that it is no loss at all. But the important thing to note here is that a system-oriented model would not offer a hospitable framework for such a detailed and comparative approach to the study of international relations, no matter what our appraisal of the decision-making approach might be.

Another and perhaps more subtle implication of selecting the nation as our focus or level of analysis is that it raises the entire question of goals, motivation, and purpose in national policy.[12] Though it may well be a peculiarity of the Western philosophical tradition, we seem to exhibit, when confronted with the need to explain individual or collective behavior, a strong proclivity for a goal-seeking approach. The question of whether national behavior is purposive or not seems to require discussion in two distinct (but not always exclusive) dimensions.

Firstly, there is the more obvious issue of whether those who act on behalf of the nation in formulating and executing foreign policy consciously pursue rather concrete goals. And it would be difficult to deny, for example, that these role-fulfilling individuals envisage certain specific outcomes which they hope to realize by pursuing a particular

---

[11] Its most well-known and successful statement is found in Snyder *et al., op.cit.* Much of this model is utilized in the text which Snyder wrote with Edgar S. Furniss, Jr., *American Foreign Policy: Formulation, Principles, and Programs,* New York, 1954. A more specific application is found in Snyder and Glenn D. Paige, "The United States Decision to Resist Aggression in Korea: The Application of an Analytical Scheme," *Administrative Science Quarterly,* iii (December 1958), pp. 341-78. For those interested in this approach, very useful is Paul Wasserman and Fred S. Silander, *Decision-Making: An Annotated Bibliography,* Ithaca, N.Y., 1958.

[12] And if the decision-making version of this model is employed, the issue is unavoidable. See the discussion of motivation in Snyder, Bruck, and Sapin, *op.cit.,* pp. 92-117; note that 25 of the 49 pages on "The Major Determinants of Action" are devoted to motives.

strategy. In this sense, then, nations may be said to be goal-seeking organisms which exhibit purposive behavior.

However, purposiveness may be viewed in a somewhat different light, by asking whether it is not merely an intellectual construct that man imputes to himself by reason of his vain addiction to the free-will doctrine as he searches for characteristics which distinguish him from physical matter and the lower animals. And having attributed this conscious goal-pursuing behavior to himself as an individual, it may be argued that man then proceeds to project this attribute to the social organizations of which he is a member. The question would seem to distill down to whether man and his societies pursue goals of their own choosing or are moved toward those imposed upon them by forces which are primarily beyond their control.[13] Another way of stating the dilemma would be to ask whether we are concerned with the ends which men and nations strive for or the ends toward which they are impelled by the past and present characteristics of their social and physical milieu. Obviously, we are using the terms "ends," "goals," and "purpose" in two rather distinct ways; one refers to those which are consciously envisaged and more or less rationally pursued, and the other to those of which the actor has little knowledge but toward which he is nevertheless propelled.

Taking a middle ground in what is essentially a specific case of the free will vs. determinism debate, one can agree that nations move toward outcomes of which they have little knowledge and over which they have less control, but that they nevertheless do prefer, and therefore select, particular outcomes and *attempt* to realize them by conscious formulation of strategies.

Also involved in the goal-seeking problem when we employ the nation-oriented model is the question of how and why certain nations pursue specific sorts of goals. While the question may be ignored in the system-oriented model or resolved by attributing identical goals to all national actors, the nation-as-actor approach demands that we investigate the processes by which national goals are selected, the internal and external factors that impinge on those processes, and the institutional framework from which they emerge. It is worthy of note that despite the strong predilection for the nation-oriented model in most

[13] A highly suggestive, but more abstract treatment of this teleological question is in Talcott Parsons, *The Structure of Social Action*, 2nd ed., Glencoe, Ill., 1949, especially in his analysis of Durkheim and Weber. It is interesting to note that for Parsons an act implies, *inter alia*, "a future state of affairs toward which the process of action is oriented," and he therefore comments that "in this sense and this sense only, the schema of action is inherently teleological" (p. 44).

of our texts, empirical or even deductive analyses of these processes are conspicuously few.[14] Again, one might attribute these lacunae to the methodological and conceptual inadequacies of the graduate training which international relations specialists traditionally receive.[15] But in any event, goals and motivations are both dependent and independent variables, and if we intend to explain a nation's foreign policy, we cannot settle for the mere postulation of these goals; we are compelled to go back a step and inquire into their genesis and the process by which they become the crucial variables that they seem to be in the behavior of nations.

There is still another dilemma involved in our selection of the nation-as-actor model, and that concerns the phenomenological issue: do we examine our actor's behavior in terms of the objective factors which allegedly influence that behavior, or do we do so in terms of the actor's *perception* of these "objective factors"? Though these two approaches are not completely exclusive of one another, they proceed from greatly different and often incompatible assumptions, and produce markedly divergent models of national behavior.[16]

The first of these assumptions concerns the broad question of social causation. One view holds that individuals and groups respond in a quasi-deterministic fashion to the realities of physical environment, the acts or power of other individuals or groups, and similar "objective" and "real" forces or stimuli. An opposite view holds that individuals and groups are not influenced in their behavior by such objective forces, but by the fashion in which these forces are perceived and evaluated, however distorted or incomplete such perceptions may be. For adherents of this position, the only reality is the phenomenal—that which is discerned by the human senses; forces that are not discerned do not exist

---

[14] Among the exceptions are Haas and Whiting, *op.cit.*, chs. 2 and 3; and some of the chapters in Roy C. Macridis, ed., *Foreign Policy in World Politics*, Englewood Cliffs, N.J., 1958, especially that on West Germany by Karl Deutsch and Lewis Edinger.

[15] As early as 1934, Edith E. Ware noted that ". . . the study of international relations is no longer entirely a subject for political science or law, but that economics, history, sociology, geography—all the social sciences—are called upon to contribute towards the understanding . . . of the international system." See *The Study of International Relations in the United States*, New York, 1934, p. 172. For some contemporary suggestions, see Karl Deutsch, "The Place of Behavioral Sciences in Graduate Training in International Relations," *Behavioral Science*, III (July 1958), pp. 278-84; and J. David Singer, "The Relevance of the Behavioral Sciences to the Study of International Relations," *ibid.*, VI (October 1961), pp. 324-35.

[16] The father of phenomenological philosophy is generally acknowledged to be Edmund Husserl (1859-1938), author of *Ideas: General Introduction to Pure Phenomenology*, New York, 1931, trans. by W. R. Boyce Gibson; the original was published in 1913 under the title *Ideen zu einer reinen Phänomenologie und Phänomenologischen Philosophie*. Application of this approach to social psychology has come primarily through the work of Koffka and Lewin.

for that actor, and those that do exist do so only in the fashion in which they are perceived. Though it is difficult to accept the position that an individual, a group, or a nation is affected by such forces as climate, distance, or a neighbor's physical power only insofar as they are recognized and appraised, one must concede that perceptions will certainly affect the manner in which such forces are responded to. As has often been pointed out, an individual will fall to the ground when he steps out of a tenth-story window regardless of his perception of gravitational forces, but on the other hand such perception is a major factor in whether or not he steps out of the window in the first place.[17] The point here is that if we embrace a phenomenological view of causation, we will tend to utilize a phenomenological model for explanatory purposes.

The second assumption which bears on one's predilection for the phenomenological approach is more restricted, and is primarily a methodological one. Thus, it may be argued that any description of national behavior in a given international situation would be highly incomplete were it to ignore the link between the external forces at work upon the nation and its general foreign policy behavior. Furthermore, if our concern extends beyond the mere description of "what happens" to the realm of explanation, it could be contended that such omission of the cognitive and the perceptual linkage would be ontologically disastrous. How, it might be asked, can one speak of "causes" of a nation's policies when one has ignored the media by which external conditions and factors are translated into a policy decision? We may observe correlations between all sorts of forces in the international system and the behavior of nations, but their causal relationship must remain strictly deductive and hypothetical in the absence of empirical investigation into the causal chain which allegedly links the two. Therefore, even if we are satisfied with the less-than-complete descriptive capabilities of a non-phenomenological model, we are still drawn to it if we are to make any progress in explanation.

The contrary view would hold that the above argument proceeds from an erroneous comprehension of the nature of explanation in social science. One is by no means required to trace every perception, transmission, and receipt between stimulus and response or input and output in order to explain the behavior of the nation or any other human group. Furthermore, who is to say that empirical observation—subject

---

[17] This issue has been raised from time to time in all of the social sciences, but for an excellent discussion of it in terms of the present problem, see Harold and Margaret Sprout, *Man-Milieu Relationship Hypotheses in the Context of International Politics*, Princeton University, Center of International Studies, 1956, pp. 63-71.

as it is to a host of errors—is any better a basis of explanation than informed deduction, inference, or analogy? Isn't an explanation which flows logically from a coherent theoretical model just as reliable as one based upon a misleading and elusive body of data, most of which is susceptible to analysis only by techniques and concepts foreign to political science and history?

This leads, in turn, to the third of the premises relevant to one's stand on the phenomenological issue: are the dimensions and characteristics of the policy-makers' phenomenal field empirically discernible? Or, more accurately, even if we are convinced that their perceptions and beliefs constitute a crucial variable in the explanation of a nation's foreign policy, can they be observed in an accurate and systematic fashion?[18] Furthermore, are we not required by the phenomenological model to go beyond a classification and description of such variables, and be drawn into the tangled web of relationships out of which they emerge? If we believe that these phenomenal variables are systematically observable, are explainable, and can be fitted into our explanation of a nation's behavior in the international system, then there is a further tendency to embrace the phenomenological approach. If not, or if we are convinced that the gathering of such data is inefficient or uneconomical, we will tend to shy clear of it.

The fourth issue in the phenomenological dispute concerns the very nature of the nation as an actor in international relations. Who or what is it that we study? Is it a distinct social entity with well-defined boundaries—a unity unto itself? Or is it an agglomeration of individuals, institutions, customs, and procedures? It should be quite evident that those who view the nation or the state as an integral social unit could not attach much utility to the phenomenological approach, particularly if they are prone to concretize or reify the abstraction. Such abstractions are incapable of perception, cognition, or anticipation (unless, of course, the reification goes so far as to anthropomorphize and assign to the abstraction such attributes as will, mind, or personality). On the other hand, if the nation or state is seen as a group of individuals operating within an institutional framework, then it makes perfect sense to focus on the phenomenal field of those individuals who participate in the policy-making process. In other words, *people* are capable of experiences, images, and expectations, while insti-

---

[18] This is another of the criticisms leveled at the decision-making approach which, almost by definition, seems compelled to adopt some form of the phenomenological model. For a comprehensive treatment of the elements involved in human perception, see Karl Zener *et al.*, eds., "Inter-relationships Between Perception and Personality: A Symposium," *Journal of Personality*, xviii (1949), pp. 1-266.

tutional abstractions are not, except in the metaphorical sense. Thus, if our actor cannot even have a phenomenal field, there is little point in employing a phenomenological approach.[19]

These, then, are some of the questions around which the phenomenological issue would seem to revolve. Those of us who think of social forces as operative regardless of the actor's awareness, who believe that explanation need not include all of the steps in a causal chain, who are dubious of the practicality of gathering phenomenal data, or who visualize the nation as a distinct entity apart from its individual members, will tend to reject the phenomenological approach.[20] Logically, only those who disagree with each of the above four assumptions would be *compelled* to adopt the approach. Disagreement with any one would be *sufficient* grounds for so doing.

The above represent some of the more significant implications and fascinating problems raised by the adoption of our second model. They seem to indicate that this sub-systemic orientation is likely to produce richer description and more satisfactory (from the empiricist's point of view) explanation of international relations, though its predictive power would appear no greater than the systemic orientation. But the descriptive and explanatory advantages are achieved only at the price of considerable methodological complexity.

IV. Conclusion

Having discussed some of the descriptive, explanatory, and predictive capabilities of these two possible levels of analysis, it might now be useful to assess the relative utility of the two and attempt some general statement as to their prospective contributions to greater theoretical growth in the study of international relations.

In terms of description, we find that the systemic level produces a more comprehensive and total picture of international relations than does the national or sub-systemic level. On the other hand, the atomized and less coherent image produced by the lower level of analysis is somewhat balanced by its richer detail, greater depth, and more intensive portrayal.[21] As to explanation, there seems little doubt that the sub-

[19] Many of these issues are raised in the ongoing debate over "methodological individualism," and are discussed cogently in Ernest Nagel, *The Structure of Science*, New York, 1961, pp. 535-46.

[20] Parenthetically, holders of these specific views should also be less inclined to adopt the national or sub-systemic model in the first place.

[21] In a review article dealing with two of the more recent and provocative efforts toward theory (Morton A. Kaplan, *System and Process in International Politics*, New York, 1957, and George Liska, *International Equilibrium*, Cambridge, Mass., 1957), Charles P. Kindleberger adds a further—if not altogether persuasive—argument in favor

systemic or actor orientation is considerably more fruitful, permitting as it does a more thorough investigation of the processes by which foreign policies are made. Here we are enabled to go beyond the limitations imposed by the systemic level and to replace mere correlation with the more significant causation. And in terms of prediction, both orientations seem to offer a similar degree of promise. Here the issue is a function of what we seek to predict. Thus the policy-maker will tend to prefer predictions about the way in which nation x or y will react to a contemplated move on his own nation's part, while the scholar will probably prefer either generalized predictions regarding the behavior of a given class of nations or those regarding the system itself.

Does this summary add up to an overriding case for one or another of the two models? It would seem not. For a staggering variety of reasons the scholar may be more interested in one level than another at any given time and will undoubtedly shift his orientation according to his research needs. So the problem is really not one of deciding which level is most valuable to the discipline as a whole and then demanding that it be adhered to from now unto eternity.[22] Rather, it is one of realizing that there *is* this preliminary conceptual issue and that it must be temporarily resolved prior to any given research undertaking. And it must also be stressed that we have dealt here only with two of the more common orientations, and that many others are available and perhaps even more fruitful potentially than either of those selected here. Moreover, the international system gives many indications of prospective change, and it may well be that existing institutional forms will take on new characteristics or that new ones will appear to take their place. As a matter of fact, if incapacity to perform its functions leads to the transformation or decay of an institution, we may expect a steady deterioration and even ultimate disappearance of the national state as a significant actor in the world political system.

However, even if the case for one or another of the possible levels of analysis cannot be made with any certainty, one must nevertheless maintain a continuing awareness as to their use. We may utilize one level here and another there, but we cannot afford to shift our orientation in the midst of a study. And when we do in fact make an original

---

of the lower, sub-systemic level of analysis: "The total system is infinitely complex with everything interacting. One can discuss it intelligently, therefore, only bit by bit." "Scientific International Politics," *World Politics*, xi (October 1958), p. 86.

[22] It should also be kept in mind that one could conceivably develop a theoretical model which successfully embraces both of these levels of analysis without sacrificing conceptual clarity and internal consistency. In this writer's view, such has not been done to date, though Kaplan's *System and Process in International Politics* seems to come fairly close.

selection or replace one with another at appropriate times, we must do so with a full awareness of the descriptive, explanatory, and predictive implications of such choice.

A final point remains to be discussed. Despite this lengthy exegesis, one might still be prone to inquire whether this is not merely a sterile exercise in verbal gymnastics. What, it might be asked, is the difference between the two levels of analysis if the empirical referents remain essentially the same? Or, to put it another way, is there any difference between international relations and comparative foreign policy? Perhaps a few illustrations will illuminate the subtle but important differences which emerge when one's level of analysis shifts. One might, for example, postulate that when the international system is characterized by political conflict between two of its most powerful actors, there is a strong tendency for the system to bipolarize. This is a systemic-oriented proposition. A sub-systemic proposition, dealing with the same general empirical referents, would state that when a powerful actor finds itself in political conflict with another of approximate parity, it will tend to exert pressure on its weaker neighbors to join its coalition. Each proposition, assuming it is true, is theoretically useful by itself, but each is verified by a different intellectual operation. Moreover—and this is the crucial thing for theoretical development—one could not add these two kinds of statements together to achieve a cumulative growth of empirical generalizations.

To illustrate further, one could, at the systemic level, postulate that when the distribution of power in the international system is highly diffused, it is more stable than when the discernible clustering of well-defined coalitions occurs. And at the sub-systemic or national level, the same empirical phenomena would produce this sort of proposition: when a nation's decision-makers find it difficult to categorize other nations readily as friend or foe, they tend to behave toward all in a more uniform and moderate fashion. Now, taking these two sets of propositions, how much cumulative usefulness would arise from attempting to merge and codify the systemic proposition from the first illustration with the sub-systemic proposition from the second, or vice versa? Representing different levels of analysis and couched in different frames of reference, they would defy theoretical integration; one may well be a corollary of the other, but they are not immediately combinable. A prior translation from one level to another must take place.

This, it is submitted, is quite crucial for the theoretical development of our discipline. With all of the current emphasis on the need for more empirical and data-gathering research as a prerequisite to theory-building, one finds little concern with the relationship among these separate and discrete data-gathering activities. Even if we were to declare a moratorium on deductive and speculative research for the next decade, and all of us were to labor diligently in the vineyards of historical and contemporary data, the state of international relations theory would probably be no more advanced at that time than it is now, unless such empirical activity becomes far more systematic. And "systematic" is used here to indicate the cumulative growth of inductive and deductive generalizations into an impressive array of statements conceptually related to one another and flowing from some common frame of reference. What that frame of reference should be, or will be, cannot be said with much certainty, but it does seem clear that it must exist. As long as we evade some of these crucial *a priori* decisions, our empiricism will amount to little more than an ever-growing potpourri of discrete, disparate, non-comparable, and isolated bits of information or extremely low-level generalizations. And, as such, they will make little contribution to the growth of a theory of international relations.

ASSUMPTIONS OF RATIONALITY
AND NON-RATIONALITY IN MODELS
OF THE INTERNATIONAL SYSTEM

By SIDNEY VERBA

I

IT is a truism that all action within the international system can be reduced to the action of individuals. It is also true, however, that international relations cannot be adequately understood in terms of individual attitudes and behaviors. Models of the international system usually deal with larger units, nation-states, as prime actors. To what extent can such models give us adequate explanations of international relations without some built-in variables to deal with individual decision-making?

It may be that some processes in international relations can be adequately explained on the level of social structure without explicit consideration of the personality, predispositions, attitudes, and behavior of the individual decision-maker. In that case, the introduction of variables dealing with individual behavior would complicate the model without commensurate payoff in terms of increased understanding and prediction. This would be true if the impact of individual decision-making on the behavior of nations in their relations with other nations were slight, or if the impact varied randomly (because, for instance, of idiosyncratic factors) among the population of international events that one was trying to explain. If, on the other hand, models of the international system that either ignore or make grossly simplifying assumptions about individual decision-making can explain international relations only very imperfectly, it may well be worth the additional effort to build variables about individual decision-making into them.[1]

This paper will deal with the place of assumptions and theories about individual decision-making in models of the international system. The individuals in whose behavior we are interested are all those whose activities either alone or with others have some perceptible impact upon

[1] We ask that a model give adequate explanation and prediction of international events, not perfect explanation and prediction. There are, however, no hard and fast rules as to what is adequate explanation. In a sense, the test is a psychological one: an explanation is adequate when the "mind comes to rest." And this will depend upon the nature of the problem, its importance, complexity, and the interests of the people working on it.

the international system. This then includes masses and elites, governmental and non-governmental figures. Behaviors that will be considered as affecting the international system range from the minimal one of holding an opinion about an international situation as a member of the public to the authoritative decision made by some major government official. If one conceives of the international system as consisting of activities involving interaction among two or more nation-states, and the act of any single state is considered an input into that system, it is clear that the main impact of the activities of individuals upon the international system takes place on the level of the internal decision-making process that determines what input a nation will make into the international system. This is the case because with rare exceptions the roles of individuals within their own nations and the norms associated with these roles outweigh in importance their roles within the international system. We shall therefore concentrate on the individual as a role-holder in the foreign policy-formulating structure of his own nation.

Theories that attempt to explain and understand the course of international relations make varying assumptions about the actions and motivations of individual actors. Two approaches can be called the rational and the non-rational. Each makes a simplifying assumption about the way in which individuals act in international situations. Non-rational models assume that when an individual is faced with a choice situation in relation to an international event (a governmental decision-maker faced with a threat from an adversary nation, an ordinary citizen hearing about an insult to his head of state), he responds in terms of what we shall call non-logical pressures or influences. These are pressures or influences unconnected with the event in question. A gross case occurs when an individual responds aggressively to an international event because of internal psychological pressures toward aggression having their root in childhood experiences. A non-logical influence is any influence acting upon the decision-maker of which he is unaware and which he would not consider a legitimate influence upon his decision if he were aware of it. The latter criterion is difficult to make operational, but inferences can be drawn from the individual's value system. In any case, the former criterion will serve as an adequate indicator of the existence of such non-logical influences.[2]

---

[2] An attitude or behavior rooted in such non-logical influences may be considered to be a "symptom," in the Freudian sense of the word; that is, ". . . an overt tension-reducing response whose relationship to an unconscious motive is not perceived by the

Rational models of individual decision-making are those in which the individual responding to an international event bases his response upon a cool and clearheaded means-ends calculation. He uses the best information available and chooses from the universe of possible responses that alternative most likely to maximize his goals. The rational decision-maker may, for instance, respond aggressively to an international event, but the aggressive response will have its source in calculations based upon the nature of the international situation. It will be directed against the real enemy—the nation threatening or inflicting damage to one's interests—and the decision-maker will have some reasonable expectation of achieving his ends through the aggressive response. Furthermore, the decision will either have no psychological side-effects on the decision-maker (he will not experience tension release or guilt because of it), or, if there are psychological side-effects, they will be irrelevant as far as the nature of the decision is concerned.[3]

In most cases, neither of these models of individual behavior represents a complete description of actual behavior. They are presented rather as simplifying assumptions about individual behavior. But the choice of assumption has serious consequences for the adequacy and usefulness of the theory of which it is a part. For even if we are interested in the behavior of nation-states, the implicit or explicit assumptions we make about individual behavior will affect our understanding of state behavior. Let us consider the non-rational models first.

II

The attitudes and behaviors of an individual often perform functions for him that are not apparent in the attitude or act itself. They may work to resolve problems that are not the overt topic of the attitude or

---

individual." See Irving Sarnoff, "Psychoanalytic Theory and Social Attitudes," *Public Opinion Quarterly*, xxiv (Summer 1960), pp. 251-79.

It may be useful to distinguish between motives that are non-logical and motives that are inappropriate. If, for instance, an individual responds to an international decision-making situation in terms of his desire for organizational promotion rather than the welfare of his nation, his motives may be considered inappropriate even in terms of his own value structure (he may feel guilty), but they are not non-logical as long as they are conscious motives.

[3] An individual may respond to an international event in terms of the event itself and still not behave "rationally," as the term is ordinarily used. (We shall consider the concept of rationality more fully below.) He may respond foolishly because of inadequate information. Or he may respond in anger and haste—not in the cool manner of the rational decision-maker—but the anger may be due to the acts of the adversary nation rather than to the previous existence of latent aggression in the individual. This type of behavior, while not rational, fits easily into the model of rational behavior, for its deviation from rationality is along the dimensions considered significant in the model of rationality.

the manifest object of the behavior. Non-rational models of individual attitudes and behaviors in relation to international affairs are built upon this insight.

These models postulate certain needs whose roots lie in innate drives or early experiences. These needs are then projected into public affairs, where their fulfillment is sought through attitudes and behaviors relevant to international events. Individuals, for instance, are described as having a need for an aggressive outlet. This need is met through the expression of aggressive feelings toward some foreign nation, going even as far as a desire for war. In this way, attitudes toward international affairs are explained in terms of certain personality-oriented pressures, not in terms of reactions to international events. The international system becomes the arena into which unresolved personal problems are projected.[4] Evidence from clinical studies of individuals as well as from correlational studies of larger groups suggests that there is indeed a relationship between personality variables and early childhood experiences, on the one hand, and attitudes on a wide range of topics, including international relations, on the other. A tendency to adopt hostile attitudes toward other groups, including other nations, has been correlated with such variables as patterns of child-rearing, level of latent aggression, scores on the F-scale, personal insecurity, and so forth. In most cases, however, the correlations—though in the expected direction—have been insufficient to explain the attitude. This fact, plus the fact that many of these studies have been of special populations, such as college students, and deal with verbal responses to hypothetical situations, suggests that one must be cautious in extrapolating to explanations of the way in which nations will behave in their relations with other nations.[5]

What we can say on the basis of these studies is that, at minimum, personality variables affect attitudes and behaviors in the international sphere. Each individual brings with him into the situations relevant to international relations in which he may be involved a set of predispo-

---

[4] For a fuller discussion of these theories and, in particular, of the origins of these personality-oriented needs and the ways in which these needs are translated into attitudes toward international affairs, see Maurice Farber, "Psychoanalytic Hypotheses in the Study of War," *Journal of Social Issues*, 1 (1955), pp. 29-35; and Bjørn Christiansen, *Attitudes Toward Foreign Affairs as a Function of Personality*, Oslo, Oslo University Press, 1959.

[5] For examples of these studies, see Christiansen, *op.cit.*; Charles D. Farris, "Selected Attitudes on Foreign Affairs as Correlates of Authoritarianism and Political Anomie," *Journal of Politics*, XXII (February 1960), p. 50; Arthur I. Gladstone, "The Possibility of Predicting Reactions to International Events," *Journal of Social Issues*, 1 (1955), pp. 21-28; and Daniel Levinson, "Authoritarian Personality and Foreign Policy," *Journal of Conflict Resolution*, 1 (March 1957), pp. 37-47.

sitions, previous experiences, and the like, all of which are irrelevant in terms of his own model of the situation. But it is more difficult to say how strong the effects are likely to be, in what direction they will operate, and under what conditions the non-logical influences are likely to be significant. And, above all, it is hard to connect theories of non-logical influence on political decisions with the way in which nations act in the international system. At best the evidence on these influences deals with the behavior of individuals and, even at this level, it is difficult to explain why one decision and not another was taken by a particular individual in a particular situation. The connection between these influences and the actions of nation-states is much more difficult to detect. The simplest model connects the hypothesized predispositions of individuals directly with the position that a nation takes vis-à-vis other nations. Thus, a high (but unspecified) proportion of individuals in Nation A have aggressive tendencies; these tendencies are displaced on an external object; for a variety of reasons, a foreign nation is a convenient object; ergo: Nation A goes to war with Nation B. This sort of model has little predictive or explanatory power, and little need be said about it. The question is not whether personality and predispositional variables determine the action of nation-states, but how these variables can usefully be fitted into models of the international system.[6]

There is, however, a previous question that can be asked—a question that begs the one just raised and that may be easier to answer. Although non-logical variables have an effect on the course of international relations, is it desirable to bring these variables into models of the international system? That they have some effect on that system is certainly insufficient reason for incorporating them into theories of the system, for to include all variables that have some effect on international relations would be to create a model so complex as to be useless. The question we raise is one of the economics of research design. Does the increase in explanatory power that would accompany the introduction of such variables into a model of the international system justify the increased complexity of the model? How significant is the impact of these non-logical influences on the sorts of events we are trying to explain in our models of the international system?

Let us assume that individuals have a variety of psychological needs

---

[6] One can distinguish between the effects on the course of international relations of the nature of man and of *the hypotheses held by men about the nature of man*. It may be that the latter have as great an effect as the former, though, of course, the two are not completely unrelated. A belief that basic predispositions are learned as a child and cannot be changed or that aggression has its roots in human nature might well affect decisions in international affairs.

and that these needs can be filled through public activities, including activities related to international affairs. For example, to take the most frequently mentioned need, assume that every individual has some need to manifest aggression. The level of the need varies from individual to individual, ranging from such a low level that there are no discernible behavioral consequences to such a high level that it dominates most behavior. Each individual is so situated that his behavior affects the international system, but he is also involved in a host of other relationships. His aggressive needs can find outlet in his behavior in relation to the international system; they can also find outlet in his behavior in relation to the other systems with which he interacts. Thus we have a simple table:

		LEVEL OF AGGRESSIVE NEEDS	
		High	*Low*
THE INTERNATIONAL	*High*	x	x
SYSTEM AS OUTLET	*Low*	x	x

People can therefore vary in terms of their level of aggressive needs and in terms of the extent to which aggressive needs find their expression within the sphere of international relations. What this table suggests is that such variables are relevant only among those individuals whose level of aggressive needs is high and whose outlet for the need is their behavior in regard to the international system. If the combination High/High is rare, one will lose little by ignoring the effects of non-logical influences.

In order to assess the probability of a significant number of individuals falling in the High/High category, one would have to develop a series of hypotheses as to the probability that an individual will be high in terms of the impact of a particular non-logical force and high in terms of its projection into the international sphere. On the first problem, it is of course possible through clinical studies to spell out the types of non-logical forces to which individuals are subject. Such studies, however, are of limited use unless they can supply us with rules, albeit rough ones, as to the likely level of a particular influence in individuals whom we cannot submit to detailed clinical analysis. Such rules would have to enable us to predict what particular non-logical force is likely to be more widespread among what groups. There is some evidence that certain non-logical forces are more prevalent among some national groups than among others, and some evidence that political elites tend to manifest a different set of non-logical forces than non-elites. But, in most cases, the research backing up these propositions is quite scanty.

In any case, the extent to which any group or individual manifests a particular non-logical need takes us into questions of general psychology and far from our consideration of political psychology. Of greater relevance to our study is the second variation—the extent to which attitudes and behaviors relevant to international affairs rather than attitudes and behaviors in other areas serve as the outlet for non-logical needs.

To what extent is the sphere of international relations likely to serve as the outlet for the externalization of non-logical needs? This will depend upon the extent to which such non-logical needs can be satisfied by attitudes and behaviors toward international affairs and the extent to which the projection of such needs into the international arena does not conflict with other more instrumental functions of attitudes and behaviors in that field.[7] The following hypotheses deal with the conditions that affect the probability that attitudes and behaviors in relation to international affairs will represent the externalization of an individual's personality-oriented needs. The first set of hypotheses deals with the relationship of the individual to the international situation:

(1) The greater the involvement of an individual in a situation, the greater will be the effect of non-logical and predispositional influences. At the one extreme, if the individual is completely apathetic to the course of international events, they can afford little or no outlet for the release of his personality-oriented tensions. But if he is deeply involved, his relations to the course of international events will be affect-laden and there will be more opportunity for the projection of non-logical influences into the international sphere. It is, of course, possible for involvement in international affairs to follow from some personality-oriented need. If the need were strong enough, one might expect search behavior in order to find an object of orientation for that need, and such an object might, for instance, be a foreign nation. But in general

[7] The underlying theory of attitude formation that we are using here is a functional one. This makes it difficult for us to ask the question that really interests us: under what conditions are attitudes toward international affairs likely to be caused by non-logical needs? We would fall into a teleological trap if we were to assume that because an attitude performs certain psychological functions for an individual, we have explained the cause or genesis of that attitude. Nevertheless, although one cannot assume causality, attitudes that do serve as the outlets for some psychological need are more likely to be determined at least in part by that need than attitudes that do not perform such functions. Theories of learning, for instance, suggest that individuals will adopt those attitudes and behaviors that perform functions for them. See M. Brewster Smith, Jerome S. Bruner, and Robert W. White, *Opinions and Personality*, New York, 1956; M. Brewster Smith, "Opinions, Personality and Political Behavior," *American Political Science Review*, LII (March 1958), pp. 1-17; and Daniel Katz, "The Functional Approach to the Study of Attitudes," *Public Opinion Quarterly*, XXIV (Summer 1960), pp. 163-204.

one would expect such needs to be oriented toward some object in which the individual is already involved.

The hypothesis that involvement will be directly related to the degree to which attitudes and behaviors in relation to international affairs perform personality-oriented functions requires qualification. Involvement refers to the degree to which an individual feels concerned and interested in an event. Involvement increases the impact of personality factors if everything else is equal. But it rarely is. Involvement tends to go along with other relationship characteristics that inhibit the degree to which personality variables affect behavior.

(2) The more information an individual has about international affairs, the less likely is it that his behavior will be based upon non-logical influences. In the absence of information about an event, decisions have to be made on the basis of other criteria. A rich informational content, on the other hand, focuses attention on the international event itself. The personality-oriented functions of the attitude would, under such circumstances, be more likely to conflict with the more cognitive and instrumental functions that attitudes also perform—functions having to do with our understanding of the world of international affairs and our manipulation of that world in the direction of our conscious interests. Such conflict might, of course, be resolved by an adjustment of one's perceptions of the international scene; one might, for instance, seek and find only that information that supported one's personality-oriented attitude. But the richer and more differentiated the informational content, the more difficult this would be.

(3) The higher the level of skill in handling international problems, the less likely it will be that attitudes on international affairs will be free to perform personality-oriented functions. Skill is, of course, closely related to information, but it is not the same. It refers to specific techniques relevant to international affairs as well as to the more general intellectual ability to deal with complex and abstract problems. Insofar as a problem is handled within an intellectual structure—a particular event related to other events and to a class of events, historical perspective brought to bear, consequences calculated, and so forth—the impact of personality on the decision will be inhibited.

(4) The more an individual values rationality as a decision-making process, the less personality factors will play a role in his decision. That an individual values rationality as a means of making decisions does not mean that he is necessarily rational in his behavior, nor does it mean that he has some complete model of scientific rationality in his mind which he mechanically follows. Rather it refers to a general tendency to

value as the basis of a decision such modes of decision-making as seeking information, controlling one's emotions (insofar as one is consciously able), trying to calculate at least some of the effects of a decision, and so forth. These modes of decision will be imperfectly observed, but insofar as they are valued, they will conflict with the formally irrelevant criteria upon which non-logical attitudes are formed.

(5) The more influence a person believes himself to have over events, the less he will orient himself toward those events in terms of personality variables. A low level of influence, especially when coupled with high involvement, is anxiety-producing. This will bring personality variables to the fore.

(6) Closely related to the degree of influence that an individual has over events is the degree of responsibility he feels for the decisions he makes. Those who are expected to be responsible for the consequences of their decisions will be more inhibited in admitting criteria that are not supposed to be relevant. Insofar as responsibility is felt, there will be greater calculation of the effects of decisions, and they will be more likely to be made in terms of the events themselves than in terms of extrinsic non-logical factors.

The second set of hypotheses as to when international relations decision-making and attitudes will perform personality-oriented functions has to do with the nature of the decision.

(1) The more detailed a decision an individual is expected or required to make, the less likely is it that personality variables will have an effect. Personality-oriented needs are non-political in origin. They have their roots in early socialization or are perhaps instinctive. The actions or attitudes that those personality factors can directly generate are, therefore, in political terms quite diffuse. They have no political content. At best they can direct a general policy one way or another; they offer little guide to specific policies.

Probably for this reason, most studies of the psychological roots of international relations have stressed rather gross distinctions—whether or not an individual's reaction was likely to be aggressive or not. More precisely, the studies have usually tried to explain the origins of war; to see under what circumstances individuals tend to choose warlike responses. But the decision to go to war is a rare one, and it is usually the result of a large number of previous decisions in which the alternative of an aggressive response vs. a non-aggressive response was not so clear. In the specific choice situations in which individuals find themselves, there may be no one alternative that better allows expression of a psychological need. To link underlying motives with an attitude on a specific public issue—atomic testing, foreign aid, and so forth—is difficult, if not impossible. The alternatives available to an individual may be so closely delimited that personality can have little or no effect.

Though general orientation toward international affairs might be linked to non-logical influences, in the process of the translation of that general orientation into specific policy choices, such cognitive factors as information and communications structure will play a part.[8]

(2) The more ambiguous the cognitive and evaluative aspects of the decision-making situation, the more scope there is for personality variables. Insofar as the "logic of the situation" is compelling, the decision-maker will have less leeway for the play of psychological forces. Thus if the values which the decision-maker consciously considers relevant to a decision are vital ones, personality will play less of a role in determining the response to an action than if the values involved are of less importance. One need not have a high level of latent aggression to respond violently to a direct attack. The level of latent aggression may, however, play a larger role in determining the reaction to some more limited provocation.

This is in turn dependent upon the degree to which the ends believed relevant in the particular situation are clear and unambiguous—i.e., are known to the participant, are few in number, and/or are clearly ordered in the participant's mind. (As will be discussed below, such lack of ambiguity is not usual.) Insofar as one has such a goal or set of goals in mind, the situation itself will be more compelling. Attention will be focused on the choice situation and the effect of unrecognized influences upon the individual will be reduced—if for no other reason than that it will be harder for these influences to remain unrecognized, since their effect on lowering the maximization of the relevant values will be more obvious. This is not to imply that where the goal is unambiguous and the way to maximize it is clear, non-logical forces might not operate

---

[8] Take the example of national stereotypes. As Boulding has pointed out, these are important components of decisions in international relations. Stereotypes of other nations tend to be long-lasting and to color interpretations of a nation's acts. But while stereotypical thinking as a mode of thought (tendency to maintain rigid categories, lack of receptivity to contradictory information, fixed evaluations) can be linked to personality variables, the particular object and content of the stereotype are harder to derive from such psychological roots. For instance, the American image of Russia changed considerably between 1942 and 1948. Such change can best be traced to the activities of the Russians during that period and the changing relations of the United States and Russia. It would be hard to trace such a specific change from a largely favorable image to an unfavorable one to the psychological roots of stereotypical thinking. See Kenneth E. Boulding, "National Images and International Stereotypes," *Journal of Conflict Resolution*, III (June 1959), pp. 120-31; and Milton Rokeach, *The Open and the Closed Mind*, New York, 1960.

and be unrecognized (by distorting perceptions and the like). But their influence would tend to be less under those circumstances.

Lastly, one can point to several effects that the social structure of the decision-making situation will have upon the probability that attitudes and behaviors in relation to international affairs will serve as an outlet for non-logical pressures. Insofar as a decision is made within a group context in which the individual's decision or attitude is visible to others, the opportunity for a decision or attitude to perform personality-oriented functions will be limited. In situations of this sort, attitudes that served such functions might be unable to perform the social adjustment functions that attitudes also perform—that is, an attitude that represented an externalization of an individual's personal problems might conflict with group expectations. The literature on group pressures for conformity is too well known to be repeated here. Suffice it to say that in group situations where attitudes are not private, and even in cases where they are, there will be both internal and external pressure upon the individual to adjust his attitudes somewhat in the direction of the group.

A group context for decision-making and attitude formation will, however, act to inhibit the effects of non-logical forces only under the assumption that these non-logical forces are idiosyncratic. If, on the other hand, a large number of the members of a group are subject to similar pressures and share attitudes that perform a personality-oriented function, the attitude in question will be reinforced by the group situation. Furthermore, personality-oriented attitudes may spread to those group members who do not share the personality need upon which the attitude was originally based. The perception, for instance, that a particular out-group is hostile may have as its origin a projection of internal aggressive tendencies, but it may also originate in the communications about that out-group to which the individual has been exposed. If the individual is a member of a group in which the general opinion of some other group is negative, he will tend to view the other group negatively. Furthermore, if all the information he has received about the other group from the members of his own group is negative, his negative view of the out-group will be quite reasonable. If this is the case, it is possible for attitudes toward international affairs having their roots in the personality characteristics of some individuals to be generalized throughout a group all of whose members do not share those characteristics. An individual in a group containing a significant number of members with personality predispositions that lead them to take hostile views toward other groups will be more likely to take such hostile views himself (even if he does not personally share the predisposition) than will a similar individual in a group with a low rate of such personality types. In this way such social-structure variables as communication networks and group norms interact with personality type to affect the set of predispositions with which a group approaches international politics.

What do these hypotheses as to the situations in which attitudes and behaviors are likely to be rooted in non-logical needs suggest about the extent to which understanding of such needs is relevant for the understanding of international relations? On the one hand, they do help to explain the popularity of non-logical models of decision-making in international relations. Attitude formation and decision-making in relation to international affairs do meet some of the conditions that, according to the above hypotheses, would tend to maximize the impact of non-logical forces. Some international issues are ones in which there is high involvement. Attachment to national symbols has a high affective content. Furthermore, the existence in international issues of an "out-group"—the other nation—presents the individual with an object toward which aggressive feelings can be directed with the minimum of such unpleasant side-effects as the guilt that might accompany aggression toward some closer object. And, lastly, international issues are often ones of high ambiguity about which information is hard to come by.

Despite these characteristics of international relations that tend to heighten the impact of non-logical influences, the non-logical models of international decision-making offer far from adequate explanations of attitudes and behaviors toward international affairs. As we have noted, the more detailed the policy situation with which we are dealing, the less useful non-logical models of decision-making become. At best they deal with rather gross distinctions and with the type of policy decision that is rarely made—the choice between a warlike or a non-warlike response. But, most important of all, the above hypotheses suggest that attitudes and behaviors in the international sphere perform many other functions for the individual than the one of serving as an external outlet for some non-logical pressure and that these other functions may be more significant.

Furthermore, the personality-oriented functions of attitudes on international affairs are probably of small significance in terms of prediction or explanation. This is largely the case because of the forces inhibiting the extent to which international attitudes and behaviors can perform personality-oriented functions for the individual. As was suggested above, the less involved an individual is in international affairs, the more information and skills he has, the greater the extent to which he accepts rationality as a valued model of decision-making, the greater his felt responsibility and influence, and the greater the extent to which his decision is made within a structured social situation, the less likely will it be that non-logical influences will play a major role in his attitude or behavior. This in turn suggests that such non-logical pressures are more inhibited among foreign policy elites than among the mass of average citizens.[9] With the exception of the degree of involvement, foreign policy elites are subject to more of the conditions that tend to inhibit the impact of personality-oriented pressures. They have greater knowledge, skills, responsibility, and influence; and, what may be most important, operate generally within bureaucratic social situations that tend to limit the scope of the decisions they can make and the criteria they can apply to these decisions. If one concentrates on explaining the behaviors and attitudes of foreign policy elites—and if one wants to explain the behaviors of nation-states as actors within the international system, this is the most strategic approach[10]—it is clear that non-logical explanations, while not completely irrelevant, are of little use. As *the* model of international relations, the non-logical model represents a great oversimplification with little explanatory power. As *part* of a broader model of the international system, the non-logical explanation of international behavior probably does not add enough to the explanatory power of the larger model to compensate for the added complexity of incorporating such variables.

[9] We mean by a foreign policy elite roughly all individuals whose activities and attitudes have a perceptible effect on the course of international relations. In most cases, this refers to a small group of high government officials, and some high communications and interest group leaders. It is important to keep in mind that on the mass level any theory of the effects of personality factors on behavior must be able to explain the modal personality in a group. Idiosyncratic variation will have no discernible effect on policy. On the elite level, as we have defined it, idiosyncratic variation might have a great effect upon policy and a study of it might prove fruitful.

[10] This is not to deny the possible impact of non-elite opinion on foreign policy. Several commentators, for instance, have described the foreign-policy formulation process in the United States as one in which mass or public opinion, dominated by mood, affective reactions, and non-logical predispositions, impedes rational decision-making by the foreign policy elite. But, insofar as non-logical factors have their greatest effect on the non-elite level, such factors can be more easily incorporated into models that assume that policy choices are based upon more rational criteria. The non-logical aspects of non-elite behavior may be considered as informational input into the elite level and a factor to be taken into account in the elite's calculations. Since one of the elite's goals will be maintenance of their position, their perception of "public opinion" may induce them to initiate policies that they might not otherwise undertake. However, in terms of the model used to explain the formation of foreign policy, it can be a rational decision-making model.

III

An alternative simplifying assumption about the processes by which individuals make decisions relevant to international affairs is an assumption of rationality. Essentially, this assumption is that the decision-maker will follow a specified set of rules in making his decisions. The particular set differs in various models of rationality, but the crucial point is that the rules can be specified. These rules indicate what information the decision-maker will use and how much further information he will seek. They specify the way in which calculations will be made, and, given the set of values that the decision-maker holds, they also specify the decision that will be arrived at, or at least the parameters within which it will fall. In this way, the varied decisional situations within the international system can be reduced to more manageable proportions. No model and no theorist, no matter how committed to holistic principles, can encompass the totality of a situation. The rationality model simplifies by specifying which variables are to be considered by decision-makers. Furthermore, by specifying the rules to be used by a decision-maker, it defines his behavior by these rules. All other behaviors—other information he seeks or receives, other modes of calculation, his personality, his preconceptions, his roles external to the international system—are irrelevant to the model. This eliminates an entire set of variables that are particularly hard to deal with in a systematic manner. Furthermore it allows one to consider all decision-makers to be alike. If they follow the rules, we need know nothing more about them. In essence, if the decision-maker behaves rationally, the observer, knowing the rules of rationality, can rehearse the decisional process in his own mind and, if he knows the decision-maker's goals, can both predict the decision and understand why that particular decision was made. Knowing, then, the process by which decision-makers respond to various turns in international affairs, the observer can concentrate on the events in the international system and greatly simplify his task of observation.

But to assess the usefulness and limitations of the rationality model in the understanding of international relations it is necessary to deal with three questions: What are the rules of rationality that are used to define the decision-making process? To what extent do individuals live up to the rationality model? And insofar as they do not live up to it—that is, insofar as the actual behavior of states in concrete situations cannot be predicted and/or explained by the model—to what extent is it still a useful tool of analysis? The answer to the last question will depend upon such factors as the extent to which deviations from the model are significant in terms of their effects on the behaviors of individuals and states and, if some of the deviations are significant, the extent to which corrections for them can be built into the model, perhaps at some later stage of analysis.

There are numerous definitions of rational behavior. These range from complete sets of rules to be followed in making decisions to more limited definitions centering around the state of psychic tension of the decision-maker (a rational decision is a cool and clearheaded decision) or specifying one aspect of the decision-making process (a rational decision-maker calculates the effects of his decisions). We will examine some of the characteristics attributed to rational decision-making and then consider the way in which such rationality models fit into models of the international system.

The most usual concept of rationality is that it is a process of means-ends analysis. The simplest case of means-ends analysis involves a single goal sought by the decision-maker. In this case, insofar as the goal is empirical (i.e., insofar as it is possible to tell if it has been attained), rational choice is the selection, among alternatives, of the action that maximizes the goal. If more than one value is relevant in the situation, it is necessary to add several steps to the model. The various values have to be listed in order of importance, and alternatives have to be compared not in terms of which maximizes one value, but in terms of which provides the best value-mix.

The means-end model, especially insofar as it specifies that one chooses the alternative that best attains one's ends, implies several other decision-making characteristics. Ideally all possible alternatives must be considered—or, if that is impossible, certainly a great number or at least all the obvious ones. Furthermore, the alternatives must be considered on their merits—that is, in terms of their contribution to the values of the decision-maker. This latter point presents some serious difficulties: if the decision-maker has a variety of goals, the alternative that would maximize the goal most relevant to the decision at hand— e.g., in a market decision, the alternative that would maximize the monetary gain—may at the same time involve great costs in terms of some other value (say, prestige or leisure) that would make it rational to reject the alternative. Since all values that may be affected by a decision are relevant to that decision, we must specify more carefully what is meant by considering an alternative on its merits. Doing so implies: (1) considering only those values that will in fact be affected by the alternative—i.e., having accurate information and making correct assessments of the outcomes—and (2) making such calculations consciously. If the individual chooses an alternative that does not maximize the goals he consciously considers to be pertinent in the situation, the decision cannot be called rational even though it maximizes others of his values which he did not consider. On the other hand—in a market situation, for instance—if an individual does not choose the alternative that maximizes monetary gain, the decision will still be rational so long as the other values relevant to the situation are consciously considered. If he refuses to drop some unprofitable activity of the family business because he believes such action would be disloyal to the memory of his father, and if the goal of loyalty is consciously invoked in the situation, the decision is rational, given his set of values. But if the relationship with family tradition is not consciously invoked and if it has effects in a situation in which it would be considered irrelevant by the decision-maker if he were aware of it, the decision will have been made on other than rational grounds. The criterion of consciousness has been added to avoid the problem of having to accept all acts as rational for which the observer or participant could, with hindsight, think of a goal that it maximized.

Thus the notion of means-ends calculations introduces the need for accurate information, correct evaluation, and consciousness of calculation. Another usual characteristic attached to this set of rational characteristics is that decisions be made coolly, with a clear head. Essentially this derives from the requirement of accurate calculations. It does not specify that the individual must avoid emotional involvement in the outcome or experience no emotion during the process of deliberation. Whether or not he does so is irrelevant as long as his calculations are not affected by his emotion. (This problem is more complex than can be gone into here, for an emotional state may change an individual's value hierarchy and thus affect his calculations. Though one can argue that emotion ought not to affect the means selected, it is more difficult to dismiss as irrational the effect of emotion on one's goals.)

The means-ends rationality model is a simplification. Individuals do not in fact make decisions in this way. However, this in itself does not make the model useless as a tool, since all theories and models involve simplification. What is necessary is to look at the nature and extent of the simplification. A growing body of theoretical and empirical work on decision-making suggests that though individuals do calculate advantages when making decisions, the method of calculation is quite different from that postulated in the means-ends rationality model.[11]

[11] The following discussion draws upon a variety of works dealing with rationality,

One set of reasons why the rationality model is not an adequate description of decision-making lies in human frailty. The type of calculation required by the model for anything but the simplest choices is beyond the powers of any individual, group, or presently designed individual-computer system. There may be too many significant variables, inadequate information, variables that are not easily quantifiable, or decisional methods that are not advanced enough. This raises serious problems for the use of rationality models, for to make the concept of means-ends rationality operational, some rules must be specified for judging whether or not such a decision-making technique has been used. Since the rules of means-ends rationality specify that one selects from the universe of alternatives the alternative that maximizes one's values, the objective observer, trying to decide if this approach to decision-making has been followed, would have to be able to make the same calculations that the method demands from the actual decision-maker. He would have to know the "right" decision, even if the actual decision-maker did not. If there are grossly different alternatives, one of which clearly maximizes the values believed by the decision-maker to be relevant to the situation while the others do not, the invocation of the "objective scientific observer" test of rationality is meaningful. But such situations are rare. They occur most frequently when one is dealing with a group that is, from the point of view of modern Western scientific thought, "foolish"—that is, a group that makes no serious attempt to approximate the rationality model in its decision-making because of lack of commitment to such an approach. Even in these situations it is often difficult to tell if the rules of rationality are being followed, for the calculations that the objective observer must make will founder on the question of the values that are operative in the situation. Usually the assumption will have to be made that there is a single overriding goal, such as increased economic production, whereas in reality a variety of other goals may be involved. But when faced with a decision made by an individual or group as highly trained and sophisticated as he is, the outside observer is probably no more able

---

including the work of Herbert Simon and James G. March and their associates on organizational decision-making (see, in particular, March and Simon, *Organizations*, New York, 1958, and Cyert and March, "A Behavioral Theory of Organizational Objectives," in Mason Haire, ed., *Modern Organization Theory*, New York, 1959); Thomas C. Schelling, "Toward a Strategy of International Conflict," The RAND Corporation, P-1648, 1959; Harold Garfinkel, "The Rational Properties of Scientific and Commonsense Activities," *Behavioral Science*, v (January 1960), p. 72; Charles E. Lindblom, "Policy Analysis," *American Economic Review*, xlviii (June 1958), pp. 298-313; and Lindblom, "The Science of Muddling Through," *Public Administration Review*, xix (Winter 1959), pp. 79-88.

to judge whether the resulting decision meets the criteria of rationality than are the actual decision-makers. Their frailty is his frailty too. And, as was pointed out in the previous section, the foreign policy elites will usually have high levels of information, be committed to rationality values, and so forth. Therefore, either one needs an objective observer whose wisdom and omniscience are much greater than those of the policy-maker or one has to assume that what the policy-maker selects is the best (most rational) alternative—a definition of rationality that is circular and gets us nowhere.[12]

But human frailty is perhaps the least important reason why the rationality model is inadequate to explain decision-making. Individuals fail to make decisions according to the criteria of the model not merely because they are foolish, or not well enough trained, or because they just do not try hard enough. Deviations from the model of rationality may take several other significant forms.

The first such deviation involves the value structure required for the rationality model. In order for a decision-maker to maximize a particular value or a set of values, he must be aware of his own values and be able to order them in terms of their significance to him. Such clear self-awareness is rare. This is true not merely because values conflict— because peace may conflict with prosperity or defense may conflict with deterrence—but because individuals do not have a clear set of value preferences that exist independently of the situation and can be matched against a variety of alternatives to see which gives the best value outcome. Instead, one's values depend in part upon the situation one is facing and what is attainable in that situation. One's preferences may change during a decision process. In actual policy decisions, as Lindblom points out, means and ends are not isolated from each other and handled independently. A policy choice is usually a choice of a set of means as well as a set of ends.[13]

---

[12] In terms of training, skills, values, and information, there is no reason to expect higher levels of rationality among detached observers than among decision-makers. There are, however, certain important structural characteristics of the situations in which decision-makers and detached observers operate that make it likely that the detached observer will more closely approximate the rationality model. This will be discussed below.

[13] Lindblom, "Policy Analysis" and "The Science of Muddling Through," *loc.cit.* This suggests why the rational model of economic man, though also inadequate, is not as inadequate as the rational model of political man. Though it oversimplifies economic choice situations to say that there is a single goal which is easily quantifiable and under which various alternatives can be rated one against another, nevertheless this is more closely approached in economic calculation, where the sphere of activity is essentially defined by its concentration around a set of values having to do with maximizing economic gain, than it is in political affairs, where the sphere is not defined by a set of values relevant to it but by the employment of certain means for the maximization of

Means-ends calculations are made more difficult by the fact that policy decisions—especially in international relations—represent collective decisions. As numerous authors have shown, if arriving at a value ordering for an individual is difficult, arriving as a joint preference ordering for a group is even more difficult, if not logically impossible. Different members will prefer different goals, and policy will often be formulated by bargaining among the members of a foreign-policy coalition. Furthermore, for any member of the foreign policy-making coalition, a particular policy decision affects both his goals in regard to the external system (i.e., what sort of foreign policy he prefers) as well as his goals in regard to the internal policy-making system (i.e., what position he wants to attain or maintain within the organization). Any policy alternative will therefore be considered in relation to a variety of goal systems that may not be consistent. It is not only that deterrence may conflict with defense, but that some members of the coalition may prefer deterrence to defense, others may prefer defense to deterrence, and others may prefer both though they conflict. And in each case the preference will be based upon both the type of foreign policy that the individual would like to see his nation follow and the effects of choosing one alternative over the other on the position he would like to attain within the foreign policy-making organization. This situation is most obvious when one considers the process of foreign policy-making in the United States, where bargaining among the various branches of the government, between government and non-governmental groups, and within the various branches of the Executive has become the normal means of reaching policy decisions.[14] But it is probable that in all decision-making systems within a bureaucratic structure (and this then applies to all modern states, democratic or non-democratic) such coalition formation is a standard part of decision-making.

One of the requirements of means-ends rationality is that a set of goals be mutually consistent. This requirement is violated both when members of the coalition have goals inconsistent with those of other members

---

any or all values held by the individual or the group. This may also explain why rationality models have been used in international relations largely in connection with military problems—more specifically, in connection with the problems of nuclear deterrence. The reason may be that the relevant goals within this limited sphere are less ambiguous (deterring an attack, avoiding nuclear destruction) and easier to place in a hierarchy.

[14] On bargaining as a process of making foreign policy, see Samuel P. Huntington, "Strategy and the Political Process," *Foreign Affairs*, xxxviii (January 1960), pp. 285-99; and Roger Hilsman, "The Foreign-Policy Consensus: An Interim Research Report," *Journal of Conflict Resolution*, iii (December 1959), pp. 361-82. On the general subject of bargaining as a characteristic of the American political process, see Robert A. Dahl, *A Preface to Democratic Theory*, Chicago, 1956, ch. 5.

(and insofar as various members each have some influence over organization policy, the organization will have conflicting goals), and when individuals themselves have goals that are inconsistent. Under the means-ends rationality model, the only way to handle such a goal conflict is to adjust the goal structure so that it is consistent. One goal must be dropped or downgraded. In such situations, however, rearranging goals to form a consistent set is not the only mechanism of adjustment; the relationship between the conflicting goals can, for instance, be denied. This can be done by separating the goals in one's mind either in terms of time (maximize X today and Y tomorrow) or in terms of spheres of activity (maximize X in relation to foreign policy, and Y in relation to domestic policy).[15] When decisions are made within a group bargaining situation, it becomes easier for a variety of conflicting values to coexist and form the basis of policy. Different goals can be pursued by different sub-groups of the organization and in this way the conflict among them obscured. Since the rationality model cannot deal with inconsistent goal structures and since such structures are not uncommon, the model is limited in explaining much organizational decision-making.

Another weakness in the rationality model is that it makes unrealistic assumptions about the way in which information, and in particular information about alternatives, is acquired. Policy alternatives are not simply presented to the decision-maker for his selection. He must seek them, a process that is difficult and time-consuming. Studies of decision-making suggest that individuals do not consider all possible alternatives and, what is more important, make no attempt to do so. Rather they scan alternatives with persistence and simplicity biases. They seek alternatives that are as similar as possible to past choices so that experience can be used as a guide. Few alternatives are considered. In fact, the process is not one of narrowing down the range of choice by eliminating possible alternatives as time goes on. Fewer alternatives are considered at the beginning of a decision than toward the end. It is only when a particular alternative is close to being accepted as policy and its implications become clear that other alternatives will be brought up by coalition members who fear injury from the proposed decision.[16]

[15] See, in this connection, Robert Abelson and M. Rosenberg, "Symbolic Psychologic: A Model of Attitudinal Cognition," *Behavioral Science*, III (January 1958), pp. 1-13.
[16] See R. M. Cyert, W. R. Dill, and J. G. March, "The Role of Expectations in Business Decision-Making," *Administrative Science Quarterly*, III (December 1958), pp. 307-40; Richard C. Snyder and Glenn D. Paige, "The United States Decision to Resist Aggression in Korea," *ibid.*, pp. 341-78; and John W. Gyr, "The Formal Nature of a Problem-Solving Process," *Behavioral Science*, V (January 1960), p. 39.

Lastly, the model of means-ends rationality treats each decision as if it were a separate entity. But a decision-maker cannot do so. He operates within a structure in which there has been previous commitment to policy and organizational vested interests in policy. A new policy will therefore tend to be not the best of all possible policies, but a relatively small variation on a present policy; it will be, to use Lindblom's word, an "incremental" policy. The choice will often be between two alternatives—the status quo or some limited modification of the status quo. And the criterion of choice will not be: "Is it the best possible action?" but: "Is it better or, at least, no worse than the present policy?"[17]

It is clear that when the decision-maker begins to search for an adequate choice rather than for the best choice—when decision-makers stop maximizing and begin "satisficing," to use Simon's term—it becomes very difficult to use the rationality model. When the operating rule was to find the best alternative, the observer, as we saw, could both predict and explain the decision that was made. There is only one best alternative. There may, however, be many adequate alternatives, and the rules of rationality do not specify how one chooses among them.

As the above description suggests, rationality models can give us only imperfect explanations and predictions of international events. Does this mean that they ought to be abandoned? Our discussion of rational decision-making should make us hesitate to do so. Like the decision-maker who accepts an adequate decision (a decision that is better, or at least no worse, than no decision), the theorist may have to accept an adequate theory (one that is better, or at least no worse, than no theory). The assumption of rationality within theories of international relations may still be a useful assumption despite the limitations mentioned above (and it will, of course, be more useful if its limitations are made explicit than if they are ignored).

Rationality models of decision-making, we have seen, would be extremely useful if only individuals behaved rationally. This suggests that the closer behavior comes to the model, and the more one is able to specify the ways in which behavior deviates from the model, the more useful the rationality model will be.

One reason for the frequent use of the rationality model in international relations theory may be that decision-making in international relations, though it deviates from rationality, approaches it more closely than does decision-making in other areas. The earlier section of this article that dealt with non-logical models of decision-making suggested

[17] Lindblom, "The Science of Muddling Through."

that there are numerous inhibitions on the sway of non-logical factors in international decision-making. Insofar as such non-logical factors are inhibited from affecting decision-making, the probability of decision-making that approaches the rationality model is increased. Of course, as our intervening discussion will have made clear, the absence of non-logical factors affecting a decision may make rational decision possible, but it does not imply that the decision will be made according to the rules of means-ends rationality. There are, however, several characteristics of international relations decision-making which suggest that the rationality model is more appropriate for this area than for, say, domestic political decision-making.

The more generally accepted the values involved in a political decision made within a group bargaining context and the simpler their structure, the more likely the decision is to approach the rationality model. Though there are many values operative in international decision-making, the fact that the decision involves an external power, in relation to which the members of the foreign policy-making coalition all occupy the same status as citizens of their nation, increases the salience of norms associated with the individual's role within the nation rather than within the sub-system of which he is also a member. In connection with foreign policy, these norms require that an individual act to further the interest of the entire nation, not his own organization. It is true that what is best for the over-all system is often equated with what is best for the unit of which the individual is a member (whether it be General Motors or the Navy or Air Force). And the over-all goals of the system, such as "maintaining the national interest," are often little better than slogans to which it is difficult to give operational meaning or, more likely, to which it is only too easy to give many different meanings. Nevertheless the existence of these emotion-laden slogans does give the system some cohesion, in that it provides a common language in which demands can be expressed and facilitates bargaining over the specific shape of the demands. Furthermore it legitimizes appeals to serve the general and not the sub-unit interest, and makes illegitimate overt invocation of sub-unit interest over the interests of the entire system. While this does not eliminate the identification of sub-unit and over-all interests, it does inhibit the extent to which the latter can be ignored in the name of the former.[18]

[18] Writing about the role of interest groups in foreign policy, Cohen has noted that "Since most foreign policy is by nature designed to deal with large national interests rather than special group interests, then it may turn out that the motivations of interest groups, the intensity of their involvement, and the extent to which they can advance legitimate claims to share official power tend to be more circumscribed in these foreign

The salience of system norms over sub-system norms in foreign policy formation is further heightened by the existence of concrete groups and organizations in the government whose explicit function is to co-ordinate and control the bargaining process among the various members of the foreign policy coalition. These co-ordinating groups and organizations—and there probably are more of them in connection with foreign than domestic policy—may be oriented to either of two types of norm: they may be oriented to the improvement of the quality of foreign policy decisions and the furtherance of system over sub-system values, or they may be oriented to the maintenance of the bargaining process among the participants in the foreign policy formation system. If they are oriented to the former, it is clear that decision-making will tend more closely to approximate the rationality model. If oriented to the latter, their effect on the degree of rationality of the decision-making process is more ambiguous, though by facilitating communications they may also increase rationality. The extent to which the mechanisms limiting parochialism will work depends in part on the nature of the policy situation. It may be suggested that the more pressing the decision, the more these mechanisms will come into play (though, of course, decisions in an emergency are affected by decisions made before the emergency). The greater the sense of stress, the greater will be the legitimacy of the over-all norms of the system and the greater the illegitimacy of parochial norms. Furthermore, the greater the emergency, the more likely is decision-making to be concentrated among high officials whose commitments are to the over-all system.[19] Thus it may be, paradoxically, that the model of means-ends rationality will be more closely approximated in an emergency when the time for careful deliberation is limited. Though fewer alternatives will be considered, the values invoked during the decision period will tend to be fewer and more consistent, and the decision will less likely be the result of bargaining within a coalition.

The ways in which actual decision-making deviates from the means-ends rationality model suggests the importance of decision-making or, at least, decision-recommending outside of a bureaucratic context. Means-ends rationality as a process of decision-making is more closely approximated in research and in decisions that are "unattached" rather

policy situations than they would be under typical conditions of domestic policy-making." (Bernard C. Cohen, *The Political Process and Foreign Policy*, Princeton, N.J., 1957, p. 283.) Though this was written about non-governmental interest groups, it probably applies as well to organizations within the government.

[19] See Hilsman, *op.cit.*, and Snyder and Page, *op.cit.*

than bureaucratic.[20] The search for policy alternatives by unattached intellectuals is less inhibited by organizational coalitions. A wider range of alternatives is likely to be considered, and the values invoked are likely to be more explicit and consistent. And, because of the over-all norms of loyalty to the system, the more explicit the values operative in a particular decision situation, the more they will tend to be non-parochial. Unattached intellectual research, therefore, can introduce a higher level of means-ends rationality into foreign-policy decision-making. And in foreign policy problems, much more than in connection with most domestic problems, there is a large amount of such work being done. But one caution: it may be just because this research approaches the rationality model that it is often not translatable into actual policy. By approximating the model of means-ends rationality—by making the values to be served explicit and by calculating explicitly the possible consequences of alternative policies—this type of policy formulation is more likely to arouse opposition among members of the foreign policy coalition whose value preferences are different.

These characteristics of international relations decision-making ought not to be taken to imply that such decision-making follows the means-ends rationality model. Such we found earlier would be very unlikely, if not impossible. It does suggest, however, that such a model may be a not inappropriate first approximation. But it will be useful only if one does not forget that it *is* an approximation. It may be useful to consider how nations would behave if decisions were made rationally, but too heavy concentration on such decisions may lead to sterile theorizing. It is important also to begin to build into the rationality model propositions as to the ways in which decision-making will deviate from the model—the circumstances under which deviation will be maximized, the types of individuals most likely to deviate, the ways in which deviation will take place. These dimensions of deviation are of course just those aspects of decision-making that were eliminated from the rationality model in order to develop a simpler and more manageable model. But their reintroduction as extensions of the rationality model does not imply a return to the chaos of looking at "raw" decisions in terms of all their aspects. One of the major values of the rationality model may be that it facilitates the systematic consideration of deviations from rationality. Some such deviations have been specified above in connection with our discussion of the factors that impede or enhance the impact of non-logical influences on decisions and in connection with our discussion of

[20] The term "unattached" is taken from Robert Merton, "The Role of the Intellectual in Bureaucracy," in *Social Structure and Social Theory*, Glencoe, Ill., 1957, pp. 207-24.

the differences between actual decision-making and decision-making according to the rationality model.

The rationality model is useful, but it is useful only if its limitations are appreciated. It may be convenient under certain circumstances to assume that nations make decisions as if they were following the rules of means-ends rationality. But if the simplification of the rationality model leads one to believe that an adequate model of the international system can be developed without consideration of the complex ways in which policy is formulated within the nations that are members of that system, the model will ill serve the cause of theory in international relations.

AGRARIA AND INDUSTRIA

Two Models of the International System

By GEORGE MODELSKI

I. THE INTERNATIONAL IMPLICATIONS OF INDUSTRIALISM

EVER since the invention of the steam engine in the eighteenth century, men have reflected upon the profound transformations being wrought in their societies by what soon came to be called the Industrial Revolution. In their own fields, historians, economists, sociologists, military specialists, and Marxist philosophers have all traced the effects of industrialization, and some of them—particularly those interested in and aroused by war—have perceived the implications of these changes for international relations. Priority in this respect seems to belong to Auguste Comte, the founder of modern sociology, for devising the first analytical-historical model of the industrial society—one moreover that explicitly, though not always convincingly, pointed to the international repercussions of industrialism. In an essay first published in 1822, Comte drew a distinction between two types (or models) of civilization: the Theological and Military, and the Scientific and Industrial (there also was a third, transitional—as he called it, "mongrel"—type, the Metaphysical and Juridical). Comte's first model is notable for the predominance of military activities: "Society makes conquest its one permanent aim." War makes it possible to found larger societies. In the transitional stage, he observed, "The two aims of activity, conquest and production, advance *pari passu*. Industry is at first favoured and protected as a military resource. Later its importance augments, and finally war is regarded and systematically pursued as a means of favouring industry." But, in the last model, "industry has become predominant. All the special relations have gradually established themselves upon industrial bases. Society, taken collectively, tends to organize itself in the same manner," renounces conquest and war, and makes production "its only and constant aim."[1]

Herbert Spencer, writing later in the nineteenth century, took essentially the same position. He too analyzed his political systems in terms of two models, the Militant and the Industrial types of society. He too held the international implications of his models to be vitally important,

[1] A. Comte, *System of Positive Policy*, London, Longmans, Green, 1877, IV, pp. 572-73; see also II, pp. 320-24, and III, pp. 48-53.

even though the analysis he undertook touches hardly at all upon international relations. He too maintained that in the militant type of society wars had had essential functions to fulfill but, he asserted, "What remains to be done, calls for no other agency than the quiet pressure of a spreading industrial civilization. . . . From war has been gained all that it had to give."[2]

Where Comte and Spencer were struck by the antagonism between war and the industrial regime, observers at the turn of the century reached almost the opposite conclusion. They argued that industrial growth caused competition and war because it set up pressures for overseas economic development and created a scramble for colonies. "La politique coloniale," wrote Premier Jules Ferry, "est la fille de la politique industrielle. L'industrialisation et la colonisation forment les deux faces d'un temps dominé par les considerations matérielles,"[3] an opinion that was repeated in more formal and sophisticated terms in Hobson's and Lenin's familiar analyses of imperialism.

These earlier models of political society which, without fully analyzing the agrarian and industrial international system as such, identified some of the international implications of differing modes of economic and social organization, seem to have been passed over by later students of international relations, most of whom were aware of and paid attention to at least some of the consequences of the industrial revolution for world politics,[4] but have not treated the subject systematically or at length.

The sudden insight that industrialization is not something that happened to Europe and North America a century ago, but a process which at this time occupies more than half of mankind, has in recent years aroused a new interest in the industrial society and its predecessors. The study of "underdeveloped" (non-industrialized, or industrializing) societies has gathered impetus, and has influenced not only sociology and economics, but also political science[5] and international relations.

[2] H. Spencer, *Principles of Sociology*, New York, 1886, II, p. 664.

[3] Cited in M. Baumont, *L'essor industriel et l'imperialisme colonial, 1878-1904*, Paris, Felix Alcan, 1937, p. 2.

[4] See, e.g., Clyde Eagleton, *International Government*, New York, 1932, pp. 10ff.; Quincy Wright, *A Study of War*, Chicago, 1942, I, pp. 199-200; H. J. Morgenthau, *Politics Among Nations*, 2nd ed., New York, 1956, pp. 357-61.

[5] See, e.g., G. A. Almond and J. S. Coleman, eds., *The Politics of the Developing Areas*, Princeton, N.J., 1960. See also F. W. Riggs, "Agraria and Industria: Toward a Typology of Comparative Administration," in W. J. Siffin, ed., *Toward the Comparative Study of Public Administration* (Bloomington, Ind., 1957), to which I owe the terms "Agraria" and "Industria" and other insights into the working of the two societies. In his paper in the present symposium, Riggs presents a deductive model, using, for example, the terms "fused" and "refracted" society. I have retained his earlier, inductive terminology, which

Authors who now spotlight the international implications of changes in the structure of national economies[6] all point out that the attainment of industrial maturity by a number of new nations has altered the character of world society, but that industrialization is as yet incomplete. Their perspective is broad; they discuss the wide range of the international repercussions of industrial growth, and pay special attention to processes of transition and to the consequences of the unevenness of those processes.

The present paper therefore sets itself a more limited task. Expanding ideas sketched briefly in an earlier article,[7] it elaborates in some detail and from a theoretical perspective the international models corresponding to agrarian and industrial societies and touches only briefly upon problems of transition. The models thus presented are seen as conceptual devices for increasing our understanding of the contemporary international system and, more generally, as a partial contribution to a broader enterprise: the comparative analysis of all known international systems.

II. Some Theoretical Assumptions

Until recently the discipline of international relations has been preoccupied almost exclusively with the international system which emerged in Western Europe at the end of the Middle Ages and which has persisted in its essential features until the very recent past. Brief textbook references to earlier, "exotic," international systems such as the Near Eastern or the Chinese have been insufficient to awaken the student to the wealth of experience in the management of international relations which was a valuable property of the earlier ages. Yet, because of this lack of comparative data, some crucial features of even the contemporary international system have remained obscure. Generalizations produced on the basis of the operation of one international system could hardly

---

seems to me more concrete and more familiar. It is compatible with the notion of a continuum and allows for an addition of "primitive" society alongside Agraria and Industria. The original terms, furthermore, appear less final and positive about the shape of the future; they leave open to question whether the few industrial societies that we now know (for instance, the United States) are in fact the "ultimate" in social development.

[6] E.g., Charles McClelland, "Systems and History in International Relations: Some Perspectives in Empirical Research Theory," *General Systems*, iii, 1958, pp. 242ff.; W. W. Rostow, *The Stages of Economic Growth*, New York, 1960; A. Organski, *World Politics*, New York, 1959. Organski believes that the present international system is still in the transitional stage and refuses to speculate about the characteristics of the future industrial international society (*ibid.*, p. 307).

[7] "Theoretical International Relations," *Australian Outlook*, xiii (June 1959), pp. 141-43.

claim universality, and have therefore remained unconvincing. In fact, so narrow has been the scholar's outlook and so great his preoccupation with the behavior of the national and independent entities of his own immediate experience that the mere notion of an international system as a system that is comprehensive, persistent, interdependent, and boundary-maintaining has remained in doubt.

The rapid changes in the structure of international society occurring before our eyes have made us aware that the international system of only a quarter-century ago does not represent the only lasting pattern in which independent states may be related. As a number of alternative patterns lie between us and the future and others have been known to exist in the past, students of international relations must seek to enrich their field of study and experience by drawing upon them. This study, therefore, assumes that (1) the proper object of the study of international relations is the universe of international systems, past, present, future, and hypothetical.[8]

If we thus extend the scope of our study to include a large number of hitherto ignored species, it behooves us to specify the properties which these entities have in common by virtue of being international systems. We therefore maintain that (2) international systems are social systems; (3) international systems have structures; (4) the same functional requirements are satisfied in all international systems; and (5) concrete international systems are mixed systems.

These assumptions are, in the main, little more than assertions of familiar structural-functional relations. Points 3-5 are in fact restatements, with respect to international systems, of generalizations made by Gabriel Almond about structure and function in political societies.[9] But so far they do not seem to have been made explicitly with reference to international systems and for that reason they seem worth restating in the context of international relations.

Our second proposition in effect declares that sociological generalizations about social systems are, *mutatis mutandis*, applicable also to the study of international systems. Like other systems, international systems consist of a set of objects, plus the relationships between these objects and between their attributes.[10] Since international systems are systems of action and interaction between collectivities and between

[8] For examples of constructs of past, present, future, and hypothetical international systems, see, e.g., Wright, *op.cit.*, II, pp. 1493-97, and M. A. Kaplan, *System and Process in International Politics*, New York, 1957, ch. 2.
[9] In Almond and Coleman, eds., *op.cit.*, p. 11.
[10] A. D. Hall and R. E. Fagen, "Definition of a System," *General Systems*, I, 1956, pp. 18-28.

individuals acting on their behalf, and hence social systems, the objects of which the international systems are composed may be defined, on the analogy of Talcott Parsons' fundamental unit of the social system,[11] as international status-roles (examples of these are the roles of a great power, of a United Nations member, or of a neutral).

International status-roles may be conceived as the outputs of the foreign-policy process of international actors (states or international organizations); they have positional (status) or processual (role) aspects. The international actors are a separate "integrative focus" of the international action system analyzable in terms of the input-output model. The input of an international actor consists in the demands facing its policy-makers and the power put at their disposal; its output is in the policy-makers' international decisions or policies or, from another point of view, their international role-playing.

In addition to the international system and the foreign policies of international actors, and pursuing further the analogy from Parsons' *Social System*, we recognize international culture as the third "integrative focus" of the total international action system. It is a concept analogous to Almond's "political culture,"[12] and is not to be confused with the term "world culture," which refers to the growing similarity of culture patterns throughout the world.[13] International culture is the set of beliefs, norms, and values engendered in diplomatic intercourse; without it, life in the diplomatic milieu would in fact be impossible. Suffice it to say that its chief makers are statesmen and their diplomatic agents, that its main symbolic vehicle is no doubt language ("diplomatic" language in particular), that it exhibits variability (for instance, in the value attached to colonies in the past century), and that it shows pattern consistency or style.

The international system (conceived to be boundary-maintaining) has an environment comprising all that is outside its boundaries, which may be geographical, political (that is, those defining non-members), or substantive (defining matters which are not international).[14]

Our third point—that international systems have structures—may be deduced from the ascertainable fact of the persistence of such systems over time; hence the need for and the evident existence of manifest or

[11] Talcott Parsons, *The Social System*, Glencoe, Ill., 1951, pp. 24-26.
[12] G. A. Almond, "Comparative Political Systems," in H. Eulau, ed., *Political Behavior*, Glencoe, Ill., 1956, pp. 36-42.
[13] See, e.g., Quincy Wright, ed., *The World Community*, Chicago, 1948, pp. 47ff.
[14] This conception of the international environment avoids the familiar difficulty of envisaging the international system as a system without an environment; see, e.g., McClelland, *op.cit.*, p. 237, and Wright, *A Study of War*, I, p. 955.

latent structures to ensure that persistence. International structures are relatively stable responses of the international system to the need for satisfying its functional requirements.

The functional requirements of international systems center upon four problems (1) allocation of personnel and material facilities to the performance of international functions, and hence international role differentiation and specialization; (2) the making of binding decisions and the allocation of rewards, and hence international stratification; (3) the maintenance of solidarity; (4) the maintenance and support of international culture and of the communication system.[15] The international system may thus be seen to comprise the structures of authority, resources, solidarity, and culture.

No matter what their size, complexity, or composition, all international systems possess standardized structures for maintaining themselves and for performing their functions. These structures may be manifest (the diplomatic network as a communications structure) or latent (scientific exchange as an international solidarity structure), fused (the imperial court as an authority-, solidarity-, and culture-maintenance structure) or specialized (the summit meeting as an authority structure), but they are found in all systems. The question asked in this paper is: what kind of international structure is consistent with, or required by, agrarian and industrial international systems?

As for point 4, an international system is a distinct system because its functions—the safeguarding of the independence of its members and the maintenance of international order by minimizing conflict and violence —are distinct from those of its objects and their relationships. If a structure fulfilling a certain function is observed in one system, the question may legitimately be asked: what structures perform this function in the other system? (Thus we might ask: how are the functions now performed by the U.N. General Assembly implemented in other systems?) Of particular interest is the way in which a set of functional requirements is satisfied in a number of systems.

In the main body of the paper, we will discuss the structures through which international functions are performed in agrarian and in industrial international systems, respectively. The four internal requirements thus serve as the conceptual framework for the comparative analysis of these two international systems. However, the four func-

---

[15] Classification based on Parsons' scheme of functional system problems; see *The Social System*, esp. chs. 1-5. See also T. Parsons, R. Bales, and E. Shils, *Working Papers in the Theory of Action*, Glencoe, Ill., 1953, ch. 5; and Parsons, *Structure and Process in Modern Societies*, Glencoe, Ill., 1960, *passim*.

tional requirements must be solved within certain limiting conditions; these conditions thus set limits to the variability permitted to structures of the international system if its international character is to be maintained (no matter whether the system is agrarian or industrial): (1) facilities (power) cannot be allowed to be fused; a segmentation of resources among at least two, but preferably more, members of the system is necessary, hence importance attaches to the number of members in the system; (2) authority may not be unduly concentrated either, and a considerable degree of equality will prevail; (3) solidarity cannot expand beyond a certain point and will in fact remain low; (4) prevalent culture patterns will stress individualism and the independence of members.

Finally, the models here introduced are presented as types marking two points along a continuum extending from primitive to industrial systems. They establish the standards with the help of which processes of change or intermediate structures may be appraised in relation to such a continuum. The models moreover are conceptual devices or constructs which draw upon and combine properties of international systems but do not in themselves necessarily represent any concrete international system. For this reason, no concrete international system is likely to be "pure" in the sense of embodying all characteristics of one model and no others. More likely it will be mixed and embody characteristics of both systems. To paraphrase Robert Redfield, in all agrarian international systems there is some Industria; in all industrial international systems there is some Agraria.

III. A Characterization of Agraria and Industria

The differentiation between agrarian and industrial international systems is intuitively clear, simple, and therefore (it is submitted) compelling. It proceeds from the basic insight that international relations of systems in which the agrarian mode of production predominates will significantly differ from those in which industry holds sway. We shall be able to keep this distinction clear in our minds as long as we continue reminding ourselves that the condition differentiating agrarian from industrial systems is not the simple presence of "factories" or "manufactures"—these have existed in simple forms in ancient Egypt, and on an extended scale in, for instance, ancient Rome and Byzantium—but the availability of tremendously increased sources of industrial energy—the consequence of the harnessing of steam and oil, of water and atomic energy. The invention and immediate widespread utilization of the steam engine in England of the eighteenth century (first of all in the textile industry and in coal mining) is the event which makes it possible for us to identify in time the origin of the industrial system; consumption of industrial energy per head of the population is still the most reliable index of industrialization.

To illuminate the concept of agrarian and industrial international systems, we shall contrast it first of all with that of "international" systems appropriate to primitive conditions. In a rough and ready sense, agrarian and industrial societies coincide with civilization. They are "civilized" structures which came into being first of all because agricultural settlement and the consequent attainment of a food surplus made possible an extended division of labor culminating in the construction and maintenance of towns. Agrarian societies are those in which "civilized" towns confront the "uncultured" and "backward" peasant; in industrial societies the towns have swallowed the peasant and the countryside, too. Contrasting with these two "civilized" systems of the historians is the primitive world of the anthropologist: the world of folk societies: of small, isolated, non-literate homogeneous and solidary communities, the prevalent form of organization of which is the extended family or tribe.[16] A few thousand years ago this was the only type of human society in existence, but even today a small, though rapidly diminishing, fraction of mankind retains these characteristics.

Traditionally, international relations has concerned itself with international systems of civilized—that is, non-primitive—societies, those with a division of labor elaborate enough to permit the emergence of such specialized roles as that of the military commander, the foreign policy advisor, or the resident representative. However, the analysis of international systems could fruitfully be extended also to relations within the primitive world. International relations are basically segmental—that is, relations between segments or structurally separate units performing essentially the same functions; examples of segments other than the nation-state (or, more generally, the political system) are families, or firms or labor unions in the same industry.[17] Segmentation is also found in primitive societies where clans or tribes may split into territorially based extended family segments, relations between which are susceptible to an international relations approach and the systems they form to international structural-functional analysis. Thus the

[16] See, e.g., Robert Redfield, *The Primitive World and Its Transformations*, Ithaca, N.Y., 1953, pp. 7ff.

[17] Segmentation occurs because limitations on the economies of scale prevent the uncontrolled extension of a given unit; cf. Parsons, *Structure and Process*, p. 263. The fact of segmentation creates the problem of relations between segments. International relations provides one set of models for understanding segmental relations.

political system of Konkomba described by David Tait[18] is essentially an international system, a usage that is borne out by the habit of referring to violent conflict between clans as war. Among the entities that they study (families, clans, tribes, tribal groups), anthropologists are now accustomed to looking for the political unit (that which sanctions the use of violence). As a complement to their extensive studies of primitive war,[19] they might on occasion find use for the concept of the international system—a semi-isolated system encompassing a number of such political units (or segments).[20]

Useful in differentiating primitive international systems from the two "civilized" societies, and also in drawing a distinction between Agraria and Industria themselves, are two properties of international systems which we shall call "size" and "homogeneity."

Through an absence of comparative studies in this field, the problem of the size of international systems has so far remained largely unexplored (except for discussions of the number of great powers in a system). It may, however, be pertinent to observe that some international systems are larger than others. Reliable indices of size of such systems remain to be elaborated, but some such elementary indicators of size as population figures, geographical scope, or trade and income figures easily come to mind. Any one of these might, with suitable qualifications, fit our purpose. Below, simple population figures alone will be used as indicators of the size of an international system. A populous international system, the figures for whose inhabitants run into billions, will be deemed to be large; a system of a few million, small. But demographic data may have to be later supplemented by more complete indices of size.

Another important system property is homogeneity. Basic to this category is the insight that some social systems are homogeneous, while others, without ceasing to form a system, are divided into a number of distinct traditions. Agrarian societies typically are non-homogeneous; their characteristic feature has been described as "the dominance of a two-class system, with the upper group enjoying prerogatives of political power and usually also religious prestige, and the lower consisting predominantly of peasants and petty traders,"[21] or, even more graphically, as the coexistence, side by side, of the "great tradition" of the court,

---

[18] In *Africa*, XXIII (July 1953), pp. 213-23.
[19] For a thorough survey, see Wright, *A Study of War*, I, ch. 6.
[20] For an extensive study along these lines, see R. Numelin's *The Beginnings of Diplomacy: A Sociological Study of Intertribal and International Relations*, London, Oxford University Press, 1950.
[21] Parsons, *Structure and Process*, p. 117.

the towns, and the nobility with the countless "little traditions" of village peasantry.[22] Agraria's political community extends to only a small portion of the population of a given state; in Deutsch's terms, the mobilized part of the population is only a fraction of the total population.[23] Agraria's foreign policy objectives are set by the interests of the ruler and his court without reference to the preoccupations of the "subjects" (who constitute the "underlying" population). In industrial societies, broadly speaking, the whole population is mobilized,[24] and for this reason the political community whose interests policymakers implement in foreign policy is coextensive with the citizen population. We would proceed further and maintain that the rate of mobilization for international interaction[25] is a property of the international system. Potentially the whole population of an international system may be mobilized for interaction (as in industrial total war) or, at the other pole, only a thin crust of the ruling elites and their retainers may in effect constitute an international society. A homogeneous system differs in essential respects from a non-homogeneous one and exhibits different behavioral characteristics.

The properties just clarified serve to draw distinctions between the three international systems that have been mentioned. Size distinguishes very small, primitive systems from small, agrarian systems and large, industrial systems. Homogeneity helps to contrast homogeneous, primitive systems with non-homogeneous, agrarian systems and, at a higher level of social and political complexity, with homogeneous, industrial systems.

Let us consider some population figures as provisional and tentative indices of size. Primitive systems encompass small, face-to-face communities in which a large portion of the adult population has the opportunity of personal acquaintance. For an African tribe which has the characteristics of an international system the population figures are given as 45,000, composed of clans of about 250 persons each.[26] On many occasions tribal war occurs in much smaller systems, but we can take the population figure of one million as the upper limit of such a primitive system, most instances seemingly falling within the limits of 5,000-

[22] Robert Redfield, *Peasant Society and Culture*, Chicago, 1956, *passim*.

[23] K. W. Deutsch, *Nationalism and Social Communication*, New York, 1953. On international homogeneity, see T. Mathisen, *Methodology in the Study of International Relations*, New York, 1959, pp. 93-95.

[24] Riggs, *op.cit.*, pp. 73-74.

[25] We might call this "horizontal" homogeneity, as distinguished from "vertical" homogeneity of units of the system—for instance, the rate of uniformity in ideological and other domestic arrangements of members of a system.

[26] Tait, *op.cit.*, p. 213.

500,000. Agrarian international systems, such as the Chinese state system of 500 B.C., the Greco-Roman system of 200 B.C. or 100 A.D., the Mexican system of 1500 A.D., and the Western system of 1300 or 1700 A.D., operated at much higher population levels, which—although difficult to estimate—seem to have ranged between the lower limit of the primitive systems and an upper boundary in the region of one billion. The classic Greco-Roman international system fluctuated between a figure in excess of 43 million in 400 B.C. to over 113 million in 200 A.D. The South American figures are uncertain, but for about 1500 A.D. may be put at least at 6 million. The Chinese system does not seem to have exceeded 100 million. Finally, the Western international system remained for centuries at a level below 100 million, rocketing only within the last hundred years above the limit of one billion.[27] (See Figure 1.)

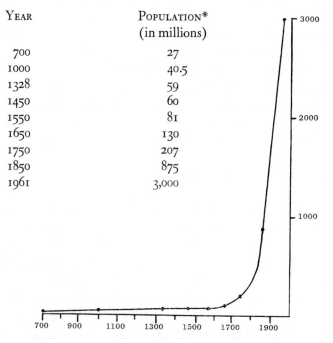

YEAR	POPULATION* (in millions)
700	27
1000	40.5
1328	59
1450	60
1550	81
1650	130
1750	207
1850	875
1961	3,000

FIG. 1. THE WESTERN INTERNATIONAL SYSTEM, 700-1961

* For 700-1450, figures have been estimated for Europe only. For 1550-1850, the following figures (estimated millions) have been added for extra-European territories: 1550—5; 1650—30; 1750—67; 1850—609. For 1961, the Western international system is assumed to contain the entire world population.

The estimates cited illustrate graphically the tremendous change in dimensions which has overtaken the Western international system in

[27] Wright, *A Study of War*, I, pp. 467, 612.

the past century. But, striking as they are, they underplay the fundamental differences which separate past systems from those toward which we are moving, for they assume the mobilization of the entire population of each system. If, on the other hand, we qualify those figures by a 5 per cent rate of mobilization factor for the Western system of 1650 and a 20 per cent factor for 1960—surely a conservative estimate—the contrasts between the two systems become even more striking, showing a change of at least two orders of magnitude—from a mobilized population of 6,500,000 to one of 540,000,000. And, as we know, both the population figures and the mobilization ratio continue to rise at a very high rate. The conclusion seems inescapable that a system so dramatically expanded must also behave in a profoundly new way.

Primitive systems are wholly homogeneous and therefore also fully mobilized for such "international" interaction as there may be.[28] But this homogeneity can be maintained only at a given level of social organization; civilization—the conquest of one tribe by another, the segregation of towns from the countryside, the expansion of societal apparatus—all these processes of increasing social differentiation work to the detriment of homogeneity. The static agricultural society is dramatically cleaved; the intensity of interaction in it is low and is always lower than the total population figures would suggest because the international system operates mainly at the level of the princes, the towns, the courts, and the warriors; it ignores the peasants, the serfs, the slaves, and the colonial populations. The underlying population suffers from wars and from the decline in public order as it does from natural disasters, but it is not actively involved in international undertakings. Industrialization means the return of homogeneity (the sentiments behind modern nationalism have justly been compared to the loyalties cementing the unity of tribe). It means either, to use the Deutschian terms again, the assimilation of the underlying population to the mobilized minority, or else the emergence of new political systems to cater to the interests of previously unassimilated peoples (for instance, in the colonies). Favorite indices of contemporary levels of mobilization are the work force in non-agricultural occupations or the rate of urbanization,[29] but they have to be used with care because in industrial states farmers and the agricultural workers are just as industrialized as the

---

[28] On the homogeneity of primitive society, see Redfield, *The Primitive World*.

[29] See, e.g., K. W. Deutsch, "Toward an Inventory of Basic Trends and Patterns in Comparative and International Politics," *American Political Science Review*, LIV (March 1960), p. 56.

employees of industry; New Zealand and Denmark are every inch as industrial as the United States. Homogeneity refers to the fact that the entire, or virtually the entire, population of a state is part of the level at which the international system operates on the political community; as more and more people partake in international interactions, the international system becomes progressively more complex.

Enough has been said to suggest that small and homogeneous international systems will tend to be primitive, small and non-homogeneous systems agrarian, and large and homogeneous systems industrial. Empirically we observe that in the past those systems which have operated in agricultural environments have been small and non-homogeneous, and vice versa. At the same time the large-scale and homogeneous system of our experience seems to be evolving out of the contemporary international society. A large, homogeneous system, moreover, can maintain itself only upon an industrial structure. The transport and communications networks which prevent a breakdown due to over-expansion and assure the system's homogeneity, the resources which feed the world-wide network of international and diplomatic connections—all these can emerge only out of a system that produces a large surplus over and above the bare necessities of life, a surplus many times greater than that of an agrarian economy. Universal and other international organizations, the projection of Great Power influences all over the earth and beyond, the total threat of nuclear destruction, these all-too-familiar features of today's large and increasingly larger and more homogeneous system could not have developed without industrialism. Industrial systems that for some reason lose size (and/or homogeneity) we would therefore expect to assume the behavioral characteristics of agrarian systems; agrarian systems that expand in size and gain homogeneity would in turn tend to become industrial (or cease to be international). And if we dare (or can bear) to contemplate a world devastated by atomic bombs, with most of its population wiped out, might not the survivors—if any—reform into associations akin to primitive tribes, creating a host of new "primitive" international systems all over the scarred globe?[30]

Size and homogeneity are two characteristic properties of international systems. Another may be identified as the membership requirements of the system: the characteristics which a political system must possess if it is to be regarded as a full member either of the agrarian

---

[30] The same connections do not hold between the size of a state and its agrarian or industrial character; a small state might be industrial because it forms part of an international system within which its special skills are accommodated.

or the industrial international system. What qualities enabled, say, the Kingdoms of Egypt and Babylonia in the fifteenth century B.C. or the Kingdom of England and the Venetian Republic in the fifteenth century A.D. to play their part in the agrarian systems of their age? What characteristics do Brazil, Ghana, or China need if they are to function efficiently in the industrial international system? Posing the question in this way, we are conditioning ourselves to view the problem from a system perspective; we are also assuming, in Morton Kaplan's terminology, a considerable degree of system dominance.

The requirements which a state should satisfy to be accepted as a member of an agrarian international system may be summarized as follows: (1) power based on land or commerce and limited in extent; (2) a narrowly based political community founded on kinship and centered on the prince and the great families; (3) traditional authority, typically focused on the landowner-merchant prince; and (4) acceptance of the great tradition as the bearer of international culture.

Like other systems, the international system too sets up pressures penalizing deviations from the "rules" of membership; it fosters growth in some members (it "levels up") and hinders undue progress in others (by "leveling them down"). Historically, in "leveling up" the agrarian international system helped to consolidate areas and political systems which were emerging out of primitiveness and assimilated unruly tribes on its fringes to the traditions of a more settled way of life. But Agraria also knows the leveling-down process: the destruction of great civilizations which might have served as nuclei of Industria. The trials and the eventual destruction of the Byzantine Empire, heir to the great traditions of the Greco-Roman state, demonstrate the fact that the international system sometimes works to defeat a state whose advanced organization and accumulated wealth may be insufficient to transform the system in unfavorable conditions, but which presents too great a temptation and also a threat to its neighbors.

The characteristics of a member of the industrial international system (hence those of an industrial state) seem to be as follows: (1) national power based on industrial organization, large in extent; (2) political community coextensive with the population; (3) rational authority of the committee type; and (4) an international culture pervading the whole society.

The industrial system also compels not fully assimilated member states to conform to its requirements: it supports the "underdeveloped" state and helps it to attain a higher level of industrialization—or else lowers its status or, on occasion, eliminates it—just as it may ostracize "colonial" powers seeking to maintain rule over areas or populations which are non-homogeneous with them. The "leveling-up" process seems strong and is most evident in the incentives and encouragement to economic growth; we may only speculate about circumstances in which "leveling-down" could come into play. The international redistribution of income in the form of foreign aid might be one of its manifestations.

We have now established the distinguishing properties of agrarian and industrial international systems. Let us see how, in the light of these properties, the systems cope with their four characteristic problems: specialization and division of labor, authority and stratification, solidarity and communications, and the maintenance of culture.

IV. THE STRUCTURES OF AGRARIA AND INDUSTRIA

If it is granted that international systems perform functions and that the performance of these functions can be traced to identifiable actors and entails the expenditure of determinate facilities, let us inquire first of all into the agrarian and industrial mechanisms which allocate actors and facilities to international functions—in short, into the division of labor of international systems.

That the division of labor is limited by the extent of the market has been the received doctrine of economists ever since Adam Smith wrote *The Wealth of Nations,* but of course the principle applies to all systems involving specialization of function. Division of labor in international systems too is directly related to the extent of the system. Grounds for believing that agrarian international systems are small and that their industrial counterparts are large have already been indicated; hence in Agraria we would expect little or, in respect of certain functions, no specialization, and in Industria a complex and elaborate division of labor. We have moreover observed that the systems differ in respect of homogeneity; hence we would surmise that the type of problem facing them would change, too. Non-homogeneous systems of low intensity of interaction are likely to produce simple demands; homogeneous systems give rise to complex new international functions, thus bringing to the international level (for instance, through UNICEF) functions which earlier were performed solely on the national level.

Agraria's international division of labor is limited and is characterized by fused role functions, performed by national actors and individuals. The functions necessary for the operations of the international system, international trade and its regulation, decision-making and the allocation of rewards, international communication and determination of the rules of international order are fused in combined roles, especially in the rulers of powerful states. Facilities invested in the performance of functions are small; there is no specialized mechanism for diverting resources to international functions.

In the industrial system role functions are numerous and specialized; they engage states, individuals, and international organizations and consume significant resources. The range of action accomplished in response to international functions is large and the number of specialized agencies great. Roles are diffused among numerous holders, and statesmen of the small powers and international agents play a more notable part as initiators of international policies. The extent of international interaction, and hence problems arising out of its regulation, change. Permanent mechanisms emerge for channeling resources to international functions: such resources may come to approximate those held by a great power (the United Nations' facilities now equal those of a small-medium power).

The extent of the market, and hence specialization, says Adam Smith, are a function of transport costs. If the commodity in question is security, then the extent of the market for it—the system within which it is bought and sold, demanded and supplied—is circumscribed by the "cost of power transmission," the ease with which power can be projected. In agrarian societies these costs are high—absolutely and relative to output. Transmission costs consume a large share of power-output; security, therefore, especially that needed by a small state against a great power, can only be had at a high price and not everywhere.[31] Industria, by contrast, has strikingly and permanently cut down the expenses of deliverable security. The time-cost of personnel movement has been nearly eliminated. The cost of nuclear weapon delivery is becoming nearly invariant with respect to location. Industria's system is thus a market in which security can be bought at a price unrelated to location; hence it is in this technical sense "perfect," tightly knit and for the first time truly world-wide in extension. In systems where security is produced on an increasingly large scale, specialization rises and costs of production and market price can be expected to fall. In the present context specialization would mean this: since security delivered at all locations can be obtained from a number of producers, brokerage mechanisms are required for the smooth functioning of the

---

[31] At times when costs of power transmission declined—for instance, during the periodic eruptions of the nomads across the Eurasian land mass or when West European seapower broke out of the North Atlantic—the state systems of the world have experienced profound changes.

"market." Functions earlier fused in one role (those of an emperor-protector or the benevolent great power granting security in exchange for loyalty, or tribute, or deference) now tend to be devolved upon a variety of actors, some of whom—international organizations in particular—specialize exclusively in the brokerage of security, or the maintenance of contacts, or the exchange of information, supplying it on a universalist (i.e., non-discriminatory) basis to all members of the system "entitled" to it, regardless of particularist attachments.

Increasing specialization and division of labor in the international system can thus be traced directly to industrialism and its amazingly efficient transport and communication facilities. However, the consequence of specialization is the increasing tightness[32] of international arrangements and declining freedom of action at least for the more powerful. The stricter, the more specialized the definition of role expectations, the less room there is for arbitrary action, by contrast with the "loose structuring" of Agraria's international relations, where constellations of powers could revolve semi-independently in their orbits, only intermittently being affected by the system's over-all functioning.

The next set of characteristics individualizing an international system concerns its structure of authority and the stratification system derived from it. We start from the axiom, grounded in the universal fact of the uneven initial endowment of the nations as well as in their varying contributions to the functioning of the system, that all international systems are stratified, that their members can at all times be ranked according to the hierarchical position they occupy within them. The position of Great Power is crucial to all international societies, and is invested with duties as well as with privileges and rewards.[33] International systems thus have a "pecking order";[34] what principles determine pecking orders in Agraria and Industria?

Agraria's social systems are built upon status and deference. Birth, rank, and position in society virtually determine a man's progress through life. Agraria's international outlook, too, centers on ranks, titles, and privileges. The ranks and titles are those of princes and sovereigns rather than of states, but diplomats contend over them and international incidents are caused by such disputes. Industria, on the

[32] On the loose or tight structuring of Agraria and Industria, see Riggs, op.cit., pp. 69ff.; looseness or tightness are corollaries of homogeneity or its absence.

[33] International stratification extends to individuals inasmuch as the standing or status of a person vis-à-vis citizens of another state depends on the position of his nation in the international ranking order.

[34] W. T. R. Fox, Theoretical Aspects of International Relations, Notre Dame, Ind., 1959, pp. 39-40.

other hand, is egalitarian; its homogeneous social system, the requirements of and the opportunities for mobility, and the high valuation of
universalism and achievement contribute to a de-emphasis of social
ranking. Despite first impressions, stratification nevertheless persists,
for facilities and responsibilities are still differentially allocated. Industria plays down rank and discourages overt manifestations of hierarchy
by such methods as precedence determination by alphabetical order or
seniority; it recognizes great powers but calls them "permanent members of the U.N. Security Council."

In both systems power is, of course, one of the determinants of
relative status. But in Agraria power rests on land and commerce, and
in Industria on the output of industrial goods and services. The value
systems emphasize, respectively, excellence of trade and estate management, and proficiency in technology and science, and put stress also on
the maintenance of the "great tradition" in one case and the promotion
of homogeneity in the other. States which fail to express these values or
otherwise neglect to meet the requirements of system membership rank
low. High status accrues to those who assume valuable functions (for
instance, as mediators and trade intermediaries or in banking, as does
Sweden, Canada, or Switzerland). The opportunities for small powers
to perform such functions are higher in Industria.

The wielders of authority hold the top of the ranking scale. The
international system, like any other, provides opportunities for collective action and for the exercise of leadership in its organization.
Agraria's joint activities are necessarily few and intermittent. At most
times leadership is equated with superior status resting on an ascriptive
quality, that of the ruler of empires to whom deference and obedience
are due by divine right or ancient tradition in exchange for such generalized duties as protection and the maintenance of order, or the dis-
semination of a "superior" culture. The Chinese "tributary system" of
the later imperial period is an example of a stable authority structure
in an international system composed of one great power and a number
of small states.[35] The great wars of the Western state system and the
peace conferences which concluded them are examples of exercise of
authority in a system composed of several powers.

Industria, too, has opportunities for such joint action. But its "tight
structuring," its interdependence, and its capacity for self-destruction
allow and indeed demand avenues of collective enterprise other than

---

[35] For a full account of its operation under the Ching emperors (1644-1911), see
J. K. Fairbank and S. Y. Teng, "On the Ch'ing Tributary System," *Harvard Journal of
Asiatic Studies*, VI (1941), pp. 135-246.

grand coalition wars. Hence leadership is called for in a number of diverse situations, each a direct consequence of the increased size of the system, its greater complexity and homogeneity. International organizations afford the most plentiful opportunity for exercising broad international responsibility, but leaders of the international system may exercise initiative also by organizing assistance to weak states and helping them to meet the requirements of system membership, by articulating world views on crucial questions, and by pioneering technological development or new frontiers of the international system (e.g., in outer space).

Agraria's international system recruits its leaders from among the most powerful of rulers, but once the leadership position has been seized and legitimized by reference to system-wide values (for instance, the sanction of religious authority), it tends to become routine and to be carried on by the momentum of tradition. Leadership roles such as those of the Holy Roman or the Chou emperors retained residual authority long after their original power had disappeared. Although agrarian leadership is initially based upon protection moving ideally towards absolute empire (which in its turn constitutes a negation of the international nature of the system), the loose structuring of the system and the leaders' limited resources prevent the actualization of the ideal.

Industria's closely knit international system calls for no ruler of rulers, no king of kings. The most powerful states compete for leadership, but their position, once reached by dint of better achievement, is held during satisfactory performance and has to be continuously reinforced by the process of nursing international support. Great powers have no monopoly of leadership either. Small states (for instance, those influential in international organizations) may act in representative roles (for instance, on behalf of the Afro-Asian bloc). The tightness of Industria makes manifold leadership necessary but also makes it unthinkable that any state's claim to absolute leadership would be tolerated or legitimized.

The means allowable in the exercise of authority vary, too. Agraria's leadership is strong, claims complete obedience, and enforces it by arms if need be. Wars are indeed the preferred means of imposing authority. Industria's leadership is more subtle; although the threat of violence ultimately still hangs over the system, the wide range of the facilities and techniques available to it makes it possible to secure collective action and carry it out by maneuvering, persuasion, bargaining, and pressure. The issues before world society are numerous, complex and specialized and the resolution of any one of them by war seems most of the time inappropriate. And in a large, tightly interdependent system the weight of the majority against the recalcitrant minority, if leadership is effective, can be heavier and more persuasive than in the small but amorphous and loosely organized Agraria.

We now turn to the structures of solidarity. Once more it is necessary to reiterate that all international systems require solidarity. For one, the hierarchical aspects of the international system just discussed set up strains which have to be counteracted by allowances in favor of egalitarianism, through the fostering of a generalized loyalty equally binding on all. The competitiveness and suspicion institutionalized in the system must be compensated by some integrative mechanisms. As is widely understood, international solidarity is chronically weak, but it is stronger than is conceded by writers who picture the international system as an universal ensemble of all the world's nations. Nearer to the truth, it seems, are those who view it at each point of time as a distinct international order with identifiable distribution of power, prestige, and other rewards, linked with an identifiable value system. To such an order those nations or ruling elites which benefit from the status quo, as it is sometimes put, feel greater loyalty and attachment than others. International solidarity is thus directed toward a particular international order and not to the system as such or in the abstract.

Agraria's international order is that of the "great tradition," usually a cultural and cosmopolitan tradition sustained by religion and radiated from the prestige centers of the age, its great courts and its great cities. The basic process of maintaining solidarity is therefore the steady stream of intercourse between courts (Agraria's "society" consists of the neighboring landowners); solidarity is a natural response to situations in which significant political and social connections are with fellow monarchical or fellow urban and commercial establishments (for instance, within the network of the Phoenician cities in the Mediterranean in 900-300 B.C.) rather than with the inhabitants of the realm. The international society of courts is small, fashioned on the model of an extended kinship group, with loyalties borne toward reigning dynasties and fortified by intermarriage. The area of royal intermarriage could be defined as the solidarity base of the system and the extension of that area—for instance, to "acculturate" unruly tribes along exposed frontiers, as the Chinese or the Byzantines used to do—as an index of system growth. Such marriage has religious sanction and coincides with areas of religious and cultural homogeneity. Marriages between reigning houses, too, formalize and consolidate alliances. Agraria's international order thus seems typically that of an extended kinship system—an "international brotherhood of kings"—with its members bound to it by the obligations of family loyalty, and its authority sanctioned by religious values and modeled on parental rights to complete obedience. In creating a feeling of European solidarity, the so-called "aristocratic international" of seventeenth- and eighteenth-century diplomacy[36] seems to have been a transient phenomenon; in earlier centuries international transactions were carried out by traders or merchants or, as in other systems, primarily by officials. To generalize for Agraria, such integration as there is seems to be the result of contacts between ruling elites rather than between their executive officials.

The network of family solidarities works well in a small, stationary system. It is ill-suited for large, rapidly changing homogeneous systems in which organizations function on universalist and achievement principles, yet in which the requirements of system integration are more pressing still. Indeed the "nationalization" of the state (that is, achievement of homogeneity in our sense, an inexorable result of industrial growth) has seemed to many to portend the disruption of the whole system, the "fragmentation of a formerly cohesive international society into a multiplicity of morally self-sufficient national communities," each given to "universalistic nationalism."[37] Is anarchy to be Industria's fate?

We may hazard the guess that the pressing demand for greater international solidarity activates processes aimed at satisfying it. The solidarity basis of Industria cannot be wholly deduced from the nature of the industrial system but it will have to be compatible with it. Thus, it must be organized around one or more of the great powers because no international order can be built without them. But in so large a system as the industrial, a single great power can no longer hold undivided sway; the loyalty to international order must be expressed on a general, preferably universalist basis (such as "the free world" or "proletarian internationalism") to which a large group of countries, and their populations, too, can subscribe. Hence the international organization, par excellence the forum of the small state, affords a wider and an increasingly potent focus for this purpose. Supplementing it are the associations articulating and in turn aggregating the variety of interests that demand an international solution.

Our last concern is with structures for maintaining international communications and culture. All international systems possess such structures for use in the expression of culture and also for its transmission to new members. As might be supposed, Agraria's international society has an international culture that is maintained in the cities and

[36] Stressed, e.g., by Morgenthau, *op.cit.*, pp. 221ff.
[37] *Ibid.*, p. 228.

principally by the courts, which function not only as foreign offices but also as agencies of integration as we have seen, and furthermore as instruments of international socialization, being places where—in addition to princes, soldiers, and officials—priests, professional men, and scholars foregather, reflect upon international life, and propagate their teachings among young and old alike, including foreign visitors. The circulation of elites through the courts, aided by the movement of merchants, pilgrims, and other inter-city travelers, ensures a minimum flow of information. Industria's system is, by contrast, complex and specialized. Its communication processes benefit hugely from the familiar industrial arts. The diplomatic and other information networks cover the whole globe with great thoroughness. Socialization processes are elaborate and include university and other elite training opportunities, the international diplomatic circuit itself which constantly absorbs new members, and the international institutional scene, with the elaborate and frequently prolonged ritual of recognition and admission to world organizations. The world press and news media, finally, through their continuous reporting and forecasting of the world climate, have come to hold an exceptionally crucial position in molding and maintaining international culture.

V. War and the Industrial International System

The analytical part of the argument is now completed. In summary, the small and non-homogeneous agrarian international system has the following characteristics: (1) limited international specialization; (2) international authority based upon tradition, inclined toward the imperial type; (3) system integration through "familial" solidarity of the rulers; and (4) small-scale, non-specialized procedures for maintaining international culture and communications.

Industrial international systems, by contrast, have (1) a well-developed international division of labor, including international organization; (2) international authority determined by achievement and a diversity of leadership and decision-making roles; (3) system integration through ideological loyalty to an international order; and (4) large-scale and specialized procedures for the diffusion of culture.

That essential system-maintaining processes are accomplished in different ways in the two systems is the reason for having the two models. Let us now specify the international societies to the understanding of which the models may contribute. The agrarian international systems we have been discussing can be identified as having operated in more or less pure form in most of Arnold Toynbee's twenty-one civilizations. The Egyptian-Near Eastern system of the fifteenth century B.C., the early Chinese state system[38] and the imperial systems, India, the Greco-Roman world, the Mexican civilization, and much of the life-history of the Western world (especially medieval Europe) furnish examples of such systems in action. The empirical referent of the industrial international system is less obvious; present-day international society is not yet a "pure" industrial system; although the First World War seems to mark the birth of this system, some of its members do not yet conform to its requirements, but in its essentials it already shows such properties of Industria as rapidly expanding size and growing homogeneity.

The period of 1648-1914, the 266 years of the modern state system, presents special problems. It is a period well-known to students of the field, well-documented, and referred to most frequently in textbooks when contrasts are drawn between contemporary and earlier systems. In that period, and after the French Revolution in particular, the Western international system could no longer be described as purely agrarian. In Western Europe the coming of the Industrial Revolution—which began in England in the mid-eighteenth century—was accompanied by striking developments in the procedures and techniques of international relations. But it is also worth bearing in mind that the world outside the North Atlantic remained essentially agrarian until well into the twentieth century, and therefore also influenced the character of the international system in that direction. The international politics of nineteenth-century Europe seems therefore to represent a transitional type, showing a particularly pronounced mixture of the two models.

Historical developments of the last two centuries, however, bear out the earlier proposition that an agrarian system that expands in size and homogeneity tends to become industrial. In eighteenth-century European Agraria, the dynamic factor was England and its Industrial Revolution. England's power and prestige rose as her economy industrialized and as her political influence spread over four continents. As the other European states in due course followed suit, the steam engine revolutionized production and transportation, unified national territories, and opened the entire world to West European expansion. New health and hygiene discoveries multiplied populations, and their survival was assured as new farming methods increased food production. By the beginning of the twentieth century, industrialism had taken root in

---

[38] R. L. Walker's excellent study, *The Multi-state System of Ancient China* (Hamden, Conn., 1953), could profitably be repeated with respect to other international systems.

Europe, North America, and Japan. The industrial powers assumed control of the whole globe and unified it by means of their superior organization. The international system was thus transformed through the growth of the industrializing states, the mobilization of their populations, the spread of Western power throughout the world and, in turn, through the increasing mobilization and industrialization of extra-European areas thus drawn into the system.

The industrial international system originated through a spontaneous change in the system, the sudden growth of industry in one state. But after one member of the agrarian system had demonstrated the feasibility and also the profitability of such change in terms of new power and prestige, the competitive functioning of the international system ensured that other states would make every effort to attain similar capability in order to avoid a decline in status. Industrial values began to percolate into international culture, and culture, in its turn, affected behavior in yet unindustrialized states. In time industrial power or affiliation with it became a *sine qua non* of national survival—that is, of membership in the international system. Thus influences emanating from all sources: from the international system, from international culture, and from individual foreign policy motivations, combined to secure the transformation of Agraria into Industria. The transition from one system to the other is not merely a process in which more and more states became industrial, as it were of their own volition; it is a change that is mediated through and powerfully reinforced by the international system, which itself changes in the process. Yet the contemporary Western system is not the only international system to which the industrial model may be fruitfully applied. The usefulness of the model resides in the fact that it helps us understand the operation of international systems alternative to the present-day Western society. A future Communist international system, for instance, would almost certainly be "industrial" in our sense of the word, but would differ markedly in other respects from the system which we now experience.[39]

One question remains, that of war. The nineteenth-century writers quoted at the beginning of this paper maintained, somewhat too smugly, but forcefully—theirs was an age free from major European conflict—that wars were patterns of an earlier civilization, incompatible with the spread of industrialism.[40] Why this should be so was never

[39] See the author's *The Communist International System*, Research Monograph No. 9, Center of International Studies, Princeton University, December 1, 1960.
[40] See also Raymond Aron, *War and Industrial Society*, London, Oxford University Press, 1958.

clearly explained except for pointing out that functions earlier performed by war would now be carried out in other ways. Although developments in the first half of our century have seemed to deny most of the Comte-Spencer argument, it may yet come to pass that those early thinkers were right, though not quite for the right reasons. They did not and could not have foreseen the development of nuclear weapons and rockets powerful enough to carry those weapons to the far corners of the earth, but it is wholly consistent with their arguments to say that industrial and scientific growth was bound to transform the meaning and character of modern war and to remove total atomic war at any rate from the category of ordinary or "normal" means of foreign policy.

It would be tempting to maintain that war is incompatible with, or inconceivable in, the industrial international system; but this is not a conclusion that can be reached from the assumptions here specified. True, wars of Agraria seem on the whole more tolerable and only intermittently bitterly destructive (the Chinese wars of the fourth and third centuries B.C., the Mogul invasions of West Asia in the thirteenth century A.D., and the Hundred Years' and Thirty Years' War in Western Europe were far from mild affairs) ; industrial nuclear war, on the other hand, imperils the survival of the whole system. However, as long as the international system persists, the threat of totally destructive war will be suspended over it; attenuated as the threat may be by inspection and disarmament schemes, it will never be entirely absent. There is no logically compelling necessity why the industrial international system *per se* should be free of war.

A relatively or largely war-free industrial international system is nonetheless arguable. Taking up Comte's and Spencer's arguments, we might say that functions efficiently filled by war in the agrarian system could now be implemented by industrial structures: the solidarity function of imposing penal sanctions on the offenders against the international order, and the leadership function of helping to enforce international decisions. The place which war has held as a test of international achievement, as a measuring rod of international status, can in Industria be replaced by productive technological or scientific competition or by space exploration. Such a world might discard the military contest for simple "status-seeking," which is equally serious, taxing, and time-consuming, and can be carried on for high stakes, but which might nevertheless be pursued without the assumption of violence. Although war as the ultimate contingency may not disappear, its share in accomplishing international purposes may greatly diminish.

A trying world, this, but also exhilarating. And for those who doubt the stability of a nuclear-armed industrial international system there is this thought of consolation: the stability of an international system (that is, its success in maintaining the independence of its members or the chances of its conversion into chaos or into a world state) is the direct consequence of the survival potential of the small powers within it. In agrarian international systems, as already explained, the "market" for security is imperfect; some states are unable to obtain the backing of a great power against unfriendly neighbors. Because of locational and other conditions certain great powers succeed in expanding at the expense of small states by swallowing them up, and in doing so threaten to overthrow the whole system. Thus perished the early Chinese and the Greco-Roman state systems; threats to the survival of small powers (as in the case of Belgium, Serbia, or Poland) served as the occasion for the great wars of the Western state system. We have already pointed out why in Industria the "market" for security may be more nearly perfect. Any power armed with nuclear missiles can safeguard the independence of a small country wherever it is situated. No state can lose its freedom against the opposition of one great power; the more such powers there are, the smaller the chance of great power collusion. Are we thus permanently frozen within the frontiers we now hold? Probably not, but change could be so manipulated that its benefits would not accrue solely or even chiefly to the great powers. By a great paradox, the overwhelmingly superior power of the nuclear-equipped states may give to the small power a new lease on life, and to the industrial international system a hope for stability.

INTERNATIONAL RELATIONS AS
A PRISMATIC SYSTEM

By FRED W. RIGGS

I. Introduction: The Inter-State System

CONVENTIONAL theories of international relations assume, implicitly, the model of an "inter-state system." According to this model, individually states possess a set of characteristics which differ fundamentally from the characteristics of a system of those states inter-acting with each other. On this basis we can construct theories about the behavior of component states in the system, and more general propositions about the nature of the inter-state system viewed as a whole. Some of the difficulties of this model will be noted here, and an alternative model proposed.

Before pointing to these difficulties, however, we need a clear image of the inter-state model. A classic formulation is contained in a speech given by former Secretary of State John Foster Dulles at a meeting of the American Society for International Law.[1] In it Mr. Dulles identified six characteristics of the nation-state: (1) laws which "reflect the moral judgment of the community"; (2) political machinery to revise these laws as needed; (3) an executive body able to administer the laws; (4) judicial machinery to settle disputes in accord with the laws; (5) superior force to deter violence by enforcing the law upon those who defy it; and (6) sufficient well-being so that people are not driven by desperation to ways of violence. The international system, Mr. Dulles pointed out, in large part lacks these characteristics. He went on to assess the limited success of attempts, ranging from the League of Nations and Kellogg-Briand Pact through the United Nations, to create such a "state system" or "order" at the international level. Mr. Dulles sadly reported that, despite notable progress in the development of international law and judicial machinery, the desired international order does not, as yet, exist.

This statement rather strikingly uncovers the implicit model of an inter-state system. In effect, Mr. Dulles depicted two contrasting "ideal" or "constructed" types. At one extreme is the political *order* character-istic of the nation-state; at the other an *anarchic* system of inter-state relations.

[1] *Department of State Bulletin*, xxxiv (May 7, 1956), p. 740.

Let us examine this model from two perspectives: first from above, the *systemic* point of view; and then from below, in terms of the component *units*, the states.

(I) THE SYSTEMIC PERSPECTIVE

The "inter-state system" is seen, in Mr. Dulles' model, as lacking the basic characteristics of a "state system," although it may have an embryonic legal system, as expressed by international law, and a fragmentary judicial machinery.

Let us imagine that the organizations of the United Nations and the specialized agencies are able gradually to extend their effective power. The U.N. becomes a primary actor in the politics of Palestine, Libya, Korea, the Congo. Its technical agencies begin to carry out agricultural and health programs in underdeveloped countries. We become aware of limited spheres of action in which it is almost possible to speak of world "public opinion," of policies which are universally applicable—for the control of epidemics or the distribution of mail—and of machinery for the enforcement of order. There may even be sufficient enjoyment of these benefits so that no state will be disposed to destroy them by violence.

Suppose that the sphere of these specialized activities gradually widens further, and the extent of world consensus together with appropriate decision-making and enforcement machinery increases, but that no unitary world government is yet formed. We should then still have an "inter-state system," but it would begin to share, however imperfectly, some of the qualitative characteristics of a state. It would not be a pure "anarchy." In other words, however anarchic contemporary world politics, is it inherent in the model of an inter-state system that it should always be anarchic? If not, then might not an inter-state system approximate the characteristics of a state system?

An alternative view of world politics takes this possibility into account. Instead of regarding international relations as an anarchy of states, it postulates an integrated "world order." Under this postulate the organs of "world government" acquire a direct relationship to individuals as actors, just as the United States government deals with individual citizens, without, of course, ceasing to deal also with the governments of its fifty component "states." In this view, world government and world law are the "ideal forms" of world politics, and our failure to achieve this condition reflects a pathological condition which must be changed as quickly as possible. Indeed, such a "world state" is what Mr. Dulles portrayed as our policy goal, to be achieved by destroying the contemporary inter-state anarchy.

This model—however good as a normative view—is as unrealistic as the model which perceives world politics in terms only of an inter-state system. Nor can the difficulty be overcome by a compromise which recognizes both states and individuals as actors in world politics. Such a formulation fails to identify many crucial characteristics of the system. We need a model that will provide a more specific picture of how states and individuals are related to each other in an international system. Moreover, there may be other entities—neither states nor individuals—which ought also to be included in our image of the system.

(2) THE UNIT PERSPECTIVE

The second perspective, viewing the system from below, in terms of its component units, the "states," draws upon our image of the Western nation-states. The model is certainly not far from reality if we use it to organize data about the United States, England, France, or a number of other Western democracies. It is when we start applying it to the non-Western world, and especially to the new states of Asia and Africa, that we run into difficulties.

We have all been struck and alarmed, I am sure, by events since the summer of 1960 in the new Republic of Congo. Here, by acknowledgment of the United Nations, a new "state" was born. If it is in truth a "state," then by Mr. Dulles' definition we must expect it to defend itself against attack from abroad and revolution from within, to adopt and enforce laws reflecting the moral judgment of the Congolese people, to organize a government, participate in the U.N., and conduct a foreign policy capable of safeguarding the "national interest" of the Congo.

But do not recent events contradict this image? What is the moral judgment of the Congolese community? Is there even such a community, or do we see rather a congeries of tribal communities brought into temporary administrative connection by Belgian imperial policy, and now suddenly released from control and expected to act like a "nation-state" in our anarchic world? The "government," recognized by foreign powers, turns out to be a group of individuals drawn from the minuscule Congolese intelligentsia, vested with formal "authority" but lacking the requisites for effective control over the population, to say nothing of a capacity to formulate laws based on public opinion and knowledge of problems and alternatives, to enforce these laws, and provide for their testing by judicial process. Nor can it be said that the population has a sufficient sense of well-being to cause it to reject violence.

If these criteria, so clearly itemized by Mr. Dulles, are not present in the Congo and are also not present in the sphere of world politics, then Congolese politics share some basic characteristics of world politics. This is a rather shattering conclusion because it suggests that if the study of inter-state and of state politics are to be differentiated, then the study of Congolese politics belongs with the study of international relations rather than of domestic politics. This seems to be a contradiction in terms. We resist the idea that the Congo is an "inter-state system." How shall we struggle out of this trap into which we have apparently slipped?

We might, first of all, fall back on the popular maxim that "the exception proves the rule." Apart from the fallacy in a foolish interpretation of this proverb which takes the word "prove" to mean "establish" rather than "test," the fact is that the Congolese case is not really exceptional except for its dramatic quality. Many new states and even some old ones qualify only imperfectly as "states" under the Dulles criteria.

The Republic of Congo, Congo Republic (Brazzaville), Chad, Niger, Nigeria, Mali, Togo, Dahomey, Ivory Coast, Upper Volta, Central African Republic, Malagasy, and Somalia have recently attained their "independence" in Africa. With many of these names we are scarcely familiar. Together with Laos and other new Asian countries—some of which come but little closer to the model of a nation-state—they have major voting power in the U.N. General Assembly. It may shortly appear that the model "state" can be used to describe only a minority of the countries in our "inter-state" system. But if they do not satisfy the basic conditions of a state, how can we call them states? Can we have an inter-state system many of whose members are not states?

(3) THE X PERSPECTIVE

How shall we escape from this awkward position? On the one hand, we discover that the inter-state system may exhibit many characteristics of a state, whereas many "states" lack these characteristics to a considerable degree. The sharp distinction between the study of domestic politics and of international relations breaks down.

The position may be clarified if we use a scale instead of a simple dichotomy. In Figure 1, let position A represent a polar type of political structure having all the characteristics enumerated by Mr. Dulles—i.e., a "nation-state." Let the opposite polar type, B, represent a structure having none of these characteristics—i.e., an "anarchy." Then a wide range of intermediate positions having these characteristics in various degrees may be imagined, as at X, Y, and Z. Perhaps the political characteristics of a state like the Congo, or an international system like the modern world, could best be classified at an intermediate point—X, for example.

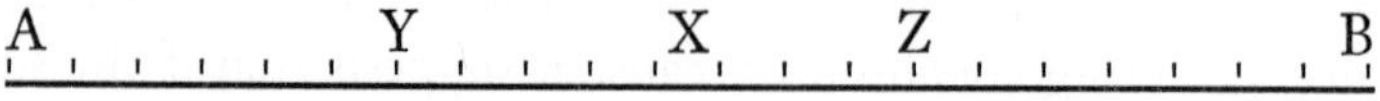

A   Y   X   Z   B
|__|__|__|__|__|__|__|__|__|__|__|__|__|__|__|__|__|__|__|__|

FIGURE I

This possibility suggests a different line of investigation. If there is any similarity between the basic political structure of government in a new state and in our international system, then perhaps models developed for one might shed light on the other. An analysis of the contemporary inter-state system might help us understand the underdeveloped country, and models for politics in these countries may illuminate aspects of international relations.

This approach, however, immediately runs into a major difficulty. We lack any widely known and accepted model suitable for the study of Congolese politics or of similar phenomena in other non-Western countries. Our traditional work in comparative government relied as heavily on the basic image of the nation-state, Western style, as did our traditional work in international relations.

However, in the last few years significant attempts have been made in comparative politics to break away from the restraints imposed by this model and to construct new typologies and hypotheses that could be used more fruitfully for the study of non-Western politics. The research and conceptualization sponsored by the Social Science Research Council, especially its Committee on Comparative Politics, played an important part in this effort.[2]

As a participant in this process I have developed a set of concepts and related hypotheses which I call the "Prismatic Model." I believe that this model is helpful as an explanatory device in studying the politics of transitional societies. In this essay I shall attempt to relate some of the elements of this model to our contemporary international system in order to discover whether or not it might provide a fruitful alternative to the "inter-state model" as a way of thinking about the subject.

(4) THE PRISMATIC MODEL

In comparing societies and political systems we have at our disposal a wealth of contrastive and developmental concepts, largely the result of sociological investigations. These include the distinction between "*Gemeinschaft* and *Gesellschaft*," "undifferentiated and differentiated"

---

[2] The latest work to reflect this new approach is *The Politics of the Developing Areas*, edited by Gabriel Almond, Chairman of the Committee, and James Coleman (Princeton, N.J., 1960).

societies, "sacred and secular" norms, "status and contract," "mechanical and organic solidarity," etc.

Each of these terms has its specific historical associations and connotations as well as precise referents established by the scholars who first proposed and defined them. I have attempted to use some of them, but have found difficulties in each case. It is unnecessary here to enumerate these difficulties; I mention them merely to explain why I decided to coin a new set of terms, having some similarity with these older ones, but yet carrying certain meanings not contained in them, and dropping some of the connotations of the earlier dichotomies.[3]

I begin with a "functional-structural" approach—*structures* being defined as patterns of action; *functions*, as the consequences of such action for the system in which the action occurs. Accordingly, we may speak of a system for which a single structure performs all the necessary functions as a *fused* model, using the terminology of light. At the opposite end of this scale is a *refracted* society in which, for every function, a corresponding structure exists. Traditional agricultural and folk societies (Agraria) approximate the fused model, and modern industrial societies (Industria) approach the refracted model. The former is "functionally diffuse," the latter "functionally specific." Intermediate between these polar extremes is the *prismatic* model, so called because of the prism through which fused light passes to become refracted.[4]

The characteristics of these three models can best be understood in terms of several variables selected from a list of "functional requisites" for the survival of any *society*, derived from functional-structural analysis.[5] Each of these functions must be performed by some structure or structures, the character of which may vary strikingly from one society to another. Accordingly, the traits to be discovered are those of the structures which perform the requisite functions in prismatic societies.

It is important to remember that these models are deductively constructed types. A parallel set of images, created by inductive inspection

[3] In an earlier essay, I used the terms "Agraria and Industria" (William Siffin, ed., *Toward the Comparative Study of Public Administration*, Bloomington, Ind., 1957, pp. 23-116). The new terminology is not a replacement for these, but sets them in a broader perspective.

[4] For a more complete explanation of the "prismatic" model, see my "Prismatic Society and Financial Administration," *Administrative Science Quarterly*, v (June 1960), pp. 1-46. The reader who finds this term awkward may substitute some such expression as "underdeveloped" or "transitional," although each of these carries unintended connotations.

[5] For a discussion of this approach and a list of functional requisites, see Marion Levy, Jr., *The Structure of Society*, Princeton, N.J., 1952, pp. 149-97.

of and abstraction from the real world, include "modern industrial society," "traditional agricultural society," and "transitional society," which roughly correspond to the refracted, fused, and prismatic deductive models, respectively.

I believe a fairly adequate beginning can be made by considering five functions selected from a considerably longer list. These five are *effective control, formal authority, communication, "sociation,"* and *economic allocation.* In a brief paper it is impossible to deal adequately even with these. Other variables, especially those relating to environmental conditions, should be included in a full treatment but cannot be considered here. For example, the psychology or motivation of individuals, demographic changes and pressures, geo-strategic considerations, and technological development all have profound consequences for social and political systems. I shall treat them as parameters for present purposes.

The procedure will be to identify a set of variables related to each of the five functions. Then we will examine the corresponding structures in the three models—fused, refracted, and prismatic—and finally examine their application to international systems.

II. Effective Control

Using Lasswell's terminology, let us call those who exercise effective control in a body politic *rulers,* and those whom they rule, the *ruled.* A political system which includes the interactions among rulers and between rulers and ruled may be called a *rule.*[6]

The distribution of effective control in a "rule" may range from highly *centralized* (autocratic) to highly *localized* (anarchic). Power in a single state may be centralized; in a tribal or inter-state system, localized. Although we normally think of a political system only in terms of relatively centralized rules—i.e., "states"—we may extend the concept to include systems with localized power distributions, such as an international system or tribal society. Indeed, it is necessary for our analysis to be able to think of such scattered power structures as a single system, linked by reciprocal interactions—whether peaceful or violent—rather than by a co-ordinating power center.

Any particular group of rulers has an area and population over which its rule prevails, which we call a *domain.* Outside the domain, however, there may be other rulers who exercise a greater or lesser degree of influence or control over the group considered, which we call a *context.* Actions which affect in any way the decisions of rulers may be called

[6] Harold Lasswell and Abraham Kaplan, *Power and Society,* New Haven, Conn., 1950, pp. 187-88.

pressures. It is apparent that such pressures may originate from the context as well as from the domain of a ruler or group of rulers. The former constitute *external pressures*, the latter *internal pressures*. If the rule considered is a nation-state, external pressures are those of "foreign powers," and internal pressures arise from "pressure groups."

It is useful to compare the relative weight of internal and external pressures in describing political systems. If the weight of external pressures is less than that of internal pressures, we are dealing with a rule which has the power structure typical of a sovereign or independent state. A preponderance of external over internal pressure is characteristic of local governments. An international system is a power structure in which the weight of external pressures approaches the vanishing point. For convenience of reference, let us call such a system a *macro-rule* and its domain a *world*.[7] Note that a macro-rule is defined by the relative absence of external pressures rather than any particular characteristic of its internal power structure. Hence all macro-rules need not be "inter-state" systems, although they may take that form. A "universal state" would also be a macro-rule.

Today the whole Earth is involved in a single macro-rule (the world), but this has not always been the case. Before the discovery of the "New World," there may have been a macro-rule centering in Mexico, a different macro-rule centering in Peru. The tribal states of the Hawaiian Islands, while interacting with each other, experienced no significant external pressure prior to European contact and hence could be considered a macro-rule. The contending states of feudal China, and the barbarian tribes with which they fought, constituted another macro-rule, as did Imperial China with its tributary tribes and kingdoms. Other macro-rules may have embraced the Islamic World, the Hellenic World, the Indic World, etc., at various times in history.

We shall now examine a number of variables relating to effective control—namely, degrees of *politicization*, power *distribution, balance,* and *tension*. In each case we shall try to identify the characteristic form of the variable in a prismatic model and then suggest the possible application of this form both to transitional societies and to our contemporary international system. Sometimes it will be necessary to modify the concepts and terminology somewhat to correspond to the qualities of a macro-rule as compared with that of a rule.

[7] Because such expressions as "state" and "local government" imply formal authority as well as effective control, it is more exact to refer to the former as an "ortho-rule" and to the latter as a "micro-rule" if we wish to designate the control system alone. In this article the terms "rule" and "ortho-rule" will be used as synonyms, and we shall not have occasion to discuss "micro-rules."

(1) POLITICIZATION AND POLARIZATION

Within a rule it is useful to distinguish the extent to which conduct is affected by the probable consequences for one's power position resulting from the conduct of others—i.e., the degree of *politicization*. This is a special case of the more general concept of socialization, referring to general sensitivity to all interpersonal relations. Obviously, in any society some individuals will be far more politicized than others. The least politicized may be called the *apolitical*. We may say that a relatively small part of the population is politicized in a fused society, a relatively large part in a refracted society, an intermediate proportion in a prismatic society. Political conduct and interest in the transitional societies fit this characterization.

It is inappropriate to use the same term, "politicization," for the comparable phenomenon in a macro-rule. The component units are not individuals but rules, whose rulers must be politicized insofar as they exercise rule. However, we might measure the extent to which such ruling groups consider the macro-rule, or other rules, in their conduct. When such considerations are of maximal significance, the rule's conduct is *polarized*; when of least significance, it is *insular*. Macro-rules, then, may be compared in terms of their degree of polarization.

Comparing types of macro-rule, we may say that a fused world is insular; a refracted world, polarized; and a prismatic world, *semipolarized*. The contemporary international system appears to fit the prismatic model, since a relatively high degree of sensitivity to global interdependencies exists, but important pockets of insular (or isolationist) perspectives also remain.

(2) DISTRIBUTION AND SEGMENTATION

By *distribution* we refer to the way power is allocated, its configuration. For example, power is highly distributed in a rule when it is allocated to many parts of the domain or shared by many members of the population, but when it is allocated to a few parts or members the "distribution index" is low, following Lasswell's terminology.[8] Thus power is *fragmented* when the distribution index is high, *consolidated* when it is low.

Power is distributed in two ways, with respect to *area* and to *function*. If we wish to speak of an areal distribution, we may say that consolidated power is *centralized*; fragmented power is *localized*. If we speak of functional distribution, we may say that consolidated power is *con-*

[8] Lasswell and Kaplan, *op.cit.*, p. 57.

centrated; fragmented power, *dispersed*. Since there is no necessary correlation between the areal and functional distribution of power, it is necessary to specify in any instance the distribution pattern in both respects. Thus, a given rule might be consolidated areally but fragmented functionally, etc.

We must also have some terms for mid-points on these scales, since particular rules may be neither consolidated nor fragmented but have an intermediate distribution index. Let us call such an intermediate index on the areal scale *federalized*; on the functional scale, *conglomerated*. The areal distribution of power is related to a rule's domain; the functional distribution, to its scope.

Turning to our models, we discover no simple correlation. Variation in power distribution can be found in all kinds of societies. Indeed, the degree of power consolidation is one of the key variables for analysis of political systems, and has largely preoccupied students of comparative politics. When we range rules on a "democratic-totalitarian" or "republican-autocratic" scale, we imply that all rules can be most significantly classified by their distribution index.

In applying this variable to the scale of refraction, can we discover any particular pattern of correlation? I believe we can, but it is not a simple correlation, and it is unnecessary to discuss it here for the fused and refracted models. Suffice it to say that the prismatic model appears to be marked by a distribution index near the mid-point on both the areal and functional scales. In other words, prismatic power tends to be both conglomerated and federalized. I believe this deduction—the arguments for which are not offered here—fits quite well the empirical facts in transitional societies in (ortho-) rules.

Does this conclusion apply also to macro-rules? We cannot use the distribution index because the units of a macro-rule are rules, not individuals. Power in a macro-rule might be distributed among many rules (fragmented), but within each unit it might be consolidated. It would be misleading to speak of a high distribution index or strong localization of power in such a system. Rather, we must adopt a new terminology to indicate the pattern of distribution of power among constituent rules in a macro-rule.

Let us call such distributions the *segmentation* pattern. When power is articulated among many units, it is highly *segmented*; when among one or a few units, the "segmentation index" is low—i.e., *unsegmented*. As with the distribution index, the segmentation pattern is oriented toward both area and function. Areal segments may be called *poles*; functional segments, *organizations*. (Kaplan's "universal" and "bloc" actors are probably "organizations.") Obviously, these are both special-ized uses of more general terms.

If power in a macro-rule is highly segmented territorially, it contains many poles; if not, only one pole. We may call the former case *poly-polar*, the latter *uni-polar*. The intermediate case of a macro-rule containing a few poles is *oli-polar*. *Bi-polar* and *tri-polar* are special cases of oli-polarity. (This is a different variable from polarization. Both uni-polar and poly-polar systems could be more or less polarized, although uni-polar systems would probably be more polarized than poly-polar systems.)

If power in a macro-rule is highly segmented functionally, it contains many organizations; if not, only one organization. We may call the former case *poly-organizational*, the latter *uni-organizational*. The intermediate case of a macro-rule containing a few organizations would be *oli-organizational*.

It is unnecessary here to characterize the complex correlations be-tween segmentation patterns in fused and refracted[9] macro-rules, but we can repeat the attribution of intermediate segmentation indices to a prismatic macro-rule. In other words, it would be "oli-polar" and "oli-organizational."

Can we attribute concrete significance to these peculiar terms? I think we can define an oli-polar macro-rule as one containing a few—two, three, or more—super-powers plus an indefinitely large number of medium and small or "infra-powers." Similarly, an oli-organizational macro-rule would contain a few functionally specialized super-organiza-tions plus many smaller "infra-organizations." Both of these character-istics apply to the contemporary international scene. The identity of the super-powers needs no specification; the super-organizations include the U.N. and its major specialized agencies, the great regional organizations with their specialized military or economic functions, perhaps the Communist international network. The infra-powers include many "new states," the infra-organizations a host of autonomous international non-governmental organizations.

(3) BALANCE

The concept of *balance of power* has been applied, as a descriptive term, to intra-state as well as inter-state relationships. A high degree of balance may be said to exist whenever efforts by one unit in a system to

---

[9] However, a refracted macro-rule would probably be federalistic, or oli-polar, in its territorial structure, but might vary within wide limits in functional structure—i.e., between unsegmented power in a uni-organizational "dictatorship," and a segmented distribution or poly-organizational "republic."

increase its power cause other units to exert countervailing power in such a way as to prevent a change in the relative power position of the interacting units. Imbalance exists when power aggrandizement by one unit is not matched by corresponding changes in other units.

I suggest there is no direct correlation between degree of refraction and degree of balance in a power system. However, a different kind of U-shaped correlation may exist, such that relatively greater balance occurs at both the fused and the refracted pole of the refraction scale, the greatest imbalance occurring at the prismatic mid-point. Figure 2 represents such a correlation pattern.

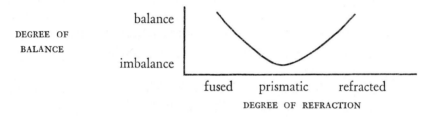

FIGURE 2

Most of the considerations which support this proposition arise from analysis of related functions, such as authority, communications, symbols, etc., and cannot be examined here. In a transitional society, power imbalance is indicated by the existence of revolutionary tensions and frequent crises, including political and social revolutions. Imbalance in the contemporary international system is suggested by major power shifts, including both the rise and fall of super-powers, often accompanied by wars.

(4) TENSION LEVEL

The degree of tension in a political system is closely related to the degree of balance but may be a separate variable. When the tension level is high, actors in a political arena are very *intense.* They tend to respond violently and tenaciously to any threat to their power position. When the tension level is low, actors are *relaxed,* and respond mildly to threatened changes in their power position. It may be that balance can be high both when the tension level is high and when it is low. In the former instance, potential aggressors are careful to avoid provocation because they fear the instant and violent reaction of their rivals. In the latter instance, aggressive drives are minimized and opportunities for negotiated settlement of disputes maximized, so that the prospects for maintaining a power balance are good.

The dangers of imbalance perhaps become most acute at intermediate tension levels, which we may call *spastic*. Spasticity implies not so much a steady tension level between intense and relaxed as it does unpredictable shifts between relatively high and low tension, moments of extreme tension succeeding extreme relaxation. When units in a power structure are spastic, it becomes difficult to predict reactions to proposed changes in power position. Hence spastic tension levels are marked by violent and apparently irrational outbursts of violence, often succeeded by apparent apathy and unconcern. Major miscalculations are likely to occur in the strategy of power-holders, and crises become frequent, leading to imbalance and probable transformations of the power structure.

If we correlate tension levels with the refraction scale, it seems probable that a direct positive correlation will be found—i.e., low tension in the fused model, high tension in the refracted model, and spasticity in the prismatic model.

Reverting to the Congolese situation, which we cited earlier to illustrate the similarities between politics in an "underdeveloped" country and international affairs, it is easy to see the spasticity in its political postures, and corresponding imbalances in domestic politics. Moreover, crises like those in the Congo and Cuba provoke indeterminate responses in the super-powers which betray a spastic tension level in the international scene that also contributes to imbalance.

III. Formal Authority

So far we have been considering only one of the constituent elements in political power, effective control. Let us now think about the other major element, *formal authority*. Authority is that aspect of power which depends on its legitimacy, on being exercised in conformity with a generally accepted *formula* which prescribes the conditions for acquiring and using power. Those who exercise authority may be called the *authorities*. A system of authority may be called a *regime*. (To distinguish the domain of a rule from that of a regime, we may call the former a *territory*, the latter a *jurisdiction*.)

The formula prescribing a regime is validated by reference to a *myth* which indicates the ultimate values of a political or social system, its final objectives, the nature of the *sovereign*. By "sovereignty" we refer to the final source of authority, whether a man, a human aggregate, or a supra-human entity, such as a god. The jurisdiction of a sovereign is its *dominion*.

When we speak of a "sovereign state" we refer to a regime whose formula admits of no source of authority outside its jurisdiction. Human sovereigns are determinate. If the sovereign is supra-human, however, its dominion cannot be assumed to be greater than the regime's jurisdiction. If the sovereign is a "universal god," then the regime claims jurisdiction over a "universal empire."

It is convenient to recognize other kinds of regimes besides a sovereign state. For example, some regimes recognize sovereignty outside their jurisdiction, as in the case of local government. We should also recognize forms of authority derived from sovereign states and claiming jurisdiction over a larger area than the sovereign, such as a league or confederation of states. Whereas a regime's jurisdiction coincides with its sovereign's dominion, a *macro-regime* asserts authority over a jurisdiction larger than the dominions of its constituent sovereigns.[10]

We may now consider the characteristic patterns of formal authority. I shall attempt in particular to investigate whether the concepts useful for analysis of prismatic regimes (a model for authority in transitional societies) are applicable to the study of our contemporary international system, considered as a prismatic macro-regime. In doing this I shall deal with: (1) the nature of consensus; (2) the content of formulae; (3) the relationships of authority to control; and (4) the implications for policies or "codes."

(1) CONSENSUS

Authority is said to be legitimate when it conforms with a widely accepted myth and formula. All those who accept a particular formula for a regime constitute its *constituency*. A constituency may, but need not, coincide with a regime's jurisdiction. In other words, some of the population over which a regime asserts authority may not accept the regime's formula or its claim to legitimacy. To the extent that a constituency coincides with a jurisdiction, *consensus* may be said to exist.

Authority in a macro-regime is affected by two considerations—the perspectives of the populations in the constituent regimes, and the attitudes of the regimes themselves. Let us call all those who accept a political myth and formula, under which authority is allocated in a macro-regime, an *ecumene*. The ecumenic myth and formula may differ from those of constituencies in the ecumene, but must be consistent with them. For example, an ecumenic myth might prescribe "self-determination" and "popular sovereignty" as a basis for authority, while a constituent myth as expressed in an "oath of allegiance" prescribes more particular norms of legitimacy for one country.

[10] We could extend this terminology by calling a regime an "ortho-regime," and a "micro-regime" one having a jurisdiction smaller than its sovereign's.

We may refer to all regimes which accept the formula of a macro-regime as its *adherents*. This formula might include criteria for admission to a "community of nations," establishment of diplomatic relations, creation of international organizations, enforcement of a law of nations, etc.

The jurisdiction of a macro-regime includes both the populations and the regimes over which it claims authority. Just as a regime's jurisdiction may, but need not, coincide with its constituency, so a macro-regime's jurisdiction may, but need not, coincide with its ecumene and adherents. The degree of consensus again varies with the degree to which these categories coincide.

The degree of consensus on a macro-regime not only affects the weight of its authority and its ability to influence the conduct of those under its jurisdiction, but also affects the weight of authority of adherent regimes. An ortho-regime is said to be *recognized* when regimes outside its jurisdiction acknowledge that it conforms to the macro-regime's formula. Thus the authority of a regime varies with the extent to which it is granted recognition by those outside its jurisdiction, as well as considered legitimate by those over whom it claims jurisdiction.

We may now apply these concepts to the analysis of our models. I offer the proposition that in both the fused and the refracted model of ortho-regimes a high degree of consensus prevails. As one approaches the prismatic mid-point between these polar extremes, the degree of consensus declines. Again, the pattern of correlation would be U-shaped.

In transitional situations, old or traditional myths and formulae are undermined, new ones are introduced, and many people are confused, accepting perhaps some parts of both symbol systems, perhaps one or the other, perhaps neither. I have called the outlook of the population under such conditions *poly-normative*. A prismatic regime's jurisdiction is therefore *poly-constituent*. Rival constituencies in the same jurisdiction adhere to different and typically incompatible myths and formulae.

Such a situation inevitably undermines the authority of a regime, and makes it *formalistic*. Several competing regimes arise, claiming jurisdiction over the same territory. Dissension, instability, inability to reach agreement on the bases of authority, to say nothing of policies and codes, become the order of the day. Charismatic leaders, military "juntas," and "bosses" seize effective control. *Naked* and *formalistic* power exist side by side.

The same model may be used at a different level for analysis of a prismatic macro-regime. The proposition is offered that consensus would prevail in the jurisdiction of both fused and refracted macro-regimes, assuring support from both adherents and ecumene. In prismatic macro-regimes, however, change from fused toward refracted myths and formulae would cause sharp differences of opinion in both the populations and component regimes. Consequently, the jurisdiction would be both *poly-ecumenic* and *non-adherent*.

Competing formulae would be offered for the establishment of component regimes, thereby reinforcing the internal crisis of authority in these regimes, especially to the extent that they are also prismatic. At the same time some of the regimes would not be recognized by others, thereby further undermining their authority. The regimes would segregate into rival "camps," each offering alternative and incompatible formulae for the establishment of a viable macro-regime. The authority of any existing macro-regime would, correspondingly, be threatened and become formalistic. Communism and capitalism, a "Comintern" and a U.N., illustrate such alternative myths and formulae.

This model may be useful in helping us understand the position of traditional macro-regimes such as the Christian Papacy and the Islamic Caliphate as well as the new Communist International, the United Nations, regional bloc organizations—such as SEATO, the Baghdad Pact, the OAS—and reliance on naked power as at a "summit" conference.

A further proposition may be offered—namely, that a regime based on plural sovereignties is inherently unstable. At best, therefore, a macro-regime is always weak. Attempts are made by the ideologists of any ecumene to create a formula which will convert the macro-regime into a regime, the existing regimes into "micro-regimes." We may assume that success in this process would occur most readily where ecumenic consensus existed; i.e., under fused and refracted conditions. But under prismatic conditions, where dissension and ideological conflict prevail in a poly-ecumenic world, no agreement could be reached on a basis for universal sovereignty. Existing regimes regard attempts by those outside their jurisdiction to change or influence conditions, views, etc., within their jurisdictions as *intervention*. They insist that authority must be based solely on considerations internal to their jurisdictions, and they insist that recognition be granted on a *de facto* basis, without reference to legitimacy—i.e., to conformity with an ecumenic formula. By contrast, under both fused and refracted conditions, extrajurisdictional interest in a regime is regarded as legitimate, and the need for external recognition is considered a key factor in the establishment of a regime's authority.

(2) CONTENT

The content of myth includes the fundamental symbols defining the meaning and purpose of a society and its political system.

The fundamental myth of the fused model relates to the problem of *order*. The basically self-contained socio-economic units of the fused society do not require concrete governmental intervention for their perpetuation. But they confront an outer world which seems to be fundamentally chaotic—the behavior of natural forces and of external human groups appears erratic, unpredictable, threatening. What the fused society requires is a principle for changing chaos into cosmos, disorder into order, disharmony into harmony. This task is obviously beyond finite human capacities, and so the creation of order requires the intervention of supra-human forces, principles of nature, great ancestors or their spirits, deities and gods. The political myth of every primitive and traditional society—and there are thousands of them, each with its particular concrete symbols—seems to reflect in some way this elemental urge for order. To re-establish order is the fundamental goal of the fused regime.

The refracted society, by contrast, takes for granted the prior existence of order. Nature and nature's God are considered to be inherently orderly. Man's task, therefore, is not so much to create order as to discover the underlying principles of nature and learn how to manipulate them and to secure and safeguard man's human needs and objectives. Nature presents a field in which countless alternative possibilities arise, and man is forced to choose among them those which will enable him to realize his creative potentialities. Refracted man sees himself as his own creator. He "makes himself" through his culture, his education, his economy, his government. Hence the fundamental myth of a refracted society relates to the problem of *decision*. The political myths of modern societies, again in diverse forms, whether autocratic or republican, all prescribe criteria for human decision-making, the goals of the regime.

The formula spells out the implications of the myth for the social order. It states how the regime is to be established and its modes of conduct.

In keeping with its basic myth, the fused regime is recruited *ascriptively*; its major task is the conduct of ritual, stressing *correct* forms of behavior; its norms are predominantly *sacred* and *particularistic*. Its relationships are *hierarchical*, based on *status*.

The refracted regime, by contrast, is recruited by *achievement* potential; its tasks are *rational*, in the sense of choosing among scarce means for specified goals; its norms are predominantly *secular* and *universalistic*. Its relationships are *equalitarian*, based on *contract*.

A fused regime is *monarchic*; a refracted regime, *republican*. A fused bureaucracy stresses *guardianship*; refracted, *merit*.

These concepts are sufficiently familiar so that I need not dwell further on them, but they have usually been posed in an exclusively dichotomous fashion. They should, rather, be viewed as polar extremes on scales, having a merely heuristic purpose. We shall not encounter such extremes in real life, however much they may be approximated. Normal conduct is better described as occurring at mid-points on these scales, usually involving a mixture of the extreme types of behavior. It is difficult to think of such intermediate points without having specific terms for them, and it is for this reason that the prismatic model is needed. Its concepts appear particularly relevant, not only for the transitional regimes of our day, but also for our contemporary macro-regime.

Consider first the prismatic myth complex. To prismatic man the need for order is still compelling in a world of chaotic and disturbing change. However, he also needs to make decisions as the products and problems of refraction increasingly impinge upon his life. No simple word seems adequate for such a confusing welter of often contradictory goals and norms. Let us tentatively call the prismatic myth *mimetic*. It involves imitation, play-acting, goals stated "as if." Old rituals are perpetuated "as if" they were still effective, but the life has gone out of them. Thus traditional regimes remain as living fossils. At the same time, decision-making forms are established "as if" they could and would be used to make and enforce decisions, but in fact they become semi-stillborn, lifeless creatures. The prismatic society, then, has two concurrent regimes, both formalistic: one a *ritualistic residue*, the other a *rationalistic embryo*.

The prismatic formula is similarly mimetic. Its modes of recruitment are *attained*; semi-ascribed in their stress on rank and station, but semi-achieved in the use of symbols relevant to competence, merit, performance. Norms are *selectivistic, syncretic*. When formal conduct is *polynormative*, effective behavior tends to become *normless, anomic*. Prismatic relationships are *kaleidoscopic*, based on a *status-contract mix*.

The application of these concepts to ortho-regimes is not difficult to make. Can they be applied also to macro-regimes? A fused macro-regime tends toward the recognition of a universal sovereign and world order, as small worlds expand and merge into larger worlds. The "emperor" is a symbol of such an "imperium" or universal dominion, whether or not it actually imposes effective control over subordinate monarchs. "Universal empires" and "feudal societies" are distinguished from each other primarily by their control structure, the character of the macro-rule, but both may have essentially the same kind of macro-regime.

As to a refracted macro-regime, I can only speculate on the form it might take in the future, since it has yet to be established. However, the League of Nations and the United Nations appear to anticipate one form of a potential refracted macro-regime. The Comintern may have been another. The stress would not be on "order" so much as on problem-solving, decision-making, "progress," or "development."

The prismatic macro-regime is more interesting because it comes closer to the current international scene. Here we clearly see the United Nations, especially the General Assembly and the Security Council, as the organs of a would-be refracted decision-making macro-regime. We also discover in the Papacy the remains of a one-time fused ordering macro-regime.

Leadership position is predominantly attained, not by traditional or religious sanctions or by universal election, but by "great-power status." There is little agreement on the norms to be applied, although the publicist of international law seeks valiantly to syncretize from tradition and modern "legislation" the customary and conventional laws to be applied to inter-state relationships.

The status-contract mix is to be found in the indeterminacy with which decisions are made on the basis of power politics and treaty obligations. Selectivism is to be found in the development of preferential norms for regional blocs, states belonging to one of several rival "camps," trading and monetary communities, treaty organizations, alliances, etc. Such norms are syncretic insofar as they include both dependence on time-honored, sacred traditions, as expressed in *jus sanguinis*, and more secular, voluntaristic norms, such as freedom of movement and rights of naturalization. *Jus soli* is an instructive syncretic compromise between the two principles of blood and free choice.

One of the distinguishing characteristics of the prismatic model is *heterogeneity*. The macro-regime is heterogeneous, first, in respect to diverse and often incompatible myths and formulae, expressed in a variety of unco-ordinated fossil and abortive "as if" systems of world order. Second, in respect to the constituent ortho-regimes, a great diversity is to be found. Some are already quite refracted in character, ranging from the democratic to the totalitarian in power structure, but all approximating the characteristics attributed to the refracted model. Many regimes also remain which still adhere to fused myths and formulae, but they flourish only in remote and isolated regions, having purely local power, and so play no significant part in our macro-regime. An increasing number of "new states," exhibiting highly prismatic characteristics in their own ortho-regimes, are beginning to play a more and more important role in the macro-regime, as expressed in their admission to the United Nations and specialized agencies, and their participation in regional blocs, sub-systems, "camps," etc.

(3) POLITY: AUTHORITY AND CONTROL

We have distinguished two basic elements of power: formal authority and effective control. To what extent are they combined or dissociated in our models? What are the corresponding implications for international relations theory? The extent to which authority and control are dissociated is indicated as degree of *formalism*. A high degree is *formalistic*, a low degree *realistic*.

A power structure considered with reference to both formal and effective power (authority and control) is called a *polity*. A polity, therefore, includes both regime and rule; a *macro-polity*, macro-regime and macro-rule.[11]

Applying these concepts to our basic models, we may attribute a high degree of realism to both the fused and the refracted model—i.e., correspondence between rule and regime. The prismatic model, by contrast, is relatively formalistic, its rule separated from its regime, its authority from its control structures.

In prismatic polities this takes the form of bossism, seizure of power by violence. The boss may prefer to rule "behind the throne," leaving the authority structure intact, or he may choose to appropriate symbols of legitimacy for himself. In the latter event, he may choose between traditional (fused) symbols and modern (refracted) ones, or he may syncretically employ both. Since neither is operational, no difficulty arises from the simultaneous use of inconsistent symbols, while the advantage is gained of attracting support from diverse constituencies, thus giving the rule at least a quasi-legitimacy.

The applicability of this model to transitional societies is not difficult to see. Can we also apply it to world politics? Here the manifestation of naked control is not boss rule attained through coup and revolution, but imperial power won through war and conquest. Domination by

---

[11] In a more complete terminology, we might speak of "micro-polity" as including micro-regime and micro-rule; "ortho-polity," ortho-regime and ortho-rule.

great powers and imperialism are the characteristic manifestations of prismatic macro-politics. But here, too, an effort is made to legitimate power. Decisions by a "summit conference" tend to give way to the caucused manipulation of a U.N. General Assembly, and the creation of a Security Council as a vehicle for great-power authority. "Imperialism" itself is a characteristically prismatic phenomenon, since colonial rule rests on neither the refracted principle of popular sovereignty nor the fused religious myths of the conquered peoples.

Formalism manifests itself as the motions of decision-making, followed by inability to implement and enforce policies; gestures of establishing order without order resulting. We see painted doves flying, hear talk of peace and high-sounding declarations about universal rights. Conferences meet to discuss disarmament, to unify dismembered peoples, to regulate the movement of goods, people, and ideas. Without questioning the value of these putative ordering and decisional activities, I wish only to point out the substantial formalism which characterizes them.

Formalism may also be seen in the character of the constituent polities in our prismatic macro-polity. Nominally independent states are recognized and admitted to membership in the United Nations, although effective control over their policies is exercised outside their jurisdiction. Such polities are "micro-rules" dressed up like "ortho-regimes," i.e., *satellites*. But there are also effective powers which are not recognized and hence not admitted to the family of nations. These are "ortho-rules" treated as "micro-regimes," i.e., *de facto* powers. The admission of "satellites" and the exclusion of "*de facto* powers" from the macro-regime compound the formalism of the macro-polity.

The extent to which the polities in our prismatic world system are themselves prismatic augments the formalism of the macro-polity. In other words, the formalism of power in transitional societies, many of which are now regarded as "sovereign states," contributes to lack of realism in world politics. In many of these states the control structure is highly precarious, its external recognition not matched by internal legitimacy and hence without effective power. Such ruling groups are often displaced by counterelites, adhering to radically different foreign policies, switching from one ecumene or "camp" to another. Hence many component units, the adherents of our macro-polity, are themselves precariously based and formalistic. We refer to them as the "uncommitted." They provide an uncertain and risky base for both decision-making and order at the level of world politics.

Another approach to the understanding of formalism in prismatic politics requires us to analyze the conditions under which control and authority can be converted into each other. In general, such conversion is readily made in a fused model but not in a refracted society. To explain this, let us distinguish political power from other forms of power based on violence, wealth, prestige, affection, skill, enlightenment, etc.—to use some of Professor Lasswell's categories.[12] In a fused model these forms are relatively undifferentiated and highly agglutinative. In a refracted model, they are highly differentiated and relatively distinct, although never fully so.

Consequently, in a fused model the elite tends to monopolize all the forms of influence. Under these circumstances it is difficult to determine whether governors (those who exercise both control and authority) have a valid claim to legitimacy. Insofar as legitimacy rests on a suprahuman basis, as in divine kingship, operational criteria to validate authority are weak. Normally, fulfillment of ritual requirements is necessary, but whoever seizes control can usually manipulate ritual performance to legitimate his pretensions.

Consider the validation of conquest. A conquering ruler asserts his authority in the name of his god, whose dominion is said to include the annexed territory. Legitimation of the claim rests upon ability to maintain control, thereby proving the extent of the divine power. Hence authority in a fused regime largely rests, in practice, upon effective control. Once announced, authority tends to reinforce control. This is the mechanism for convertibility of authority and control in a fused society.

In refracted society, by contrast, the various forms of influence are clearly differentiated, and political authority can be gained only by determinate means, based on procedures for the delegation of authority from a regime's constituents—voting, majority rule, etc. Moreover, other forms of influence, such as wealth, popularity, prestige, skill, etc., are protected and limited. They tend to block generalization of the scope of control to include formal authority. Political power comes to be exercised in an institutionally distinct sphere, as do the other forms of influence. (It is this characteristic of relatively refracted societies, incidentally, which enables us to study "politics" and the subjects of the other social sciences as though they were virtually autonomous spheres of behavior.)

In a prismatic model the differentiation of a political sphere is both present and not present; it exists formalistically but not effectively. In other words, authority is differentiated and the criteria for establishment

[12] Lasswell and Kaplan, *op.cit.*, pp. 55-57, 83-92.

of a legitimate regime become relatively operational. At the same time, the consensual basis of support for constituted authority is lacking, so that control falls into the hands of military and bureaucratic specialists who wield non-authoritative but effective means of control. In both the fused and the prismatic model, power may be seized by several means; but, whereas in the fused model it is readily legitimized, in the prismatic, legitimation is precarious.

For this reason, prismatic rulers use *ad hoc* rationalizations to lend some color of legitimacy to their rule. In particular, they rely on *charismatic* leadership myths and doctrines of *tutelage* to justify temporary exercise of power, pending the establishment of a more permanent and viable regime.

I believe this model is readily applicable to the description of many contemporary transitional societies. Is it also useful for study of the macro-polity? I believe it is, once we translate some of the terminology to a different level of analysis. The units are no longer individuals but groups, especially polities in the macro-polity. The phenomenon of convertibility appears if we consider that, whereas in traditional systems of international relations, conquest could readily be converted into legitimate imperial authority, today the barriers to recognition of conquest are far greater. At the same time, there has come into being embryonically an institutionally distinct sphere of formal political authority—under which, for example, the boundaries of new polities could be drawn, through the principle of "self-determination," under plebiscites supervised by a world regime. Hence control, in the form of superpower domination, largely prevails but increasingly lacks legitimate authority. The macro-political equivalent of charismatic leadership and tutelage is the concept of a *leader* nation and its "civilizing" or *developmental* mission.

These considerations help us to clarify an inadequacy of the term "world politics." It presupposes a refracted model in which political institutions and behavior can be meaningfully distinguished from non-politics. On a refracted basis we can conceive of distinct spheres which, in addition to world politics, might include world law, world trade, world sociology, world religions, world geography, etc., each as significantly differentiated subjects of inquiry. Such concepts would provide a valid basis for a set of approaches to the study of international relations in a refracted world paralleling the existing academic disciplines. If my hypothesis is valid, however, we do not have a refracted world today but something like a prismatic one. These formal spheres arise only formalistically. In practice each *overlaps* extensively with the others.

Hence none of these approaches can be very useful without concurrent study of the impact of other spheres upon them.

By this I mean to say that "world politics" is unintelligible except as an analytic aspect of a whole which includes social, economic, religious, and ideological aspects as well as the political.

The fused model also helps us to understand why traditional imperial and feudal systems resist analysis under the categories of "international politics." In them political power was largely undifferentiated from other aspects of the society and economy. Hence any concrete interaction combines uniquely political, economic, social, and religious implications or aspects. It is clearly anachronistic to use current disciplinary concepts of politics and economics for those societies. What we do not so generally recognize is that it is almost equally anachronistic to project these same concepts onto our own international system. Although these differentiated structures exist formalistically, the effective basis of interaction remains, to a considerable extent, undifferentiated.

(4) POLICIES AND CODES

So far we have considered only myth and formula in relation to authority in political systems. We must add now the concept of *codes*, referring to the more specific policies and norms adopted by a regime for the regulation of affairs.

Codes occur in every society, but the structures for formulating and adopting them vary sharply. Only in the decisional framework does conscious adoption and enforcement of codes become a major preoccupation. In a refracted model, where consensus on myth and formula is assumed, major political controversy revolves around matters of law and administration—i.e., codes. Even great political struggles, such as national elections, involve, not changes in the formula, but general orientations toward maintaining or changing codes, tendencies which are spelled out in rival "platforms." Thus, the focus of refracted politics is not "power" per se, but policies, codes.

In the fused model, by contrast, decision-making is minimal, and codes are taken for granted as given by tradition. They have a sacred basis. Thus they hardly enter into political controversy. The power struggle becomes a quest for power for its own sake—i.e., those who aspire to elite status seek the perquisites which go with fused power, not only authority and control but also respect, wealth, affection, etc.

In the prismatic model decisional structures are introduced, but work imperfectly. Consensus on myth and formula does not exist, as we have seen. Hence the power struggle primarily concerns the character of the regime itself, what the dominant myth and formula are to be. Although codes and policies are considered, they are given a lower priority than the more fundamental ideological struggle. Insofar as "legislative" structures are institutionalized, they become embroiled in ideological and constitutional rather than policy questions. Because of this, in considerable part the society falls back on traditional codes and normlessness or the mere will of the rulers.

The relevance of these three models to modern, traditional, and transitional societies is fairly apparent. Can they be applied to macro-polities and contemporary international affairs?

The fused macro-polity provides an arena for the international power struggle and "balance of power" politics par excellence. Here the traditional codes of component polities are not questioned. The chief issue is simply the desire for power for its own sake, the "outs" against the "ins," the conquering vs. the conquered. Instead of elites seeking power, we have states, each attempting to maximize the perquisites which go with power—wealth, prestige, authority. The fused model seems to fit not only much of medieval and early modern European politics, but also the inter-state struggles of classical Greek, Indian, and Chinese states, as well as the politics of universal empires.

On my assumptions we have not yet attained a refracted macro-polity, but we can imagine that it might involve a world government, resting on general consensus on a myth and formula for the global regime, but entailing also acute political struggles concerning policy questions, the allocation of resources, rules for trade, population movements, currency systems, the cultivation of the arts, etc.

The contemporary world system, however, fits more nearly the prismatic model. It is neither an arena of simple power struggle nor a field of battle over policies. Rather, it is an arena torn by deep ideological questions of far-reaching significance. Hence the power rivalry concerns mainly the question of what the ultimate myth and formula for a world order will be and what the corresponding allocation of values, wealth, power, prestige, etc. Power can no longer be sought for its own sake, nor is it sought as a means to decide between alternative policies. It is primarily prized as a means to determine which of several competing formulae will be used to organize the world.

What is the character of this ideological issue which rends the prismatic macro-polity? The issues are surely complex and defy simple explication. At the risk of oversimplification, however, I will offer a guess about the deeper implications of this struggle.

In a fused world the primary issue, as I have already suggested, is *order.* As refraction occurs, two other issues come to the fore as decisive: *freedom* and *justice*. Neither is perceived as a basic issue in a fused society, but the processes of development (refraction) make them crucial. The process of refraction is speeded by freedom which permits not only certain social groups but also certain self-selecting societies to advance more rapidly than others. The price of this advance for the *elect* is corresponding regression for the *reject*.[13] Hence a countermovement arises to limit freedom in the interest of justice. This movement draws its mass base from the reject, but its leadership comes from a *counterelect*. The danger of this reaction, however, is that tyranny can be imposed in the name of justice, and further development suppressed. The prismatic role of a revolutionary leadership in a polity is played by a revolutionary state in a macro-polity.

In practice a developing (or refracting) society must strive for a balance between freedom and justice. A fundamental point at issue in the myth and formula is the precise balance to be struck between these goals, one being weighted more heavily than the other, especially for the many situations in which they conflict with each other. Indeed, it is precisely in the prismatic situation that the goals of freedom and justice are most incompatible. It is only a refracted society which can attain a sufficiently high level of productivity—the "affluent society," as Galbraith so aptly names it—to enable it to be just to all without sacrificing freedom.

But patently, however affluent some societies in the modern world may be, they constitute but a small minority of the world population. Thus the "free" minority adopts a slogan for world order which cannot but appear to many as a rationalization of their self-interest. But the countervailing symbol of "justice" appears to the free minority as a rationalization for those who would establish a world tyranny.

The ensuing ideological struggle is exceedingly painful for all participants, and its issue appears to be an all-or-nothing choice. One response to this revolutionary crisis is the *ritualization* of means. I have already mentioned ritualistic survivals of traditional regimes. Let us observe that one reason is precisely the inability of ideological adversaries to agree on ultimate goals and a political formula. The main sphere in which agreement can be reached is the importance of scarce means which, of course, can be used to achieve diverse and incompatible ends. One such means is *wealth*. Economic development can be seized on as

---

[13] The "elect" differ from the "elite" in that they rank high in all values, not merely in power; correspondingly, the "reject" are deprived with respect to all values. See *ibid.*, p. 62.

an orienting concept if one refuses to answer the prior question, "Development for what?" Only the traditionalists, the remnants of a fused era, question the norm of raised productivity as a primary goal. The modernists, whether capitalist or Communist, agree on the ritualization of this means, even where they disagree violently on the uses to which enhanced production should be put.

Another such means is *power*. It is a paradox that in fused societies, where power, in large measure, provides the essential rationale for political struggle, it is rarely used as a shibboleth. A pure power struggle, rather, is waged in the name of ultimate supra-human goals, for the "glory of God," or the creation of Order.

In a prismatic macro-polity, however, marked by poly-ecumenic ideological strife, it becomes fashionable to advocate a pure power struggle as, virtually, an end in itself. This occurs precisely at the time when increasing imbalance in the world power structure, improved techniques of mass destruction, and inability to create an effective world authority combine to heighten the risks of utterly devastating total war. It is this risk which creates a fascination with the idea of power per se, even though power struggles are at their most ideological level.

IV. COMMUNICATION NETWORKS

On the premise that no society is possible without communication among its members, we may examine the characteristic patterns or structures of communication in diverse societies. In doing so, it is useful to distinguish two key variables, social *mobilization* and *assimilation*.[14]

By *mobilization* we refer to the extent to which a population participates in wider networks of communication made possible by territorial and social mobility, literacy, the spread of mass media, etc. In a relatively fused society, mobilization would be minimal, whereas a refracted society is conceivable only under the assumption of extensive mobilization. A fused world is, then, segmented into innumerable little communities inhabited by an "underlying" or non-mobilized population. A refracted world would be integrated into a global community inhabited by a fully mobilized population.

By *assimilation* we refer to the extent to which the mobilized population in a society adheres to the myth and formula of its elite. A refracted society is possible only by virtue of extensive assimilation, since otherwise the consensus and intensive co-ordination required could not be achieved.

[14] This discussion is based on the analysis furnished by Karl W. Deutsch in *Nationalism and Social Communication*, New York, 1953.

When a polity embraces a mobilized and assimilated community, we may speak of a *nation*. Hence *nationalism* is a movement aspiring to or reflecting the creation of a nation. The logical extreme of refraction is a mobilized and assimilated macro-polity; hence, a world order and a world community. The question of assimilation does not arise in a fused society inasmuch as it is un-mobilized.

In a prismatic society, however, assimilation and mobilization both take place, but to a limited degree and not necessarily at the same rate. Hence a population may be more mobilized than assimilated—i.e., *differentiated*.

(1) POLY-COMMUNALISM

A differentiated polity contains a *dominant* community from which the elite is recruited, plus one or more *deviant* communities—differentiated in terms of language, religion, status, and other symbol systems—assuming postures of relative hostility and opposition to the dominant community. The most mobilized members of each deviant community must choose betweeen attempting to assimilate to the elite of the dominant community or, alternatively, forming a *counterelite* determined to modify, infiltrate, or replace the elite, or to demarcate an autonomous zone for occupancy by members of its deviant "minority." When a society is divided into differentiated communities, we may call it *poly-communal*. A movement to control the polity on behalf of one community at the expense of others is often called "nationalism," but it would be more accurate to term it *communalism*.

The relevance of the concepts of differentiation and poly-communalism to many contemporary non-Western societies is apparent and justifies the imputation of prismatic features in their communication nets. Do these concepts apply equally well to our contemporary macro-society, the "world system" of our times? At least one major distinction must be made between the level of macro- and ortho-analysis with respect to communication; namely, whereas a single dominant community supplies a single elite for an ortho-polity, a set of communities provides the corresponding elites for the set of polities in a macro-polity. A more complicated set of possibilities, accordingly, must be considered.

Let us call a community which is "dominant" at the level of a single society a *prime community* at the macro-polity level. The prime communities of the super-powers may be called *super-prime* communities, the Americans, Russians, English, French, and Chinese being examples. Correspondingly, prime communities of "infra-powers" could be called *infra-prime* communities, examples being the Burmese, Arabs, Turks, Greeks, Koreans, etc. A deviant community seeking independence, autonomy, or revolution within a polity may be called, from the perspective of the macro-polity, a *proletary* community. The counterelite of a proletary community may be termed *rebels*. After a successful revolution resulting in the partition of a polity (empire), the former rebels become the elite of a new prime community.

Tensions arise, at the macro-political level, from a variety of intercommunal struggles. For example, elites of the "super-prime communities" are likely to regard each other as rivals for control over a unified world order, and hence engage in a relentless struggle for power in which the infra-powers become their pawns, as they seek to form alliances with them or bring them under control. Apart from the military and economic strategies open to them, they may strive to assimilate members of the infra-communities, whether prime or proletary, to their own community. Educational and informational programs are designed to promote these objectives. If the infra-prime elites resist such assimilation, communication with proletary communities and rebel groups will be encouraged.

From the side of the infra-powers, insecure elites require external assistance to maintain their security both against hostile neighboring powers and against their own restless rebel groups. They may also wish economic and technical aid and insofar as they may already have partially assimilated to the dominant language and values of one of the super-prime communities, they will also desire to strengthen communication with them. For similar reasons proletary communities and rebels, seeking assistance in their own struggles, open up communication with foreign communities. The flow of information and ideas begins to reinforce demands and capacity to carry out revolutions, partitions, annexations, etc.

The foregoing analysis sounds rather similar to conventional accounts of power politics, imperialism and nationalist movements, etc. Obviously it is related to them, but it differs in its reliance upon communications theory to explain and predict relationships which arise in the process of social mobilization and differentiation. It assumes a dynamic perspective and "evolutionary" sequences rather than a "billiard ball" model in which power centers interact in a repetitive and unpatterned way. The focus is on communities and communication rather than states and power.

(2) PROLETARIANIZATION

In this analysis we have thought of communities as large-scale systems. We can also use communications analysis as a framework for examining the relations of the individual to his society and polity. In our refracted model the fully mobilized and assimilated individual is highly *socialized* and *politicized*, in that his behavior reflects a high degree of sensitivity to social and political forces in society and polity. In the fused model, by contrast, the unmobilized remains highly *privatized* and *insular*, his responsiveness being largely to his primary, face-to-face family and neighborhood setting.

At the former extreme the individual—whether controlling or controlled—is deeply enmeshed in governmental and administrative processes. We may call him a *citizen*. At the opposite extreme the individual is, to a considerable extent, self-contained and indifferent to government, which impinges only incidentally and tangentially on his life. We shall call him a *subject*. (This usage differs from the contrast between *free* citizens in a republic and *unfree* citizens in a totalitarian despotism, although the words "citizen" and "subject" are sometimes also used to make this distinction.) Relative stability marks the relationships of citizens to refracted polities and of subjects to fused polities.

In the prismatic model, relations between the individual and his polity are more ambivalent and unstable. Mobilization means that each individual becomes increasingly aware of, concerned about, and influenced by the political and social events of his larger milieu. At the same time he experiences a sense of helpless inability to direct these events, but he simultaneously resists direction by others so that the elite feel equally helpless in their efforts to co-ordinate or change the social order. As a result, the individual feels himself to be "in but not of" his society, and may be properly called a *proletarian* in Toynbee's sense of the word. The proletarian becomes concerned but non-participant; he is contacted but not controlled; both frustrated and frustrating.

The predominantly proletarian composition of the population in a prismatic society contributes to its restless, unstable, unintegrated, intermittent, and spastic quality. It becomes subject to violent explosions, mob demonstrations, and anomie, jeopardizing the security of government—to say nothing of its effectiveness. The rise of proletary communities and rebellions not only increases tension within prismatic polities, but contributes to the characteristic fragility of a prismatic macro-political world.

(3) INTELLIGENTSIA AND COSMOPOLITANS

Of the various proletarian types, one is particularly worth examination—namely, those who are most learned. The intellectual in a "transitional society" is typically a man of strong ambivalence, since he is torn between the values and lore of his traditional heritage and the new learning of an incipient "modern" world. A familiar designation for this group is the *intelligentsia*. It plays a major role in both the elite and the counterelite of the prismatic polity, since it possesses the technical knowledge and facility in communication with the external world needed to establish and maintain autonomy. At the same time, it can communicate with the traditionally minded majority of its own semi-mobilized community. This very ambivalence, however, makes the intelligentsia a restless, unstable, and often vacillating type, haunted by a sense of alienation and a lack of identification, both at home and abroad.

When we look at our contemporary macro-polity as a prismatic system, we ask whether there is any global equivalent of the intelligentsia. I think there is, and I would call him the *cosmopolitan*. Here again we find an ambivalent intellectual, torn between a new perspective which has been called "world-mindedness," and a more traditional view which puts national identifications above all others. His home, however, is characteristically in the more refracted rather than the prismatic societies of our world. In his work he vacillates between identification with national goals and programs and more utopian endeavors to advance the causes of world peace and development. Just as the intelligentsia plays a crucial role in the evolution of a prismatic polity, so the cosmopolitan has a historic mission in the travail of a prismatic macro-polity. A theory of international relations which concentrates on nation-centered behavior leaves out one of the most hopeful elements in the dynamics of world politics.

V. "SOCIATION"

We have space only for a cursory look at one aspect of the solidarity system of our prismatic model—namely, the organizational structure. Organizations may be classified on a scale ranging from "primary" or familistic types, which are highly ascriptive, particularistic, and diffuse, to "secondary" or associational types, which are achievement-oriented, universalistic, and specific. These types play a corresponding and fundamental role in the fused and refracted models respectively.

In studying the prismatic model we discover that, to some extent, organizations of both types flourish, and hence the mixture of contrasting organizational forms is characteristic. However, I think we can distinguish also an intermediate type of organization which is semi-associational and semi-familistic in character. A religious order which enters politics, provides schools, and engages directly in economic activity is one example, as is a "family-name association" which unites all those who happen to bear the same surname in programs for educational, social, political, and religious objectives. For brevity I refer to such organizations as *clects*.[15]

(1) CLECTS

A "clect" makes use of modern techniques of large-scale organization, but its goals are relatively particularistic or perhaps "selectivistic." Poly-communalism undergirds the growth of clects. Interest groups formed in each community not only seek the implementation of their specific interest, but they typically seek to restrict the benefits of governmental activity to members of their community, to deny the same benefits to members of rival communities. A government based on clectic organization, therefore, aggravates the deep hostilities between communities, finds it increasingly difficult to "aggregate" interests, to arrive at shared or compromise programs which would provide something for each group. In a prismatic polity one clect may dominate, eliminating and forcing its will upon rival clects as in a ruthless, single-party dictatorship. The Communist Party, indeed, is in organizational form a clect.

Alternatively, a politically impotent "coalition" system is established which cannot make definitive decisions because every crucial choice is sure to alienate one or more of its constituent clects.

This hypothesis, which I find applicable to many of the "less-developed" countries, applies equally to our contemporary macro-polity. Again, we face the unhappy dilemma of choosing between a world dictatorship established by one of the super-powers or a coalition regime—symbolized by the veto-ridden Security Council—which is politically impotent.

(2) SUPER-CLECTS

An organization which may be associational in the context of a polity becomes a super-clect in a macro-political context. Instead of having

---

[15] The word is onomatopoeic, based on sounds common to such words as "clique," "club," "sect," "collect," "eclectic." We seem to lack an established word for this concept.

a global chamber of commerce, for example, we have a set of national chambers. Each one, in seeking to strengthen the economic development of one country, may impair the development of others. Through tariffs, exchange controls, quota systems, regional markets, and other restrictive devices, selectivistic policies are enforced, favoring and subsidizing the politically powerful segments of the macro-polity at the expense of the politically weak, the great powers at the expense of the small.

The most important super-clect is, of course, the nation-state. From an ortho-political perspective, the modern nation-state may appear as a gigantic association, offering all its advantages to its member-citizens. But from a world-wide perspective it has all the essential clect characteristics. Considered as a whole, it is very diffuse in its functions. It is selectivistic in that most members are born into and cannot leave the organization, nor do they make an initial, contractual agreement to accept the obligations of membership, although they may periodically recite "oaths of allegiance." Only "naturalized" citizens effect such a formal adherence, but the rules of immigration and emigration tend to restrict sharply access to and separation from membership. From a macro-political viewpoint, the "national interest" is a highly particularistic goal.

At the same time, the nation above all makes use of associational principles of large-scale organization, and forms innumerable subsystems which are highly specific, achievement-oriented, and universalistic in character. The nation as a super-clect, in other words, is the organization par excellence which confronts us with an apparently tragic choice between world empire dominated by a single nation (domi-nation!) and a feebly indecisive coalition of powers—the essential dilemma of every prismatic polity.

VI. Economic Allocation

Modern economic structures, whether based on the market, as in free enterprise societies, or on state planning, as in the Soviet model, all employ fundamental "economizing" or "rationalizing" concepts and institutions. Traditional systems, whether "reciprocative" or "redistributive," even when utilizing trade and market places, subordinate economic to religious, political, and social considerations.[16]

These concepts of economizing and traditional systems help us to explain "adaptational" characteristics of fused and refracted societies.

---

[16] For a fundamental review of economic concepts in this connection, see Karl Polanyi, Conrad Arensberg, and Harry Pearson, *Trade and Market in the Early Empires*, Glencoe, Ill., 1957.

An intermediate concept is needed to deal with the prismatic model, and I have proposed the *bazaar-canteen* as an appropriate tool.

The key point about the "bazaar-canteen" is that, although transactions in it assume, in part, an economizing dynamism, they also partake of traditional political, social, and religious functions to a substantial degree. This leads to such phenomena as "price indeterminacy," a "status-contract mix," "pariah entrepreneurship," "intrusive access to the elite," etc. It is unnecessary to explain these characteristics here, since they are fully described elsewhere,[17] but they may be illustrated by reference to the "canteen," whose prices are typically higher or lower than those to be found outside.

(1) CANTEENS AND SUPER-CANTEENS

When canteen prices are low, we may speak of a "subsidized canteen," and when high, of a "tributary canteen." Admission to the subsidized canteen is a privilege open only to elites, whereas customers in a tributary canteen are captives who cannot buy elsewhere. Such phenomena are numerous in transitional societies, whether we think in terms of exchange controls, import permits, taxation, or bank loans.

These and the related concepts identified in the model are applicable, I believe, to contemporary international economic relations, i.e., to our macro-polity. Economists often speak of the "infrastructure" which is necessary for economic development to occur. By this they refer largely to such facilities as schools, roads, health programs, transport, and power, which reduce the costs necessary for profitable investment. They give less attention to the political and administrative prerequisites of economical production.

Markets, especially when organized on a large scale and over extended periods of time, are highly explosive. They produce socially disruptive tensions, competition and conflict, which can only be contained if the political-administrative environment is adequate, and such an environment is costly to establish. In particular, the temptation to abuse power by confiscating wealth must be overcome by a legal system which protects property and contracts. (Such a system, incidentally, is as necessary to protect "public" and "socialized" property, as it is to protect private property.)

Transitional (or prismatic) societies typically lack the political and administrative, as well as the material, infrastructure for profitable

[17] For an extended treatment, see my "The Bazaar-Canteen Model," *Philippine Sociological Review*, VI (July-October 1958), pp. 6-59. A more succinct treatment is given in my "Prismatic Society and Financial Administration" (cited in note 4 above).

investment. The result is that their costs of operation are much higher, including the costs of "buying protection," and they need to make large profits in anticipation of future costs—i.e., to take account of enormous risks.

To use the bazaar-canteen model, then, we can see that in some countries the potential customer for capital enjoys a heavily subsidized *super-canteen*—even at low rates of interest (prices), more than enough capital is readily available. In other countries, the market for capital is a highly tributary *super-canteen*—the costs (interest and profit rates) of capital are inordinately high, and hence capital is scarce and few investments can be made. Capital will be found only for industries in which anticipated profit rates are very high—raw materials and extractive industries, for example.

The result of the world super-canteen situation—a model which may fit the contemporary macro-polity much better than the market model—is that capital, including the savings of entrepreneurs in "underdeveloped" countries, is strongly attracted to the markets (subsidized super-canteens) of the more developed countries, and it is extremely difficult to induce investment in the less developed markets (tributary super-canteens). Imperialism was in part, at least, an effort to convert some tributary into subsidized canteens.

Now, I stated that in the prismatic model the bazaar-canteen involves strong overlapping of economic and political considerations and functions. We can see that the world super-canteen does have its strictly economic aspects, which can be properly understood in the context of world trade and classical economic theory. But a purely economic study of this subject fails to expose its equally important political and social aspects.

(2) NEGATIVE DEVELOPMENT

The socio-political implications of the bazaar-canteen can be better understood if we examine its characteristic consequences. In considering development we normally lump together two kinds of variable which by no means necessarily change in direct ratio with each other.

The first variable is degree of *marketization*, involving increasing specialization, exchange, reliance on prices, work for wages and salaries, etc. The second variable involves economic *welfare* factors—namely, changes in productivity and capital formation, distribution of wealth, and security or predictability of future income.

In the industrialized countries we may assume that both types of development have taken place.[18] But even in the West these two processes did not advance at uniform rates. Indeed, it stands to reason that capital formation, the prerequisite for great increases in productivity, can be achieved in a poor country only by substantial savings, i.e., reduction of real consumption standards. Labor conditions in nineteenth-century England and the liquidation of the kulaks in Russia provide striking illustrations of the social costs of industrialization.

In the underdeveloped countries, however, increasing marketization is taking place at a rapid rate, reinforced by pressures from powerful industrialized nations, but no corresponding improvement in "welfare" values is occurring. Let us call this *negative development*. Development is *positive* only when increasing marketization is accompanied by capital formation and rising per capita income, enhanced security, and more equitable distribution of wealth.

Negative development affects both the mass of population and the mobilized intelligentsia or elite. Among the elite it increases the hostility and envious resentment felt toward industrialized countries, which are viewed as the cause of this disastrous trend. But, simultaneously, the elite in these countries desire for themselves and their people the benefits of industrialization and recognize that if they are to acquire them, they must rely on the assistance—both in technical "know-how" and in capital investment (or grants)—of the very people they blame for their predicament. Their attitude, naturally, becomes highly ambivalent and emotional. Indeed, the response to this "economic" situation parallels the more direct response to the "political" situation of conquest and imperial dependency. Under colonialism a counterelite forms which, while demanding independence from foreign rule, welcomes the new institutional weapons of politics and administration put in their hands by foreign conquerors. Similarly, prismatic elites, while attacking "economic imperialism," seek to attract foreign investments and assistance.

The human response to victimization by a tributary canteen is naturally intense resentment and anger. This is translated into politics as xenophobia and insecurity. Prismatic rulers are caught in a tragic dilemma since, if they reveal their hostility, they may be cut off from possible sources of help which might enable them to overcome their economic difficulties. But in the act of accepting assistance, they also weaken their domestic position by playing into the hands of new

[18] Kenneth Galbraith in *The Affluent Society* (Boston, 1958) has convincingly shown the relationship between these variables in contemporary American economic development.

counterelites who accuse them of treason through collaboration with the imperial enemy.

For the "developed" countries the dilemma is equally tragic, for they are torn between the frustrations of basically unsuccessful efforts to provide assistance and the knowledge that failure to furnish such aid will only aggravate international political tensions. Furthermore, how can one plan a sound foreign policy—economic or political—when the government with which one negotiates today may be replaced by a hostile regime tomorrow?

The political consequences of bazaar-canteen phenomena in the world economy are therefore of the utmost significance and cannot be overlooked in any study of international politics. If one views international economics from this point of view, it is clear that the world economy is as much influenced by political considerations—trade barriers, political insecurity, dumping, grants, etc.—as by strictly economic forces. The present macro-polity, if viewed as a single system, may then be better studied in terms of the bazaar-canteen than in terms of the market model.

But this model requires the juxtaposing or overlapping of economic and political spheres. What is needed is not just an "inter-disciplinary" approach in the conventional sense—i.e., the parallel examination of political and economic structures as though they could exist in relative autonomy—but rather a joint approach to the examination of a unitary phenomenon which, however, has both economic and political implications.

VII. Conclusion

The foregoing discussion represents but a fragmentary and preliminary look at five of the crucial functions whose analysis provides an image of the prismatic society that is applicable to contemporary world politics. A full treatment would deal also with such environmental factors as the population explosion, psychic insecurity, technological changes, geo-strategic considerations, etc. Obviously, this cannot be done in a brief paper, and yet a complete assessment of the utility of the prismatic model for the study of world politics is impossible without completion of this task.

At the psychological level, for example, we might look into the inherent insecurity of the prismatic personality, based on the collapse of traditional values, motivations, and satisfactions, combined with the inadequacy of new norms, resulting in inferiority fears, aggressiveness, preoccupation with power and wealth, normlessness and opportunism, anomie and xenophobia. Equivalent manifestations would be found in the behavior of states in a prismatic macro-polity, as well as in individual behavior. Indeed, the most prismatic orientations might be found among the super-powers, which appear threatened by revolutionary developments elsewhere that undermine their accustomed roles of primacy and their wealth as well as their power.

Among the other associated environmental factors, none is more striking than the demographic. Both fused and refracted models would be characterized by relatively stable population levels, with birth rates approximating death rates, although both rates would be high in the former model, low in the latter. The prismatic model, by contrast, is marked by rapid population growth, with death rates declining much more rapidly than birth rates. Inability of economic development to keep pace with population growth means growing poverty for prismatic populations. If this is taken as a characteristic of transitional societies on the ortho-political level, it is also a feature of the modern world as a whole, considered on the macro-political level.

Thus, each of these prismatic configurations would have points of correspondence in contemporary world affairs that amplify and fill in the skeletal outline provided above. What emerges is not a model for world *politics*, but rather a "holistic" or total picture of "world affairs"—perhaps a "macro-society"—which might be studied in terms of its political, economic, social, and ideological aspects but would not have distinguishable and autonomous effective structures corresponding to these labels.

In conclusion, therefore, I suggest that not only does the traditional "inter-state" model fail to provide us with an adequate theoretical framework for the analysis of contemporary world politics, but the prismatic model does provide us with a framework that throws light on several dimensions of the tragic situation which faces our generation. Hopefully, it may provide some fruitful hypotheses for research and possibly even lead to suggestions about how to advance our quest for a secure world order and peaceful development.

THE ACUTE INTERNATIONAL CRISIS

By CHARLES A. McCLELLAND

ACCOUNTS of the acute crises of international politics occupy a substantial place in the diplomatic history of the past hundred years. These compounded events have been interpreted as manifestations of international rivalries among the Great Powers. Intermittently, they have drawn intense public attention and have generated heavy anxieties over the possibility that they may lead into general warfare. After the fact, they have become subjects of historical reconstruction, with students and commentators attempting to describe "what really happened." Thus, both scholarly and popular interest has persisted in the "inside stories" of the several crises belonging to three historical periods: from 1870 to World War I, the interwar period, and the era since World War II.

There is, consequently, a large descriptive literature of the crises, mainly connected with the diplomacy of opposing coalitions and of interstate conflicts during these three periods. The depth and quality of this literature vary greatly, most often according to the recency of the events and the amount of available and relevant historical documentation. The Moroccan crisis of 1905 and the circumstances of the *Anschluss* of 1936 are, quite naturally, better known and more firmly established factually than the inner details of the Suez crisis of 1956. However, the accumulated knowledge of the series of crises of the post-World War II period, uncertain and impressionistic as it still is, has a great deal to do with our understanding of current international affairs. Take away the facts and meanings commonly associated with the crises of Berlin, Korea, Indochina, Suez, Quemoy, the Congo, and Laos and, obviously, the usual estimates of the scope, intensity, and workings of the Cold War will greatly change. Despite this fact, acute crises have not often been made the focus either of theorizing or of intensive analytic research. Students of international relations have not found it important or necessary to consider these events as if they constituted a significant class of phenomena in the international field. The reasons for passing over the acute international crisis as a focus of explanation are worth consideration.

Since the main purpose of this essay is to advance ideas which put the occurrences of acute crises in a more central perspective, it will be useful to identify, at least cursorily, the conceptual settings which ordinarily have operated to keep systematic approaches to these events in a secondary role.

I

There are, first of all, certain common sense and *ad hoc* interpretations to consider. International crises tend to appear as first-order realities. They seem to be givens of history and, therefore, do not call for particular identification or definition. "Everybody" knows when one happens. The labeling has become virtually instantaneous and world-wide in the Cold War period, but it is interesting to note in passing that the term "crisis" appears also as a "natural naming" in passages of the diplomatic correspondence of the pre-World War I period.[1] The crises fit easily into the major conventional images of the situation of international conflict. What more is there to explain beyond the apparent facts that the foreign policies of certain states are in opposition and that, from time to time, a confrontation or challenge involving these states becomes intense enough to constitute a crisis?

On the same level of common-sense interpretation is the notion that a crisis is but a concrete manifestation of the international clash of public ideas or values. Although the connection is by no means made regularly, this meaning has roots in theoretical inquiries into the general nature of conflict.[2] The Spanish Civil War was seen popularly as a battle between fascism and democracy and the Korean War was regarded as a contest between democracy and communism or, from the Communist angle, between imperialism and socialism. Both were conceived of as crises in the conflict of ideologies.

Still more elemental is the outlook which seizes on the motives and interests of political leaders and elites for an explanation. Leading men plan and execute strategies and tactics of international conflict during "no war" periods. Thus, the accounts of crises have been cast, not infrequently, in terms of Bismarck against Gambetta or Boulanger, Bülow against Delcassé, Izvolski against Aehrenthal, Hitler against Chamberlain, Truman against Stalin, etc. The simplicity of the plan is

[1] See, for example, quoted passages in Sidney B. Fay, *The Origins of the World War*, 2nd ed., New York, 1935, I, pp. 31, 205, 290, 336, 435, 451, etc.

[2] Jessie Bernard, "The Conceptualization of Intergroup Relations with Special Reference to Conflict," *Social Forces*, XXIX (March 1951), pp. 243-51; Jessie Bernard, "The Theory of Games of Strategy as a Modern Sociology of Conflict," *American Journal of Sociology*, LIX (March 1954), pp. 411-24; Samuel Stouffer, "An Analysis of Conflicting Social Norms," *American Sociological Review*, XIV (December 1949), pp. 707-17; Raymond W. Mack and Richard C. Snyder, "The Analysis of Social Conflict—Toward an Overview and Synthesis," *Journal of Conflict Resolution*, I (June 1957), pp. 212-48.

concealed frequently by the dramatic quality of the events: Leader A initiates his line of action, Leader B responds to the challenge with his own brand of action, and Leaders C, D, and E then do various things in reaction to the situation. The concept of crisis is easily transformed into the image of a contest between prominent individuals.

Yet another *ad hoc* type of explanation has been manifested in the notion of the "power vacuum." The idea had a certain popularity in the years immediately following World War II. Although it, too, may be traced to deeper roots—in the traditional power theory—it is able to stand alone in terms of the physical analogy. Strong aggressive states always will move into weak and poorly defended areas unless they are forestalled by other powerful forces which will oppose such expansion.[3] The situation of a "power vacuum" is considered to be crisis-provoking.

The last of the simple conceptions of the reasons for the phenomena of international crises that will be mentioned here is the "problem-seeking-a-solution" idea. In a later passage, it will be proposed more fully that complex modernizing societies are regularly beset by so many chronic problems that there is a normal propensity to become preoccupied only with those which erupt in an acute form. Then, certain instrumental values take control so that it is assumed that the "reasons" for the problem should be exposed, the causes should be removed, and the needed remedies and reforms should be instituted. The problem-solving blanket is thrown over the flames of conflict in the expectation that they will be smothered. Underlying is the faith that no problem can fail to have a relevant solution. The devoted pursuit of causes and remedies will succeed.

Beyond the *ad hoc* level are at least two current explanations which place the acute crisis in a general setting but do not allow it more than a dependent or subordinate role. Both are doctrines which are influential in shaping the meanings of contemporary international relations. These are the Marxist-Leninist theory of international relations and the traditional power theory.

In the Marxist-Leninist perspective, the prevalence of acute crises in the post-World War II period is an expression of the processes of the world revolution. A limited number of changes are rung on the themes provided mainly by Lenin's writing on the theory of imperialism and war.[4] No details need be given here on the ideas of the capitalist encirclement of the "camp of socialism," the impending collapse of capitalism,

[3] For example, George C. Marshall, "Assistance to European Economic Recovery," *Department of State Bulletin*, xviii (January 18, 1948), pp. 71-72.

[4] V. I. Lenin, *Imperialism, the Highest Stage of Capitalism*, New York, 1940.

the "final" conflicts between capitalist states, and the crusade against "capitalist, war-mongering, imperialist" aggression. In this framework, the series of acute crises is represented as part of an inevitable playing out of historical processes and, also, as the consequence of Soviet resistance and counteraction against the imperialist moves of the "capitalist camp." Endless illustrations and examples are at hand. A remark of Khrushchev at the time of the Lebanon crisis typifies this outlook: "The imperialists are prowling around the fence of the socialist camp like wolves around a sheep pen, but our defenses are strong and the defenders are reliable."[5]

The anti-Communist version of the doctrine accepts as true and correct the Marxist teachings concerning the Communist drive for world revolution and world domination. On this basis, the meaning of the recent crises is located in the strategy and tactics of Soviet foreign policies, which are considered to be concentrated exclusively on conflict and expansionism. The interest in the crises lies not in their patterns, in their relationships to decision-making, or in methods of control of their processes and effects, but in specifications and plans for foreign policies which would contain or defeat the aggressive designs of the Communists.[6] In a word, no great mystery or problem of knowledge is seen in the occurrences of crises. Rather they are perceived as rather obvious and expected manifestations of the main line of current international conflict.

If signs of relaxation appear in the conflict or if there is a lengthening of time between major crises, the causes can be found readily in some domestic problem or circumstance. At the time of this writing, for example, commentators whose views reflect the opposing versions of this theory of international conflict and crisis are speculating on the possibilities of a *détente* in the relations of the United States and the Soviet Union on the basis that both countries now need a lull in the conflict in order to carry out large-scale programs of industrial automation.[7]

By far the most important reason for the relative absence of systematic and intensive study of the acute international crisis is to be found in the traditional power theory. As in the case of the Communist theory of

[5] Speech at Smolensk on August 13, 1958, *New York Times*, August 24, 1958.

[6] Robert Strausz-Hupé *et al., Protracted Conflict*, New York, 1959. See also Harold F. Smiddy, "Manageability and Crises," *General Electric Defense Quarterly*, IV (January-March 1961), p. 23.

[7] Jacob Morris, "Profit, Automation, and the Cold War," *Science & Society*, XXIV (Winter 1960), pp. 1-12; and Institute for the Study of the USSR, Soviet Affairs Analysis Service, "Reference Paper," No. 16, pp. 1-3, and No. 17, p. 4 (1960/61), mimeo.

international relations, there is no need to review the fundamental concepts of the power approach. It suffices to note that, under this explanation, significant occurrences in international politics are regarded as consequences of the distribution of power among the members of the existing international system. Variations from this attributed regularity are regarded as contingent and accidental developments, aberrations in interstate relations brought about by the participating actors' lack of skill, or conceptual and ideological misconceptions of the "reality." The basic construct delineates the play of power among member states around points of equilibria with the outer limits of action set by physical capabilities and such other control factors as conventional rules, norms, and laws. Empirical flesh is put on the skeleton of the theory mainly through specific studies of the foreign policies of states. As a consequence, the phenomena of acute crises are accommodated in the scheme in several ways.

First, it is apparent that any acute crisis always can be located and explained with reference to the operation of the balance of power. A crisis is an occurrence in history which reflects the state of the balance or some change in it. Hans J. Morgenthau remarks simply: "At the bottom of disputes that entail the risk of war there is a tension between the desire to preserve the existing distribution of power and the desire to overthrow it."[8] In the context, it is clear that Morgenthau includes under the headings of disputes and tension those encounters which otherwise are called crises. He proceeds to declare that the disputes which involve tensions are not open to rational evaluations of claims, to concessions and compromise, or to orderly problem-solving in the terms of the dispute.

A place for the crisis in the power explanation is provided also in another conceptual corner. The calculation of relative power is held to be extremely difficult in practical situations so that decision-makers may become persuaded, from time to time, to allow "field tests" of the status of the balance. Hence, limited and controlled assaults or campaigns are launched to test the strength and will to resist of the competitor or enemy. If an armed clash takes place in the field, a crisis may be brought to life. A fumbling technique on the part of either protagonist may lead to a much larger and more serious engagement than was originally anticipated. Progressive commitments of forces and the involvement of national prestige through a process now fashionably called "escalation" may expand such an affair into a major war. An interpretation of the Korean War suggests that the genesis of the crisis

---

[8] Hans J. Morgenthau, *Politics Among Nations*, 3rd ed., New York, 1960, p. 428.

was a *Kraftprobe* which was mismanaged and so became a stalemated limited war.

Although the statement is somewhat dispersed, a further proposition on the occurrence of crises may be noted in Quincy Wright's *A Study of War*. The concept, which is categorized properly within the balance-of-power theory, takes this form: the polarization of opposing alliances of an international political system into rigidly structured armed camps results in a series of acute crises, the last leading to war between the armed camps. This indicates a condition in the system which inhibits adaptation to change and creates serious restraints on its members' freedom to act. The crises are symptoms of non-adaptiveness and war is a means for breaking the structural rigidity of the system. This is, perhaps, the most competent conceptual formulation in support of the widespread notion that a series of acute international crises is the prelude to general war. One finds in *A Study of War* an experimental expression of the idea: "The probability of war between two states during a period of time is not the product or the sum of the probabilities of war in all of the crises anticipated in their relations during the period, nor is it the probability of war in the most serious crisis. Rather it is one *minus* the probability of war being avoided during the period. This is the product of the probabilities of war being avoided in each crisis. . . . Assume that A and B during a period of ten years passed through three crises of which the probable eventuations in war were, respectively, 50, 60, and 70 per cent and that states C and D had, during that period, only one crisis with a war probability of 94 per cent. It should be said, at the beginning of the period, if these probabilities were known, that the probability of the members of the two pairs being at war with each other within ten years was equal. With A and B the probability of avoiding war in the successive crises was 50, 40, and 30 per cent. The product of these percentages is 6 per cent, giving a war probability of 94 per cent. If p_1, p_2, p_3, etc., indicate the probability of war in successive crises in the relations of two states and P indicates the probability of war for n crises, then $P=1-(1-p_1)(1-p_2)(1-p_3) \ldots (1-p_n)$. . . . Even though p is very small, as n approaches infinity the probability of war approaches certainty."[9]

If, as Harold Lasswell has suggested, long-term expectations of highly probable future outcomes feed back and influence current conduct and goals in the manner of a self-fulfilling prophecy, there may be some validity in the idea of the march to war under the conditions of a rigid

[9] Quincy Wright, *A Study of War*, Chicago, 1942, II, p. 1272n.

balance and of recurring crises.[10] On the other hand, a more sanguine interpretation of the relationship between a series of crises and the eventual outbreak of general war is contained in the hypothesis that the growth of experience with the tension-ridden and "short of war" events of acute crises may be, actually, a substitute and replacement in the system for general war itself. Raymond Aron has raised the question as follows: "Is the 'cold war' a preparation or a substitute for total war? If the former, the two camps are simply maneuvering for position until the day of final settlement. If the latter, the propaganda battles, the struggles among national parties, the fighting localized in Greece and Korea, constitute the war itself—inevitable because of the incompatibility of the two worlds but limited so as to reduce the ravages of violence."[11]

On the ground that the "cold war" represents some kind of change in the structure of the international system, it may be argued that the long series of crises since 1946 is a part of the process of experimenting with and learning a "new politics" of international relations. In a word, the crises can be conceived as leading, step by step, away from general or total war. Wright's formula might well be reversed to indicate that exposures to crises carrying some probability of general or total war lead progressively to reduced probability of the eventual occurrence of the terminal event. Thus, where P_i is the probability of general war at any time after a number of crisis exposures (i) and p_1 is the probability of war at the first crisis exposure:

$$P_i = \frac{p_1}{i}$$

The trouble with both of these formulations is that they yield too little in the way of meaningful suggestions for a study of crises which would link concepts and hard data. Indeed, we see that the more systematic approaches which have been discussed to this point do not offer appreciably more guidance than do the *ad hoc* explanations to fruitful investigations of the role of the crises in international politics. There is a conceptual tangle of popularized ideas and vaguely applicable hypotheses. The crises are thought to be connected with the international struggles for ideas and also for power. They are seen as indicators of the state of the international system, but they are regarded as prime operations in the system, as well. They seem to be related to

[10] Harold D. Lasswell, "Inevitable War: A Problem in the Control of Long-range Expectations," *World Politics*, ii (October 1949), p. 6.
[11] Raymond Aron, *The Century of Total War*, Garden City, N.Y., 1954, p. 226.

going to war and to staying at peace. If the international political system has remained fundamentally as it was in 1870, the crises probably play one kind of role—possibly, as stepping-stones on the path to general war—but if the international system has been transformed lately, the current crises may be symptomatic of emerging processes and structures which do not belong to past experience.

In order to move ahead with inquiries into a subject which common sense indicates is important in international affairs, it appears that some setting and orientation different from the conventional perspectives must be provided. A new start for the investigation of acute international crises has developed in the upsurge of research interest in the nature and meanings of social conflict.

II

A judgment made by Karl Deutsch in 1955 has proved to be correct: "There are some indications that at the present time the problem of interstate conflicts is ripe for a concerted research attack, combining the methods of several of the social sciences. The aim of this research would be to develop techniques to do three things: to identify generally those conflict situations and states which are likely to lead to war; to evaluate particular conflict situations and the probable lines along which they are likely to develop if left to themselves; and to suggest further possible techniques for controlling or containing such conflict situations so as to prevent them from breaking out into war."[12]

So many probings into the general subject of conflict have been undertaken in the last few years that it should be emphasized that the hypothetical formulation which is to be developed here concerning international crises is but one alternative approach among several, dependent on the body of "new thought" on the subject of conflict. Starting with the ordinary apperception that acute crises are concrete phenomena of international history with distinct time and place boundaries, we are able now to pick and choose from a number of research suggestions.

One of these suggestions is that an international crisis marks the time of a turning point in a conflict and a period when major decisions are likely to be made.[13] The advent of studies which analyze such crucial

[12] Karl W. Deutsch, "Mass Communications and the Loss of Freedom in National Decision-making: A Possible Research Approach to Interstate Conflicts," *Journal of Conflict Resolution*, 1 (June 1957), p. 200.

[13] Jacques Freymond, *The Saar Conflict, 1945-1955*, London and New York, 1960, p. xiv.

times in international politics according to the conceptual schemes of decision-making promises important gains in knowledge of the "internal behavior of actors" on occasions when the purposes and procedures of states are revealed at their most fundamental level.[14] The data of crises may be re-examined under the hypothesis that the actions of decision-makers may be narrowed progressively under the impact of mass communications and popular opinion until there can be no turning back from war.[15] By noting the definition of international conflict as a bargaining situation in which the participants operate according to mixed motives in the range between full conflict and full collaboration, we may take advantage of the insight concerning the "impure" character of moves and countermoves in the exchanges during a crisis.[16] We may reconsider the detailed events of the histories of crises as sequences of strategic plays and treat these histories as if, virtually, they were clinical records to be used eventually for comparison with synthetic data derived from experimental games of strategy.[17] "Richardson effects," which are believed to abound in a great many social conflict situations, probably are in evidence in the internal sequences of crises.[18] Some of the data of crises might be open to categorization and arrangement according to short-run developmental effects of interaction of the Richardson type without resort to mass behavior data and the formulations of "social physics."[19]

Other avenues to crises studies can be conceived within the framework of suggestions by Quincy Wright for "a study of international conflicts from four different angles: the relations between the opposing parties, which implies particularly an examination of the 'distance' separating them, from the technological, strategic, legal, ideological, social, cultural, and psychological points of view and from the point of view of their attitudes toward recourse to war; the internal structure and policy of the states under consideration; procedures available and used for

[14] Richard C. Snyder and Glenn D. Paige, "The United States Decision to Resist Aggression in Korea: The Application of an Analytical Scheme," *Administrative Science Quarterly*, III (December 1958), pp. 341-378; Allen Whiting, *China Crosses the Yalu: The Decision to Enter the Korean War*, New York, 1960; Bernard C. Cohen, *The Political Process and Foreign Policy*, Princeton, N.J., 1957.

[15] Deutsch, *op.cit.*, pp. 200-11.

[16] Thomas C. Schelling, *The Strategy of Conflict*, Cambridge, Mass., 1960, pp. 5-6, 21-80.

[17] See Thomas C. Schelling's paper in this symposium; Harold Guetzkow, "A Use of Simulation in the Study of Inter-Nation Relations," *Behavioral Science*, IV (July 1959), pp. 183-91.

[18] Kenneth E. Boulding, "Organization and Conflict," *Journal of Conflict Resolution*, I (June 1957), p. 132.

[19] Anatol Rapoport, *Fights, Games, and Debates*, Ann Arbor, Mich., 1960, pp. 88-99.

the adjustment of opposing interests; and the state of international relations during the period under consideration."[20]

The conceptual framework of decision-making[21] is extremely attractive because it so readily encompasses many of the aspects of international conflict and crisis which were noted above. In addition, there is a possible framework of inquiry whose virtues are not so apparent and whose potential has been developed but little in the study of international relations. This is system interaction analysis.[22] Decision-making and interaction analyses represent different investigative interests and preoccupations. A study of data such as that of an acute crisis can be focused according to one mode of analysis as well as the other.

The subject matter of the acute international crisis is almost ideal for the application of the interaction approach. Prominent international crises are complexes of events which can be dissected, up to a point, to yield numerous sequences of related acts. A crisis temporarily narrows the focus of international politics and accelerates events in the public view so that there is very little difficulty in tracing sequences of action in which Event A calls forth Event B which calls forth Event C, etc., until the track is finally lost. After a number of such sequences have been traced and studied, similarities or identities of form in some of them may appear.

Diplomatic historians are perfectly familiar with the tracing of related events in this manner but, on the whole, they have not been concerned to take particular note of recurring forms in the sequences of interaction. In the second place, historians normally divide their attention in order to search out the motives of actors and the concurrent deliberations and decision-making which occur within the foreign offices of involved governments. Thirdly, published diplomatic history cannot possibly include more than a small selection of the interaction sequences because the recounting of interminable detail would clog and divert the narrative. Hence, the collected materials for interaction analysis, as conceived here, often exist in the files of the historian's research notes but not in the published history.

The concept of conflict as a bargaining process leads one to expect that bargaining going on during intense crisis periods will appear in the details of the interaction. If there are "turning points" or important

[20] Freymond, op.cit., p. xvii.

[21] Richard C. Snyder et al., Decision-making as an Approach to the Study of International Relations, Princeton, N.J., 1954.

[22] Robert Bosc, "La sociologie américaine des relations internationales," Revue de l'action populaire, cxlv (February 1961), pp. 207-14; C. A. McClelland, "The Function of Theory in International Relations," Journal of Conflict Resolution, iv (September 1960), pp. 323-26 and references.

decisions in crises, these, too, will take shape under observations of the sequences. There is a possibility of learning a great deal about a "system" from the record of its performance, even in the absence of much knowledge about its main working parts: not always must one be concerned over the motives and capabilities of the "actors." Two additional points are important.

Verbal descriptions of a series of related events of a crisis are unwieldy and, after a few score have been collected, the recognition of recurring forms and patterns becomes more and more difficult. A technique of recording more efficient than the ordinary description is required. Block diagrams similar to those used in other fields can be adapted for the purpose.[23] Further, the block diagrams, when correctly formed and refined under hypothesis, become a definition of the system which is under study.[24] The crisis is demarcated and traced by the chains of acts which, in translation, become inputs and outputs between blocks, the latter standing for the "units" of the system.

How the multifarious data of a crisis system can be recorded for analysis may be shown readily. Block diagrams of actual interaction sequences, one from the Berlin blockade crisis of 1948 and the other from the Korean War period, are shown in Figs. A and B.[25]

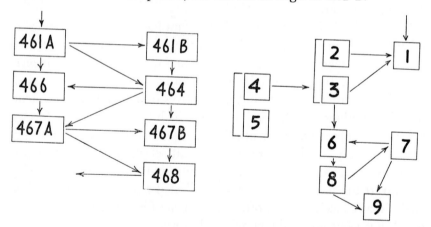

A. "Trade-off" pattern with bids and counterbids; Berlin crisis sequence, February 16-March 3, 1949.

B. Minimal collaboration with mild bargaining; Korean War sequence, June 23-July 8, 1951.

[23] W. Ross Ashby, *An Introduction to Cybernetics*, New York, 1957, chs. 2 and 6, in particular; Robert Rosen, "A Relational Theory of Biological Systems, 1," *General Systems Yearbook*, v (1960), pp. 29-35: first published in *Bulletin of Mathematical Biophysics*, xx (1958), pp. 245-60. See also Mervyn L. Cadwallader, "The Cybernetic Analysis of Change in Complex Social Organizations," *American Journal of Sociology*, LXV (September 1959), pp. 154-57.

[24] Russell L. Ackoff, "Systems, Organizations, and Interdisciplinary Research," *General Systems Yearbook*, v (1960), pp. 1-8.

[25] The arrow direction indicates output from a block. The "receiving" block at the

Without any reference to the setting of a crisis or to its larger meanings in the politics of international relations, the coding of the events of a crisis in chains of interaction sequences makes possible the identification of patterns and the comparison of forms of crisis behavior. Almost immediately, inferences are drawn and labels for several kinds of sequences are brought to mind. In the due course of an analytical study, a mapping of the complete crisis from its dramatic initial "input" event to its tailing-off into the "normalcy" of routine international relations becomes possible. Studies which are limited to such charting and immediate analysis will have value in putting historical data to a new use and in developing limited explanations of an aspect of international behavior. The ambition is greater, however: we wish to cope with the matter of peace and war and with the problem of control, as Karl Deutsch has indicated. In other words, we shall want to study the structures of many block diagrams according to some assumptions and hypotheses which relate to the more general state of affairs.

The variations in international conduct must arise from one or a combination of three sources of variables at any given passage of his-

---

arrowhead stands for an action-in-response (i.e., "it" processes the output and sends its related, "answering" input—the latter indicated by the outgoing arrow). The numbers in the blocks correspond to numbered items in a chronology of events. "A" diagram items are from the writer's "Chronology of Events in the 1948 Berlin Crisis," SFIS 60-17 (ditto), and the "B" diagram uses materials from William H. Vatcher, Jr., *Panmunjon: The Story of the Korean Military Armistice Negotiations,* New York, 1958, pp. 20-25. The relevant chronology items are as follows:

For A—(461a) General Clay requests withdrawal of Soviet repatriation mission at Frankfurt by March 1, 1949. (461b) Soviet Military Governor protests that the mission is still needed and that Clay has no right to order its withdrawal. (464) Soviet note protests Clay's order for removal of Soviet repatriation mission as violating the Crimea agreement on the matter. (466) US authority announces that if Soviet repatriation mission does not leave at once, the premises will be blockaded and the utilities disconnected. (467a) Soviet repatriation mission headquarters blockaded and utilities turned off. (467b) Sokolovsky protests that the action is illegal and breaks repatriation agreements. (468) Soviet authority announces that it has ordered the repatriation mission to leave Frankfurt but, as a reprisal, has cancelled the permits of two US search teams looking for war graves in the Soviet Union.

For B—(1) Yakov Malik broadcast on June 23, 1951, suggesting discussions between Korean War belligerents on cease-fire and armistice. (2) Truman challenges Soviet Union to make Malik's suggestion an official proposal. (3) Truman announces that the United States is prepared to join in talks on peaceful settlement in Korea. (4) Dr. Rhee demands withdrawal of the Chinese and a guarantee of the unification of Korea as prior conditions of an armistice. (5) Dr. Rhee declares against a cease-fire at the 38th Parallel, (6) UNC Commander-in-Chief, General Ridgway, by radio, proposes a meeting with the Communist command in Korea on Danish ship, *Jutlandia.* (7) Generals Kim II Sung and Peng Teh-huai, North Korean and Chinese commanders, agree to meeting but counter with proposal to meet in the area of Kaesong. (8) General Ridgway agrees to Kaesong site to expedite end of fighting and to show good faith. (9) Meeting of liaison officers of both sides at Kaesong on July 8, 1951, to prepare for full meeting.

The foregoing interaction sequences are very simple, brief, and of little independent significance and are included here only for the purpose of illustrating the technique.

tory: from the traits and characteristics of the participating actors, from the effects produced by their contacts and interactions, and from factors of the environment which are external to the first two sources. Our conception is, further, that information concerning conditions created at a certain moment by the effects of interaction and by factors of the environment is returned to the participating actors. The latter are presumed to receive and process such "output" information and to feed the processed results (as inputs) into the next phase of participation in the particular and relevant "system of action." It is the decision-making approach which inquires into the finer detail of the "internal" processing of the incoming streams of "outputs" and of the fabrication of new "inputs" to the system.

Since the strategy of interaction analysis is to exploit a different sector of this unceasing and spiraling process, the investigator of interactions will prefer to deal with approximations and generalizations about the traits of participating actors that would be too inexact and too hypothetical for the purposes of the student of decision-making. In other words, the research bet of an interaction approach is that a large amount of the work of decision-making study can be by-passed safely in arriving at explanations of international behavior. The contention is that the performances of the participants—the interaction sequences— are reliable indicators of active traits of participating actors. Hence, we are free to build hypothetical constructs concerning these pertinent actor traits and to make tentative statements about the patterns of interaction to which the traits are coupled. Then, a series of studies of interaction patterns, recorded in block diagrams, may establish whether we have been right, in any reasonable degree, in the formulation of this structure. If it turns out that we are wrong, we have, at least, the hedge of our detailed tracings and arrangements of interaction sequences which will remain intact for use in further attempts to establish an explanation of the processes of the international crisis phenomena.

In this essay, the testing of a hypothetical structure against the interaction data cannot be reported but only promised for the future. The concluding section, therefore, sets forth no more than several propositions about certain overriding traits and characteristics of participating actors in a crisis system and about the course of the current series of crises between the poles of peace and war.

III

Our basic assumption is that the kind of social organization developed in a nation-state fundamentally conditions its crisis behavior. This assumption is of interest, first of all, because it has appeared so many times in the past. Secondly, it does not accord fully with historical experience and, therefore, is at least partially untrue. Thirdly, the only responsible alternative is the assumption that the fundamental traits of nation-states which have bearing on international conduct are fixed and are identical in all times and places:[26] we reject this assumption for the fairly casual reason that we doubt intuitively that there exists any strong linkage between the assumption and the empirical world. In the fourth place, the assumption requires attention because we shall make use of no more than a selected aspect of the general hypothesis.

Plato explained the occurrence of warfare between city states on the basis of the progressive elaboration of social function and structure with particular emphasis on the division of labor for the carrying out of economic functions.[27] Between Plato and Comte, the idea reappeared many times. Since Comte, the world has been treated to a whole series of explanations of war and international relations—concerning causes, occurrences, and trends—on the basis of changes in social organization. These doctrines, brought to the fore by Comte, Marx, Spencer, Hobson and the Continental socialists, Lenin, and Schumpeter, have been reviewed many times[28] and most recently by Raymond Aron.[29]

The impulse toward change in social organization (and, consequently, toward change in international conduct) has been attributed most often to the forces generated in business and industry. Thus, capitalism and industrialization have been key terms. It was Joseph Schumpeter, however, who made a major attempt to depart from previous conceptions and, in particular, to counter Lenin on war and imperialism with a more competent explanation.[30] Since Schumpeter's ideas were the intellectual point of departure for the central hypothesis of the present work, it will be well to recall his main points.

Schumpeter argued that history shows two main methods of giving and getting goods and services between independent societies: trade and conquest. By far the more common method has been conquest. Social structure and culture have adapted in a thoroughgoing way to the prime function of conquest. In dozens of societies, war became a way of life,

[26] See Morgenthau, op.cit., pp. 4-5; and his "Another Great Debate: The National Interest of the United States," American Political Science Review, xlvi (December 1952), p. 972.

[27] Plato, Republic, Book ii.

[28] E. M. Winslow, The Pattern of Imperialism, New York, 1948; Klaus Knorr, "Theories of Imperialism," World Politics, iv (April 1952), pp. 402-31; Eduard Heimann, "Schumpeter and the Problem of Imperialism," Social Research, xix (June 1952), pp. 177-79.

[29] Raymond Aron, War and Industrial Society, London, Oxford University Press, 1958.

[30] Joseph Schumpeter, Imperialism and Social Classes, New York, 1951.

permeating all social strata and affecting all thought and practice. In the modern world, the other method—trade—has become increasingly dominant, causing basic reorderings of social organization and culture. The practice of war departs as the practice of peaceful exchange according to comparative advantage arrives. Only survivals of the social values and structures of the older martial practice among elites continue to bring about war between nations. In current sociological terms, we should say that as social functions changed, social structures became dysfunctional and required reconstruction. In the contemporary historical process, international war may be predicted to diminish both in intensity and frequency of occurrence. Schumpeter, by the 1940's, was quite aware, along with everyone else, that he had been wrong in 1919. Let us now attempt to reshape Schumpeter's idea and at the same time provide a fresh conceptual setting for the occurrence of international crises.

There is in progress, as there has been, in some measure, throughout the modern era, a monumental reordering of national social structures. At different times, presumably because of peculiar concatenations of historical circumstance, societies have been launched on transformations of the social orders which, in due course, have produced behavioral traits of "advanced modernizing nations." The severe phases of transition between old and new appear to take about two generations. Two main waves of modernizing have swept the world during the past century: one in the late nineteenth century and the other presently in progress.[31]

Schumpeter considered that the mode of international exchange was the pivot of national social modernization, while others have named the domestic growth of capitalism and industrialization. The contemporary social science outlook, which is seasoned to the basic ideas of pluralistic phenomena and multiple-factor causation, would hold that a movement as massive as national modernization becomes an intertwining of causes and factors which might be labeled variously as political, economic, psychological, ecological, and cybernetic, with causes changing into effects and ends into means in an endless chain. Single factor analysis is suspect and multiple factor analysis of so complex a change is tremendously difficult. Either the orderly matching of social functions with

---

[31] Hugh Seton-Watson, *Neither War nor Peace: The Struggle for Power in the Post-war World*, New York, 1960; Cyril E. Black, ed., *The Transformation of Russian Society: Aspects of Social Change Since 1861*, Cambridge, Mass., 1960; Reinhard Bendix, "Industrialization, Ideologies, and Social Structure," *American Sociological Review*, xxiv (October 1959), pp. 613-23; Kenneth Boulding, *The Organizational Revolution*, New York, 1953. A very large literature, beyond the possibility of citation here, exists in recent sociological, anthropological, and economics writings.

social structures or empirical applications of "requisite analysis" become Herculean chores, perhaps beyond any hope of practical execution.

But, in any case, through multiple and varying processes of organizational change and development, nation-states move through their transitional stages and, as they emerge as advanced modernizing societies, they exhibit many similar or at least comparable traits. Some manifestations— the multiple appearances in many societies of small groups of nihilistic teen-agers-in-revolt, for example—have very little connection with international conduct, except contingently. Other traits which appear to be vitally important in international relations can be distinguished in advanced modernizing societies. We venture to point out one set of traits constituting virtually a "cultural focus"[32] of these nation-states in their international relations.

With the exception of China, the nation-states that play dominating roles in international affairs in the present day are either in a final transitional phase or already equipped with advanced modernizing social organizations. The two chief protagonists of the cold war, the United States and Soviet Union, are, without question, in the advanced condition. The "principal actors" of contemporary international relations have become urbanized, secularized, and industrialized. Moreover, they have created and multiplied whole banks of social sub-systems, marvelously intricate, intertwined, and interdependent, within their national boundaries. These sub-systems have a "high metabolism" and ceaselessly undergo change, modification, and reorganization. The services of large numbers of men with technical and specialized skills are required to keep the sub-systems in order and running. Further, a great many persons must become habituated to performing services in different roles virtually as if they were standard replaceable parts of a complex mechanism. Modernizing societies favor and propagate social values which are instrumental and supportive of problem-solving activities.

Whether the modernizing society is open or closed, Asian or European, totalitarian or pluralistic, Communist or democratic, it develops, invariably, ever larger and more differentiated networks of administration in public and private sectors alike. This "progressive mechanization" of the advanced modernizing national society works after its fashion; it invents hordes of novel "needs," both corporate and individual, and then struggles to gratify them. But everything cannot be attended to at once; a great many "problems" can receive little attention before they burst into acute "trouble." The response to "trouble" is a behavioral manifestation with obvious bearing on international crises.

[32] Melville J. Herskovits, *Man and His Works*, New York, 1948, pp. 542-49.

Social attention and social activity are focused most readily on trouble-spots but usually the response has only a brief duration.

"Problems" become legion in an advanced modernizing society, for the simple reason that its sub-systems are complicated and must mesh properly and with the appropriate timing. The structure is forever threatening to collapse in some of its parts and the latter must be braced, patched, repaired, and replaced in endless succession. The cultural focus of the modernizing society is its preoccupation with maintaining its own increasingly complicated structures against breakdown. The strain toward structural-functional consistency is precisely here. In the absence of countering influences, the modernizing society would turn progressively inward on itself, concentrating on its never-finished business of problems and reducing the distractions and difficulties of its external environments.[33] The implications of these observations for international relations are very important.

The pull of domestic interests and practices and, with these, the concomitant system of emergent public values of a modernizing nation-state will cause the international environment to be perceived increasingly as a burden and distraction to the society. Relations with other countries and peoples may be acknowledged to be beneficial or, in some matters, essential for national survival, but the maintenance demands of the national organization set up strains in the contrary direction. The most desirable international situation would be one in which all goes smoothly, with minimum effort, minimum cost, minimum attention, and maximum national benefit. A proper system of international relations would resemble the day-to-day operations of a well-run industrial plant or government bureau. Multitudes of difficulties and problems would be received and dispatched in the work-flow by specialists in handling such business, while the organization as a whole, buffered against shock, surprise, and major disruption, would continue its struggle for self-maintenance and self-organization.

The dominating goals and values of modernizing societies, it is argued, are becoming increasingly those of a bureaucracy rather than those of commercial enterprise, as Schumpeter proposed. Further, the modernizing national society tends to behave toward news of important departures from international "normalcy" very much in the way the shop or office reacts to the information of the cancellation of a large

[33] Karl W. Deutsch, in "Shifts in the Balance of Communications Flows: A Problem of Measurement in International Relations," *Public Opinion Quarterly*, xx (Spring 1956), pp. 143-60, shows data for relative shifts of intake-output ratios which lend support to our general hypothesis of progressive self-concentration of advanced modernizing societies.

contract, a major personnel reorganization, or any other drastic change in procedure. In general, the larger the threat to the stability of routines, the greater the concentration of interest, attention, anxiety, and restorative resources on the impending "problem." All this leads to three summarizing propositions.

(1) Advanced modernizing societies strain progressively toward conservatism[34] in international relations.

(2) "Outputs" received from occurrences and situations in the international environment and from sequences of international interactions are processed by the advanced modernizing social organization according to their perceived characteristics: if these outputs are recognized as familiar and expected experiences met repeatedly in the remembered past, they will be treated in a highly routine fashion.[35]

(3) Those environmental and interactional outputs that, phenomenologically, are unusually novel, unexpected, and threatening will tend to overflow the routine processing channels, to spread into normally inactive and inattentive parts of the organizational structure of society, and to generate extraordinary inputs which are returned to the international environment. When, in this situation, a succession of extraordinary inputs begetting new outputs begetting new inputs, etc., passes some point in volume and intensity, the whole phenomenon begins to be called an international crisis.

The consequences which follow from these three propositions are straightforward. An international system consisting of but two advanced modernizing nation-states as the actors would be one of progressively routine action whose crises would be of diminishing intensity and frequency of occurrence, assuming, of course, that the domestic social structures of each actor suffered no major breakdown or disruption. The system might be expected to evolve toward minimum action and a maximum regulation of the surviving relationships. International relations between the two nations would, in large measure, become administrative.

It is not suggested, however, that the dominant mode of interacting behavior would shift necessarily. Conflict relations would not have to turn into collaboration or accommodation. On the contrary, if relations

---

[34] Conservatism is intended to refer here to behavior toward policies, lines of action, and preferred values which supports and reinforces "time-tested" social practices, frameworks, and objectives. It is an outlook which tends to resist variation from familiar content or established routine but which, under the pressure of power, persuasion, or innovation, may tend to yield to compromise or a *modus vivendi*. In this sense, conservatism is only a type of conduct, characterized neither by a systematic "falling behind the times" nor by a relationship to a particular political ideology or public philosophy.

[35] James March and Herbert Simon, *Organizations*, New York, 1958, p. 140.

were founded primarily on competition, the competition would fall, more and more, into expected patterns and, perhaps, would be brought under self-enforcing rules of the game. It is even conceivable that chronic warfare could be waged under normal conditions and within controlled behavioral boundaries. It might well drift into the agonistic form which tended to develop in earlier centuries.[36]

When we approach the historical records of acute international crises and begin the analyses of interaction sequences, we shall be on the watch for signs of "routinizing behaviors" and for the rise of "standard" techniques for managing situations which, with the passing of time, have become familiar types. The interaction patterns ought to show much evidence of bids countered by bids, claims countered by claims, stalemates, standoffs, postponements, and no-win, no-solution outcomes; barring upheavals in the system or environmental innovations, the general trend should be toward repetitions of such patterns of action but with a decreasing volume of interaction in succeeding crises (i.e., less action in the mobilization and demobilization of the crisis). If such phenomena appear in the record, they will be taken as evidence in support of the hypotheses of the conservative behavior, the routinizing tendencies, and the spillover effects of crises in advanced modernizing nation-states. Such phenomena would be revealed by the block diagrams discussed above.

We shall anticipate that, in the mobilization of a crisis, many sectors of the national social organization not usually involved in the "normal work-flow" of international relations will become agitated and active, while in the demobilization of the crisis there will be a rapid falling-off of such activities and a return of affairs to routine channels. These processes should take place whether or not issues are settled, problems are solved, or relations are "improved," although we may find that crises recede behind a veritable smokescreen of conflict resolution promises and of problem-solving talk. On the whole, we should anticipate that the actors will become more and more reluctant to resort to escalation of the means of violence as they acquire greater experience with crisis systems. We expect that the level of violence will not be raised readily above the level existing at the time the actors perceive that they are "seized" by an acute crisis.

At this point, we have considered a simple model of international behavior which focuses on crises and which also brings a suggestion of

---

[36] Johan Huizinga, *Homo Ludens: A Study of the Play-element in Culture*, Boston, 1950, ch. 5; Hans Speier, "The Social Types of War," *American Journal of Sociology*, XLVI (January 1941), pp. 445-54.

why repeated exposures to acute crises may reduce the probabilities of an outbreak of general war.[37] A mechanism has been isolated and identified—the bureaucratic processing of "problems"—and a view has been expressed that the mechanism will be found to have been operating in historical instances of international relations. It would be quite foolish, however, to imagine that so simple a model will be efficient in establishing satisfying correspondences with the empirical complexities of international relations. To improve the situation, we shall now add other elements to the two-actor system. In fact, we shall bring it close to what is thought to be the current reality: a bipolar system under stress.

The system is expanded to include a number of other participating actors, some of whom have achieved an advanced and modernizing form of social organization and some of whom are still in social transition. Of these, some are bound with one or the other of the two principal actors of the system in opposing coalitions, while some remain free from the coalitions. Thus, the system is dominated by conflict which polarizes in the two principal actors at the head of opposing camps. For reasons already given, these principal actors, being advanced modernizing nation-states, have behavioral traits which would allow the system to run down to a minimum-action, maximum-regulation state of affairs. Although they are committed to "permanent" conflict and mutual opposition, they share (covertly, at least) some common problems. Their conservative propensities lead them to put high value on maintaining their respective leadership positions in the opposing coalitions. Each must stand ready to act to preserve solidarity and cohesion in the coalition it leads. Each must be willing to take vigorous action in local clashes and embroilments which involve commitments or interests of members of the coalition. Cleavages and quarrels within the camp must be attended to, while the modernizing tendencies which influence some allies toward lukewarm and perfunctory adherence to common tasks and causes must be countered. Further, neither principal actor dares to fail to respond to demands and problems arising in the non-aligned and non-committed areas for fear the other side will steal a march, gain an advantage, or otherwise weaken leadership and solidarity in the home camp.

Even were there no ideological complications and no special problems of military technology, the stresses in the bipolar structure would introduce structural-functional ambiguities and induce significant strain (and conflict) within the social organizations of the principal actors.[38] The

[37] See above, p. 188.
[38] Gideon Sjoberg, "Contradictory Functional Requirements and Social Systems," *Journal of Conflict Resolution*, IV (June 1960), pp. 198-208.

latter may, in fact, be said to be victims of the "double bind" in several dimensions.[39] Both have vested interests in maintaining their leadership positions and in preserving the system (the prospect of a radical transformation in the organization of the international system would be repugnant to both, in anticipation, and the dislocating effects domestically would be unwelcome). Yet the exertions and cost involved in such maintenance run against the grain of the ascending social values of increasingly bureaucratized societies. Since both principal actors occupy similar positions and experience similar difficulties, they might drift gradually toward collaboration, except that such a movement is blocked by the essential conflict structure of the international system.

Under these circumstances, the mobilization of an acute international crisis may not be as repellent as it seems on the surface. The tension and excitement of a mounting crisis may provide some relief and respite from the "double bind" situation. One of the weaknesses of a system of conflict is the problem of maintaining tension and a sense of motion in the system. Conflicts are subject to obsolescence.[40] The acute crises may play a role here. The waging of a crisis refreshes the stream of conflict interaction, almost as a transfusion to the system. Faltering or wayward members of the coalitions may be jolted into new allegiance by a crisis. The fear of war and the need for national solidarity and efficiency are brought home to domestic publics by the spillovers of information and action connected with major crises.

As long as the leaders of the coalitions can control the interplay of conflict in the mobilization of a crisis, general war, which would be as destructive to the vested interests of the principal actors as any other conceivable eventuality, may be averted. Hence, in the detailed historical records of crisis interaction sequences, we should expect to find evidences of anxious attention to control problems, even to the extent of hidden collaboration on the part of the principal actors, during the early phases of a crisis. A proposition which may be too risky to entertain at full value is that an international crisis, not transformed into a general war during the first week or so of its mobilization, will not lead to such a war.

A more reasonable prediction is that the record will show progressively refined techniques of crisis demobilization on the part of the principal actors as experience with the system grows. The trend toward the routinizing of acute conflict operations and toward the growth of

[39] Gregory Bateson, Don D. Jackson, Jay Haley, and John Weakland, "Toward a Theory of Schizophrenia," *Behavioral Science*, I (October 1956), pp. 253-56.

[40] Quincy Wright, "The Nature of Conflict," *Western Political Quarterly*, IV (June 1951), p. 207.

specialized skills of crisis demobilization can be interrupted and reversed in any of three predictable situations, however. First, under the competitive drive to preserve leadership and solidarity, the leading actors will tend to seek out new theaters and new forms for the interplay of their main-line conflict, with the possibility that unexpected control problems will arise. Secondly, the associated actors of the international system whose countries are in the labors of transformation of their social organizations, whether within or outside the coalitions, may create novel crisis situations in unfamiliar arenas. "Standard" demobilization techniques may then fail to work. Thirdly, the bipolar structure of the system may begin to crumble gradually, causing the principal actors to face the difficulties of reorienting their strategies and devising new control techniques.

In any of these eventualities, the duration and intensity of an acute crisis may be increased and the confidence in the demobilization of crises without general war may be decreased. The view may be ventured that crises connected with the third eventuality—the gradual crumbling of the bipolar system—will come closer to precipitating general war than any other. A further thought is that an abrupt and drastic reorganization of the international system into a new form might prove more favorable to the cause of the preservation of general peace than the process of gradual and piecemeal evolution toward the new system.

One obvious device for facilitating crisis demobilization is to allow the affair to be played out under the guidance and auspices of a third party, either an international organization, a non-involved group, or a single non-aligned actor. There are serious liabilities in the third-party device, however. The third party, particularly if it is an international organization, is not likely to survive a series of crisis exposures without losing mutual trust in its non-involvement and non-commitment in the conflict. This shock-absorber technique tends also to work against the leadership interests of the principal actors. It is better if a crisis is demobilized by the efforts of the principal actors themselves. The vitally important sense of controlled motion directed by leaders is thereby preserved.[41]

Some of the complications of the operations of a bipolar system under stress have now been considered. We have, in other words, noted certain

[41] The protagonist who deliberately loses control of his responses in a conflict situation may not be behaving in a wildly irresponsible manner but, rather, may be paying discreet tribute to the underlying reliability and stability of the system he is attempting to exploit by his tactic. See Herman Kahn, "The Arms Race and Some of Its Hazards," *Daedalus*, LXXXIX (Fall 1960), pp. 756-57; and Schelling, *The Strategy of Conflict*, pp. 37, 137, and elsewhere.

modifications which must be taken into account in the functioning of the simple model first hypothecated. Of course, it will be understood that such a model, even with its modifications, will not begin to account for the complexities of actual experience. The model is a tool expected to be helpful in the study of international behavior during crises.

Two criticisms are sometimes raised, apparently for the purpose of discouraging efforts toward systematic analyses of patterns and recurring forms in international relations: the first objects that unique events and non-patterned influences are controlling in the unfolding of international affairs, making the search for behavioral regularities and reappearing patterns virtually fruitless;[42] the second trusts in the actual existence of controlling or dominating trends and regularities of behavior but insists on perfectly isolated and specified variables along with the recipe of the exact relationships among such variables. The scholar who takes either advice and who prefers the simple investigation of international phenomena to practical policy-advising is left unemployed. It seems better, therefore, to ignore the criticisms and the problems of precise methodology merely in order to plunge into the work, equipped with little more than some rough approximations about how actors behave and some reasonable techniques for empirical investigation. This essay has sought to establish such a framework as a prelude to later reporting of empirical analyses.

In the case of the present subject, there is now no reasonable basis for declaring that international crises will or will not occur more frequently or more violently during the coming decade than during the last ten years.[43] Intuition and past performances notwithstanding, it remains impossible to say whether the prospects of general war have become stronger or weaker according to the number of exposures to acute crises since the close of the last major war. We have emphasized above that historical behavior as complex and multidimensional as that of contemporary international relations should be examined in different perspectives and through several investigative approaches. We have chosen one among the many with no guarantee of its truth-producing efficacy.

[42] Stanley Hoffmann, ed., *Contemporary Theory of International Relations*, Englewood Cliffs, N.J., 1960, pp. 177-78.

[43] A field of study as future-oriented as international relations might be expected to give much attention to the bases of prediction, whether by officials, commentators, or scholars, but little is, in fact, given to the matter. For a discussion, see Hans H. Toch, "The Perception of Future Events: Case Studies in Social Prediction," *Public Opinion Quarterly*, xxii (Spring 1958), pp. 57-66.

INTERNATIONAL SYSTEMS
AND INTERNATIONAL LAW

By STANLEY HOFFMANN

THE purpose of this essay is twofold. First, it proposes to undertake, in introductory form, one of the many tasks a historical sociology of international relations could perform: the comparative study of one of those relations which appear in almost any international system, i.e., international law.[1] Secondly, this essay will try to present the rudimentary outlines of a theory of international law which might be called sociological or functional.[2]

International law is one of the aspects of international politics which reflect most sharply the essential differences between domestic and world affairs. Many traditional distinctions tend to disappear, owing to an "international civil war" which projects what are primarily domestic institutions (such as parliaments and pressure groups) into world politics, and injects world-wide ideological clashes into domestic affairs. International law, like its Siamese twin and enemy, war, remains a crystallization of all that keeps world politics *sui generis*. If theory is to be primarily concerned with the distinctive features of systems rather than with the search for regularities, international law becomes a most useful approach to international politics.

This paper will examine the relations between international law and international systems, first in general terms, and subsequently in more concrete form, with evidence derived from history. Finally, in the light

---

[1] See some suggestions in my *Contemporary Theory in International Politics*, Englewood Cliffs, N.J., 1960, pp. 174ff.

[2] These adjectives are borrowed from Julius Stone, "Problems Confronting Sociological Enquiries Concerning International Law," *Recueil des Cours de l'Académie de Droit International*, Vol. 89 (1956), 1, and Hans J. Morgenthau, *Dilemmas of Politics*, Chicago, 1958, ch. 11, respectively. The only additional recent works which try to establish a political sociology of international law are Charles de Visscher's *Theory and Reality in Public International Law*, tr. by P. E. Corbett, Princeton, N.J., 1957; Percy E. Corbett's *Law in Diplomacy*, Princeton, N.J., 1959; B. Landheer's "Contemporary Sociological Theories and International Law," *Recueil des Cours ...*, Vol. 91 (1957), 1; and, to some extent, John Herz's *International Politics in the Atomic Age*, New York, 1959, and Morton A. Kaplan's and Nicholas Katzenbach's "The Patterns of International Politics and of International Law," *American Political Science Review*, LIII (September 1959), pp. 693-712—the last two pieces being more concerned with politics than with law. The present essay, which supplements an earlier piece on "Quelques aspects du rôle du Droit International dans la politique étrangère des Etats" (Association Française de Science Politique, *La Politique étrangère et ses Fondements*, Paris, 1954, pp. 239-77), will itself be expanded into a volume on *International Law in World Politics*.

of such a historical presentation, I will examine briefly two of the main politico-legal problems raised by international law.

I

Most theories of domestic politics start from the ideal-type of (1) a community—i.e., an unconditional consensus on cooperation, a belief in a common good (however vague) and in the precedence of this common good over particular interests; and (2) an organization, the State, which has created this community or was established by it, and is endowed with the monopoly of the legitimate use of force. The theory of international politics must start from the ideal-type of a milieu in which (1) the behavior of the members ranges from, at best, that of partners in a society (who cooperate on a limited number of issues, rarely unconditionally, and give primary allegiance to themselves, not the society) to that of accomplices in chaos: the social group made up of the states is always on the verge of being a fiction; and (2) there is no monopoly of power, over and above that possessed by the members. Thus, whereas procedures for cooperation, for the creation and expression of consent, exist both in domestic and in world politics, the permanent possibility of free and legitimate recourse to violence remains the mark of international relations.

This simple and banal point of departure is of decisive importance both for the understanding of international law and for the delimitation of international systems.

(a) Law is a body of rules for human conduct established for the ordering of a social group and enforceable by external power. Domestic law orders the national group by acting directly on the individual citizens and by regulating all the problems which are deemed to be of social importance; it is enforced by the power of the state, exerted directly on individuals. By contrast, international law suffers from three forms of precariousness. The first is its low degree of institutionalization. The second is its unique substance. In the domestic order, which regulates a great mass of individuals, law is an instrument of homogeneity. The international legal order regulates a small number of subjects. Consequently, its law is a law of differentiation, which vacillates from the Charybdis of universality at the cost of vagueness, to the Scylla of precision at the cost of heterogeneity. The scope of the subject matter is limited by the reluctance of the subjects to submit themselves to extensive regulations and by the inefficiency of premature regulations: hence the numerous gaps in the body of rules. The third weakness is the

limited amount of solidity or authority in international law. I do not
refer here to efficiency in Kelsen's meaning of the term, for it is true
that most forms of international law are obeyed, but to the effect of the
following factors: the obscurities or ambiguities which mar existing
rules, since they are established by the subjects themselves; the fact,
analyzed by de Visscher, that the greatest solidarities exist in matters
which least affect the power and policies of the subjects and vice versa;
the fact that, in Julius Stone's words, international law is the one legal
order which provides for its own destruction by the mere force of its
own subjects.[3]

(b)   An international system is a pattern of relations between the
basic units of world politics, which is characterized by the scope of the
objectives pursued by those units and of the tasks performed among
them, as well as by the means used in order to achieve those goals and
perform those tasks. This pattern is largely determined by the structure
of the world, the nature of the forces which operate across or within the
major units, and the capabilities, pattern of power, and political culture
of those units.[4]

One of the main tasks of a historical sociology of international politics
is the delimitation of such systems: where does one system begin or end,
in space and in time? It is with the limits in time that I am concerned
here. As Raymond Aron has observed, periodization is always both
necessary and dangerous: the historian is free in his choice of criteria
but should refrain from attributing to those he chose consequences
which only empirical evidence could prove.[5] The criteria I would
propose are what I would call the *stakes of conflict*. A new system
emerges:

(1)   When there is a new answer to the question: what *are* the units
in potential conflict?—i.e., when the basic structure of the world has
changed (as in the passage from the city-state system to the Roman
Empire; from the Empire to the medieval system; from the medieval
hierarchy to the modern "horizontal" system of multiple sovereignties).

(2)   When there is a new answer to the question: what *can* the units
do to one another in a conflict?—i.e., a basic change in the technology

[3] *Legal Controls of International Conflict*, New York, 1954, p. 1.
[4] Such a definition corresponds to accepted definitions of domestic political systems,
which are characterized also both by the scope of the ends of politics (the limited state
vs. the totalitarian state, the welfare state *vs.* the free enterprise state) and by the methods
of organizing power (constitutional relations between the branches of government, types
of party system).
[5] Raymond Aron, "Evidence and Inference in History," *Daedalus*, Vol. 87 (Fall 1958),
pp. 11-39.

of conflict. Such a change may also bring about a transformation in the basic structure of the world: as John Herz has reminded us, the gunpowder revolution ushered in the era of the "impermeable" territorial state. Even within the same type of basic structure, a fundamental innovation in the technology of conflict changes the nature of the international system: the atomic revolution has rendered obsolete previous "multiple-sovereignty" systems because it meant the passage from a relative to an absolute power of destruction, and consequently the end of great-power "impermeability." An effective diffusion of nuclear power would mean another system still.

(3) When within a single state of the technology of conflict there is a new answer to the question: what do the units *want* to do to one another? Here, we try to distinguish systems according to the scope of the units' purposes, and to the techniques the actors use in order to meet their objectives or to prevent their rivals from achieving theirs.

If we combine those sets of criteria, we come to a fundamental distinction between two types of systems: stable ones and revolutionary ones. A stable system is one in which the stakes of conflict are limited, because the relations between the actors are marked by moderation in scope and means. Whatever the world's basic structure and the state of the technology of conflict, the units act so as to limit the amount of harm they could inflict upon one another. In a revolutionary system, this moderation has disappeared. When one major actor's decision to discard it coincides with or brings about a revolution in the technology of conflict, or a change in the basic structure of the world, or both, the system is particularly unstable.[6] In other words, a stable system is one in which the life or the essential values of the basic units are not constantly in question, and the main actors agree on the rules according to which the competition will take place; a revolutionary system is one in which the incompatibility of purposes rules out such an agreement.

For each kind of basic structure in the world, and each kind of technology of conflict, we may obtain the ideal-type of a stable system by asking what are the conditions from which moderation in scope and means is most likely to follow. Actual historical systems at times meet

---

[6] The *number* of violent conflicts does not intervene in these definitions. A stable period may be marked by frequent wars as long as they remain limited in objectives and methods. A revolutionary period may not necessarily be marked by all-out, general war, if the technology of conflict introduces a mutual interest in avoiding the total destruction such a war would entail; but as long as this restraint does not bring back moderation in the purposes and means of conflicts other than all-out war, the system remains largely a revolutionary one, although it disposes of an element of stability—a fragile element, given all the other circumstances.

all those conditions, but often they do not; and they are, of course, marked by constant change in all their elements. Those changes (1) do not affect the system at all if they do not hurt or remove the essential conditions of stability; (2) merely weaken the system by making it operate in less than ideal conditions, if they do cripple some of those conditions but without destroying the moderation in scope and means; (3) ruin the system altogether if such deterioration, instead of leading to temporary disturbances, brings about a breakdown in moderation, a revolution in the technology of conflict or in the basic structure of the world.

Whether a change which affects the essential conditions of stability damages the system decisively or not depends on the circumstances. A breakdown requires the collapse of a large number of such conditions. This can happen either (1) when one of the main actors decides to overthrow the system, and succeeds in removing so many of the conditions of stability that the system does indeed collapse—i.e., when this actor's move leads not simply to *any* kind of conflict, but to a revolutionary one; or (2) when a previous deterioration leads to a conflict which might not start as a revolutionary one, but becomes one because it develops into a decisive additional factor of disruption. In both cases, the end of a stable system is marked by a general war.[7]

In the world of multiple sovereignties before the invention of absolute weapons, it was the balance-of-power system which brought stability into international politics: i.e., a pattern of relations among states which through shifting alliances and the use of various diplomatic techniques tends to limit the ambitions of the main actors, to preserve a relative equilibrium among them, and to reduce the amount of violence between them. The ideal conditions for such a system are as follows:

(1)   Conditions related to the structure of the world: a greater number of major states than two; a relative equilibrium of power among them; the existence of a frontier, a prerequisite of the kind of flexibility that a balancing system needs.

(2)   Conditions related to transnational forces: technological sta-

---

[7] Besides making the fundamental distinction *between* stable and revolutionary systems, we have to distinguish *among* stable and *among* revolutionary ones. Here our criteria should be, in addition to the basic structure of the world and the state of the technology of conflict: (1) in the case of stable systems, the kind of *means* used by the actors in their competition and co-operation: cf. below, the distinction between the stable system which preceded the French Revolution and the stable system which followed the Congress of Vienna; both were "balance of power" systems, but the latter was more institutionalized than the former; (2) in the case of revolutionary systems, the type of *objective* for which the conflicts take place (religious allegiance, form of government).

bility; a common outlook among the leaders of the major states, provided either by a similarity of regimes, or by a common attitude toward religion, or by similar beliefs about the purpose of the state. Such an outlook allows for horizontal ties as strong as, or stronger than, the political ties which attach those leaders to their domestic community; a common conception of legitimacy can thus develop.

(3) A condition related to the domestic situation within the major actors: the existence of a political system in which the state exercises only limited control over its citizens' international loyalties and activities.

(4) The outcome of these conditions is a system in which the objectives of the major actors remain limited to moderate increases in power or prestige, and in which many of the tasks which can be performed through the processes of world politics remain beyond the pale of those politics. The means used by the major units in their mutual relations are coalitions designed to prevent any single actor from disrupting stability, either by rewarding him for his cooperation or by punishing him for his misbehavior, without, however, making it impossible for him to cooperate again.

The ideal conditions for stability can be defined as *evenness* in the situation of the major units—just as a large degree of identity in the members of the state is necessary for the emergence of the general will. Conversely, the process of deterioration which leads to disturbances within the system and might provoke its breakdown beyond a certain point can be summed up as the reintroduction of unevenness or *heterogeneity*.[8] This process includes the appearance of the following conditions:

(1) In the structure of the world: irrepressible ambitions of individual rulers;[9] ambitions kindled by a disparity in power between a major actor and its neighbors or other major units; the end of the frontier, which increases the likelihood of, and the stakes in, direct clashes between the major units.

(2) In the forces which cut across those units: a technological revolution, which leads to instability when it produces a race; the destruction of transnational ties, either under the impact of domestic integration which inevitably submits diplomacy to greater internal pressures, or

---

[8] See the little-known but brilliant analysis by Panayis A. Papaligouras, *Théorie de la Société internationale*, Geneva, Graduate School of International Studies, 1941.

[9] They do not, by themselves, destroy the balancing system but they make its operation uncertain, and increase the likelihood of "in-system" wars, which may in turn destroy the system if other essential conditions for an ideal balance have also disappeared, or if the logic of war destroys previous limitations on the instruments of conflict.

because of an ideological explosion set off by a disparity of regimes or beliefs.

(3) In the domestic situation of the major units: strong integrative trends leading to nationalism; the expansion of state control over the foreign activities of the citizens either for economic or for ideological purposes.

(c) Let us turn now to the relation of international law to various international systems. International law can be studied as a product of international systems and as a repertory of normative theory about each one of them. On the one hand, it is shaped by all the elements which compose an international system:

(1) It reflects the structure of the world. The nature of the actors determines whether the law of the system is the "law of coordination" made by territorial states, or the external public law of an empire, or whether it will disappear altogether as it did during much of the medieval period. The size of the diplomatic field determines the degree of universality of the legal order. The degree of unity of international law and the efficiency of a good deal of its provisions depend on the existence, duration, and seriousness of a relationship of major tension.

(2) International law reflects the forces which cut across the units. Technology is of considerable importance: the intensity or density of legal relations between the actors depends largely on the state of the arts. The unity and authority of the legal order depend on the presence and number of transnational ideologies and conceptions of legitimacy.

(3) The domestic situation of the major units is relevant here also. International law has always reflected the pattern of power and the political culture of the main actors.[10] The development of law by treaties and the reception of rules of international law within the various units depend on the provisions of constitutions and on the decisions of domestic courts.

(4) Finally, international law reflects the relations among the units. It is shaped by the scope of those relations: the breadth and the nature of the subject-matter regulated by law vary according to the range and character of the goals which the units try to reach and of the tasks they try to perform. In particular, the rules of law often express the policies of the major units. Moreover, customs and treaties always both reflect the methods by which the units try to meet their objectives, and regulate at least some of the techniques used in the process.

On the other hand, if we turn from empirical systems to normative theory, we find in theories of international law a critical assessment of

---

[10] See Corbett, *op.cit.*, especially chs. 1-3.

international systems from the viewpoint of world order. In any political system, order is achieved if the following three requirements are met: (1) security—i.e., dealing with the problem of conflict by assuring the survival and safety of the members of the system; (2) satisfaction—i.e., dealing with the problem of assent, and obtaining it through constraint or consent; (3) flexibility—i.e., dealing with the problem of change (which is crucial, since assent is never definitive or total), by establishing procedures capable of absorbing shocks and of channeling grievances. In a world divided into numerous units, order is always threatened. Legal theorists have constantly asked whether order was possible at all; if so, whether the system was capable of ensuring it; and if not, what kind of measures were necessary to obtain order. On the whole, in each period, there have been three types of reactions: the deniers, who question either the possibility or the desirability of a stable legal order; the utopians, who also question the effectiveness of the existing system but propose to substitute a radically different one; the adjusters, who try to show how and to what extent order can be established or preserved within the existing system. We learn a great deal about the nature and operation of a given international system if we study the range of disagreements among those three groups; the more stable the system, the narrower this range.

Since international law constitutes the formal part of whatever kind of order reigns and expresses the more lasting interests of the actors—their long- or middle-range strategy, rather than their daily tactics—the link between the solidity or authority of international law and the stability of the international system is both obvious and strong. The basic function of international law is to organize the coexistence of the various units: this presupposes that their existence is assured. In stable systems, it is possible to distinguish three kinds of international law:[11]

(1) The law of the political framework—i.e., the network of agreements which define the conditions, and certain of the rules, of the political game among the states. By conditions, I refer to such provisions as the settlement of borders after wars, the main alignments expressed in treaties of alliance, the holding of periodic conferences among major powers; by rules, I refer to provisions which determine the mutual commitments of states, or the procedure for the settlement of major disputes.

(2) The law of reciprocity, which defines the conditions and rules of interstate relations in areas which affect less vitally the power and

---

[11] See George Schwarzenberger, *Power Politics*, New York, 1951, ch. 13; and Hans J. Morgenthau, *op.cit.*, pp. 228-29.

policies of the states. This is the large zone in which states can be assumed to have a mutual and lasting interest in common rules: the zone of predictability, on which the competition of the actors in politically more sensitive areas rests and depends. We can distinguish two kinds of laws of reciprocity: first, the law of delimitation which defines the respective rights and privileges of states, in peacetime over such matters as diplomatic relations, territory, and people, in wartime over weapons, military objectives, non-combatants, etc.; second, the law of cooperation, which regulates joint interests, particularly in commerce.

(3) The law of community, which deals with problems which can best be handled, not on the basis of a reciprocity of interests of states understood as separate and competing units, but on the basis of a community of action independent from politics: problems of a technical or scientific nature for which borders are irrelevant.

This distinction is sound and legitimate in a stable period, for when the survival of the players is insured, a hierarchy of interests becomes possible. The law of the political framework deals the cards with which the players try to reach such objectives as greater power, or prestige, or the triumph of ideals; the law of reciprocity provides the underpinning of national security and defines those functions and attributes of the state which are not put at stake in the political contests. But in a revolutionary system, the distinction between these two kinds of law becomes extremely fuzzy, for when survival is not assured, the limits which the law of reciprocity sets to states' privileges or jurisdiction become obstacles to their quest for greater security and power, while cooperation over joint interests is replaced by conflict or competition which challenges previous rules. In such a system, the power and policies of states are directly involved in almost every aspect of international activity.[12] Thus, in a revolutionary system, the great bulk of international law partakes of the somewhat shaky authority of the law of the political framework.

The difference in the solidity of law in revolutionary and stable systems is reflected in the contrasting impact of political change on law. Changes which do not destroy a stable system have no lethal effect on

[12] Scholars may argue that important mutual interests still exist and that states have little to gain by turning the zone of predictability into a battlefield. The trouble is that what seems irrational to the scholar from the viewpoint of international society seems rational to the statesman from the viewpoint of his own national calculation, given the peculiar logic of such calculations in fiercely competitive situations. An "objective" common interest might not be perceived by the antagonists and, even if it is, there remains an abyss between such understanding and a formal legal agreement which would sanction it. On these points, see Kenneth Waltz, *Man, the State, and War*, New York, 1959, pp. 192ff.

the legal order, precisely because customs and agreements express, as I have put it, strategic rather than tactical interests. To be sure, the body of rules reflects such changes if they are of sufficient magnitude: in particular, the disappearance of some of the essential conditions for an ideal stable system has repercussions on the law of the political framework, which is the most sensitive to such tremors; it may also leave its mark on the law of reciprocity, because certain kinds of agreements become increasingly rare, or codification more troublesome, or difficulties appear in the discharge of treaties. However, the law of reciprocity may continue to develop even when the ideal conditions for stability are not present anymore (as was shown by the flowering of such law just before World War I), precisely because it reflects mutual interests which the fluctuations of politics do not impair so long as the stable system lasts. Also, while the essential moderation in the scope and means of international relations continues, the gaps and uncertainties of law do not become factors of disruption: in the areas which are not regulated or in which the rules are ambiguous, a purely political decision or interpretation by the states concerned will be needed but, given the system, no destructive effects are likely to follow.

In a revolutionary system, however, gaps and ambiguities become wedges for destruction or subversion of the international order in the interest of any of the actors. The absence of any agreement on the rules of the game, the increase in the stakes of conflict, the reign of insecurity for the actors, mean that political changes will have the following impact on international law: (1) just as old theories and concepts outlive the system which justified them, old regulations which have become obsolete nevertheless continue to be considered valid (although they are less and less respected) because of the increasing difficulty in agreeing on new rules, or because the old ones serve the interests of some of the contending units; (2) new problems thrown up by political or technological change often remain unregulated, for the same reasons; (3) new regulations appear which constitute attempts to deal with some of the changes but turn out to be incompatible with the new system; and (4) since international systems change essentially through general wars, the collapse of previous laws of war is usually the first effect of the change on the legal order.

This conglomeration of ruin, gaps, and "dysfunctional" old or new rules denotes the major areas of friction and tensions in world politics during the lifetime of revolutionary systems and particularly in periods of passage from one system to another.

Thus, it is in balance-of-power systems that the authority of international law has been greatest: as Oppenheim has stated in his treatise, the existence of the balance is a condition of the flourishing of authoritative international law. However, this condition is at the same time a limitation.

(1) Even when the balance functions under optimum conditions, the political framework may remain largely unregulated. We have to distinguish between systems in which the balance is more or less automatic or mechanical, and systems in which it is institutionalized to a greater degree—a distinction among stable systems based in particular on the law of the political framework (see n. 7).

(2) Even when the balance functions under optimum conditions, it operates sometimes at the expense of law. In a system of "sovereign" states, the principles of equality and consent are essential to the legal order. But the daily practices of the balance may conflict with these norms: a preponderance of power often forces small or even isolated large states to assent to measures which go against their objectives or detract from the formal equality of all the units.

(3) Among the many power configurations which characterize the relations of the major units in balancing systems, there is one which threatens the solidity of international law (especially that of the political framework) more permanently. When the optimum conditions are met, the most likely resulting combination is the "mechanism of imbalance"—a coalition of a majority of the main actors against an isolated would-be disrupter; but when those conditions are not all present, there may come into being an opposition of blocs of comparable strength, so that alignments stiffen instead of remaining flexible, with a tendency to shift. The authority and unity of international law may then be imperiled.

II

I will try now to support the preceding generalizations by examining briefly three concrete examples of relations between international systems and international law.

(a) The first example, which I want to mention very briefly, is that of international law during the balance-of-power system which lasted from the Peace of Westphalia until the French Revolution.

The balance could operate effectively because the treaties of Westphalia had redistributed territory in such a way as to create a number of major states capable of neutralizing each other, and had also removed the poisonous element of religious conflict. Within the main units, mercantilism and absolutism weakened gradually. New transnational ties developed: the "corporate identity" of monarchs, diplomats, and officers across borders led to a consensus on the legitimacy of the balance, just as the community of European intellectuals produced a consensus on the values of the Enlightenment. The result, politically, was a mechanical balance, with frequent disturbances due either to the fact that a state could never be sure in advance whether or when others would try to stop it, or to individual ambitions. Hence numerous limited wars occurred: stylized wars of position which affected only rarely the civilian population.

Although there was little international law of the political framework, the law of reciprocity developed in a way which reflected both the moderation and the volatile character of a balancing system. On the one hand, in the area of trade, statesmen came to realize that law was the best technique for obtaining an increase in national wealth and power (as in past mercantilist practice), but with safety; the idea of a harmony of interests replaced the previous expectation of conflict, hence numerous measures to protect commerce at sea, especially in wartime. Neutrality became for the first time altogether possible, a good bargain, and a subject of legal regulation. On the other hand, the balance imposed limits to the development of law. The preservation of the system required at the end of wars practices which restored the equilibrium among the major powers at the expense of small states; those compensations proved that the norm of territorial integrity was efficient only as long as it was backed by force, and that it was subordinated to the operations of the balance. Also, there were gaps wherever rules would have restricted state power too sharply: maritime warfare remained anarchical, and no adequate procedure for the settlement of disputes developed, except for rare and delicate instances of arbitration.

The response of theory to these developments was most interesting. In the previous revolutionary system, a big gap had separated destroyers of the medieval dream of unity, like Machiavelli, creators of new dreams like Crucé or Sully, and the numerous would-be rescuers of the medieval theory, who reasserted the supremacy of natural law and the doctrine of just war, but secularized the former, hedged in the latter with qualifications, and came to recognize the existence of an international law created by the will of states. Now, in a system of increasing moderation, the gap narrowed. Even deniers of the efficiency of "covenants without the sword" showed that self-restraint might prevent a war of all against all. At the other pole, the Kantian utopia also reflected a new optimism: the problem of establishing order among the states was going to require essentially a change in the regimes but not the end of the division of the world into separate units, and it would be solved by the invisible hand of history. The theorists in the middle, still trying to save the idea of a legal community of mankind, gradually gave up natural law as its cement—a retreat which would have been taken as an invitation to and a confession of chaos in the preceding period, but which could now be accepted without anguish, for a positivistic emphasis on the fundamental rights of states as the foundation of order did not seem necessarily self-defeating any longer. The expectation of a harmony of interests had been fed by the system.

Its collapse was sudden and took the form of a swift chain reaction. (1) The decisive factor was the change in France's regime—a fact which shows that the study of international systems must extend to the analysis of the political ones they include. (2) The revolution, in turn, destroyed previous transnational links: the heterogeneity of regimes introduced an explosive element into Europe, and after a brief period of idealistic pacifism—a revulsion against the balance, that sport of kings—the revolutionaries, turning to Messianism, lit the fuse. (3) This attempt to destroy old regimes everywhere in turn removed another essential condition of the balance: nationalism in France led to the imposition of full government control on its citizens' acts and thoughts. (4) Next, the previous equilibrium among the major powers was destroyed by the French victories—an incentive to exploit unevenness even further. (5) Then, Napoleon's ambitions produced the first modern instance of total power politics, based on an ideological inspiration, and waged by total domestic and international means. (6) A further series of changes in the previous conditions of stability resulted: constant shifts in the map of Europe, a transformation of the domestic order of many of the actors, who moved away from feudal absolutism to defeat France's nationalism with its own weapons, the creation of two opposed ideological camps. Consequently, previous international law was thoroughly disrupted: the law of neutrality collapsed; wars of total mobilization, movement, and extermination of civilians replaced the ballet of limited wars. We have here the example of a system breaking down because of the deliberate attempt by one of its major actors to destroy it, and because of this actor's capacity to succeed for a while by exploiting the dynamism of revolution.

(b) Let us examine now the international system of the nineteenth century, its fate and its impact on international law. The defeat of the force which had destroyed the previous system—France—and the apparent collapse of French-inspired ideals seemed to make a return to stability possible. The victors of 1815 decided to restore a balancing system, for they saw in it the pattern which could best ensure such stability, by giving security to the main powers, providing the greatest amount of flexibility, and obtaining the assent of all, including France, on whom only a far tighter organization of her enemies than they were capable of maintaining could have imposed a punitive peace with any chance of success.

Some of the victors, however, wanted a new kind of balancing system; what is interesting here is the discrepancy between intention and performance. Specifically, although England was willing to return to a mechanical balance, Austria and Russia wanted to extend the scope and means of world politics: whereas the eighteenth-century balance had excluded intervention in domestic affairs, Metternich and Alexander now wanted an organized balancing system which would include in its concept of legitimacy a formula for domestic order, and dispose of means of enforcement against the rise of liberal and nationalist forces. The international law of the political framework would have become an explicit and powerful instrument of the big powers' common policy of preserving the Vienna order, both in its international *and* in its internal aspects. But this was not to happen, for it soon appeared that a voluntary system of cooperation was too weak to control developments within nations which a previous balancing system had already been powerless to prevent. In other words, so extensive a community could not be created by superstructural means alone: the failure of the Holy Alliance proved that an effective new balancing system could be obtained only through a return to moderation in scope and means, not through an ambitious extension.

In the beginning, almost all the conditions for a successful balance were present. (1) The structure of the world was marked by a double hierarchy: first, there was a distinction between a civilized core and a frontier; secondly, within the core, there was a hierarchy between small and large states. No permanent relation of major tension emerged until after 1870. (2) In the core area, technology expanded but never to such a degree as to give to one major actor power of life and death over another. Despite the clash of political ideologies, supranational ties persisted: the dominant ideologies were themselves either supranational or favorable to the maintenance of bonds between national elites; the "Internationale" of diplomats allowed for a consensus on the rules of the game. (3) Although regimes were far from identical, the limited state developed everywhere. The conduct of foreign affairs could be divorced from domestic passions. Constitutionalism, marked by the legalization of public affairs and by the growth of the judicial apparatus, made notable advances. Liberalism led to a separation between state and society.

Consequently, the relations among states were once again characterized by moderation in scope and means. The moderation in scope was twofold. First, the number of tasks performed by the processes of world politics was limited to conflict and political accommodation. The failure of Metternich's hope meant that, within the core area, domestic developments were not a legitimate object of international politics: the "neutrality of alignment"[13] necessary to the effectiveness of the balance required neutrality toward regimes as well, which remained possible as long as internal revolutions made no attempt to disrupt the international system. The separation of state and society removed another vast zone from world politics—the field of private transnational activities, especially economic ones. Secondly, the objectives of the major units also remained moderate in scope: they sought limited increments of power and influence within the core area; they avoided on the whole the destruction of the actors' value systems or national existence in this area. As for moderation in means, it was shown by the return to limited wars, the practice of non-intervention within the core area, the multiplication of international conferences of all kinds.

In this system, international law—the law of the European core area—played all three of the roles described above, within the limits previously defined. The law of the political framework was the law of the Concert: as the instrument of the society of the major powers for the supervision of small states and the control of the individual ambitions of each member, it consecrated the power relations which developed for such purposes. Hence the prevalence of the legal techniques of neutralization and internationalization. They implied an agreement on common abstention from, or common action in, a given area or problem; they resulted from the consensus on moderation and cooperation rather than all-out isolated moves.[14] But since this law was a balancing technique, not a way of overcoming the balance, its development was hemmed in by the usual limitations. Many rules merely expressed the independence of states in such a system: for instance, the principle of unanimity in Concert meetings. Law was violated whenever the maintenance of the system required it—i.e., at both ends of Concert activities: the composition of the meetings violated the principle of equality, and

[13] See Kaplan and Katzenbach, *op.cit.*
[14] For a more detailed analysis, see the author's *Organisations internationales et pouvoirs politiques des Etats*, Paris, Colin, 1954, part I.

the process of enforcement often twisted the independence, integrity, or free consent of small powers. Finally, there were major gaps in the law of the framework, as exemplified by the purely voluntary character of Concert meetings and by the total freedom to resort to war. Moreover, these limitations and violations became far more dangerous for world order during two periods: the 1860's, when the balance was too fluid— i.e., the mechanism of imbalance did not function, owing to the divisions or passivity of a majority of the big powers—and the last years before World War I, when the hardening of the blocs produced arteriosclerosis in the Concert.[15]

The law of reciprocity was a projection of the constitutional state into world affairs, a reflection of mutual interests, and a product of the balancing system, which curtailed states' objectives. The law of delimitation became firmly established. The law of cooperation progressed considerably in two areas: commerce, where the retreat from mercantilism opened a "depoliticized" zone for free trade and for the free establishment of aliens; the settlement of disputes, as states became willing to resort to judicial procedures in a variety of cases: either cases involving private citizens in the "depoliticized" area, or even cases which involved state interests directly, but which the actors found convenient to send to arbitration because the balance had made resort to force less profitable, or because the development of domestic legal institutions had given greater prestige to legal than to diplomatic mechanisms. But in all its branches the law of reciprocity suffered from the same weakness as the law of the political framework. The different standards for the treatment of foreigners applied by the major states to "civilized" nations and to backward areas showed the limit of the norm of equality. The treatment of debtors by creditor nations proved that the law often identified right with might. "Depolitization" came to an end either whenever citizens ran into trouble abroad and appealed to their country of origin, or when a dispute fell within one of the numerous areas excluded by reservations in arbitration treaties. Spectacular failures at the Hague Conferences left many gaps in the laws of war and for the settlement of disputes. Again, these weaknesses became more severe when the Concert did not function well; at the end of the period, a return to protectionism, tariff wars, and the failure of the London Conference on maritime warfare were signs of deterioration.

The branch of the law of reciprocity which reflected best all the elements of the system was the law of war and neutrality. First, since

---

[15] It was in 1871 that Russia denounced the Black Seas provisions of the Paris Treaty, in 1908 that Austria annexed Bosnia-Herzegovina.

war was a legitimate method of settlement of disputes, and law did not try to curtail the ends which sovereignty served but only to regulate the means which it used, war was entitled to a *status*: it received a legal framework, which distinguished sharply between peace and war (hence the need for a declaration at one end, a formal treaty at the other), and between international and civil strife. Within this framework, both the means and the various categories of war victims were regulated. Secondly, since total war practices were banned by the balance, and war had once again become a method of settlement of disputes but not a way of eliminating one's antagonist, war was considered to be merely a *moment*; it was a dispute between states, not between individuals: hence the customs and court decisions on the effect of war on treaties and, more importantly, the crucial distinction between the combatants and non-combatants in war, between the duties of the neutral state and those of neutral citizens. Furthermore, it was a political dispute, not an interruption of economic processes: hence the protection of the neutral trader, who was maintaining the continuity of these processes, and the inviolability of as much of the belligerents' private property as was possible, both at sea and in occupied territory.

The law of community expanded also through countless conferences, conventions, and even institutions; it regulated an increasing number of administrative and technical functions.

Consequently, the law of the nineteenth-century balancing system presented two sides. In matters which affected directly the power and the policies of the major states, law was the transcription of the balancing process in normative terms, the expression of a system in which each state submitted to law insofar as the rules were backed by the pressure of superior force. In other matters, law grew out of the restrictions to which power, in a liberal century, consented for the development of non-political forces of reciprocity and for the devaluation of borders. One result of this double role of law was a fairly effective system of world order. Security was achieved in the core area, especially for the major actors; lesser ones bought survival at the cost of supervision, and, often, partial sacrifices of sovereignty. The Concert tried to preserve flexibility by acting to legalize and harness revolutionary changes. Assent was never complete, but as long as the major powers preferred, or had no choice but to prefer, the maintenance of the system to the gains they might hope to reap by destroying it, this was enough.

Another result was a new rapprochement among the three groups of theorists who coexisted in this period. They agreed on three crucial points: first, the possibility of avoiding chaos; secondly, the basic character of the state as the foundation of world order (and the definition of the state in terms of will); thirdly—and paradoxically—the weaknesses of international law in the world as it was: an admission which, as in the previous stable period, could be made because of the general moderation of world politics. Even deniers such as Hegel believed in a European family or a "higher praetor" which would prevent the warring states from turning inevitable war into inexpiable hate. Even the visionaries no longer dreamed of supranational utopias: they thought that the world was moving toward a community of harmonious nation-states, thanks to free trade and public opinion. The positivists could deal with the previously avoided problem of the basis of legal obligation, and come up with auto-limitation, *Vereinbarung*, or an indivisible community of interests, without feeling that these were circular answers. At the end of the previous period, the positivists, stressing the differences between international and municipal law, and the individual rights of the state, had sounded almost like the cynics. Now, on the contrary, it was the positivists and the visionaries who were close, as Walter Schiffer has shown.[16] Both groups saw a new world almost without power, and failed to realize that the retreat of power from certain spheres had been the result of a highly political balancing process—which was at its most rigid, and in its death throes, just when the theorists believed that the millennium was arriving.

The deterioration of the system had, once again, started with a change in the domestic order: but this time it was a change which occurred in most of the major units, and the deterioration was gradual, not sudden, and not deliberate. (1) The emergence of the modern nation state weakened some of the essential conditions for an ideal balance: for in such a unit, the population is mobilized around national symbols, and the development of the machinery of the state re-enforces internal integration at the expense of transnational ties: after 1870, the army's weight in domestic affairs increased everywhere, and pushed the nation toward imperialism. (2) Consequently, there came about a change in the structure of the world which almost obliterated the difference between disturbances within the system and destruction of the system: the end of the frontier. (3) The horizontal links between the major powers were progressively weakened by the rise of mass nationalism, the success of philosophies of conflict and of national or racial superiority, and the acts of nationalities' movements which sought

---

[16] *The Legal Community of Mankind*, New York, 1954.

allies among the major powers. The legitimacy of states which were not based on the national principle was being challenged: thus international legitimacy concerned itself again with domestic affairs, and with this new dimension heterogeneity returned to the system. (4) As a result, the relations between states took on new and threatening aspects. The very frequency of disturbances, due to the uncertainty of the balance, created a climate of dissatisfaction in which small powers tried to escape from the control of bigger ones. The big states, also looking for an exit, could agree only on temporary adjustments which would not tie their hands for the future, but which in turn infuriated the small powers. In such a climate, the freezing of the balance after Bismarck's departure meant the end of "neutrality of alignment" and the replacement of the hierarchical system of the Concert with a vertical one, in which blocs composed of large *and* small states were facing each other. Hence a switch in means—the decline of the Concert, the return to arms races— and an increase in scope: the sphere of economic affairs became vital again for international politics. It was another change in means: the resort to general war, which dealt the death blow to the system: for the "technical surprise" of World War I, to use Aron's expression, destroyed all remaining restraints on means, and the logic of the war made the objectives of states once again incompatible and increasingly more universal.

(c) Lastly I would like to discuss the relation of international law to world politics in the present revolutionary system.

The essential elements of the present system are as follows: (1) The structure of the world is characterized by one consolidation and two deep transformations. On the one hand, the diplomatic field, which had been gradually extended and unified by the previous system, embraces the whole world for the first time. On the other hand, two conflicting movements have destroyed the double hierarchy of the nineteenth century: bipolarity has replaced the multiplicity of major actors (and put an end to the mechanism of imbalance); the splintering of the former frontier into a large number of new units has obliterated the distinction between the core area and the rest.

(2) A gigantic technological revolution has led to a race toward industrial power, and not been accompanied by the restoration of any universal transnational links. The diversity of regimes, "isolationist" reactions in many nations (especially the new ones) against the intrusion of foreign affairs into all spheres of life, the tendency of the major forms of regimes to project and promote themselves throughout the world have resulted both in the absence of any clear and extensive con-

ception of international legitimacy, and in huge ideological rivalries. New transnational links have emerged as a consequence of the latter, but they are divisive, competitive, and often negative solidarities.

(3) The spiritual and temporal control of the state on the citizens has increased everywhere. Just as the old territorial essence of sovereignty was becoming obsolete, the spreading ethics of nationalism and the universal practice of public welfare have given to sovereignty an incandescent "personal" core.

(4) The outcome is a series of revolutionary changes in the scope and means of world politics. Concerning the former, there is no longer any "depoliticized" zone of major importance. The collapse of empires has made the question of economic development, once dealt with by private investment or behind the walls of the empires, one of the biggest issues of world politics. Nor is there any more a separation of domestic and international affairs: the logic of intervention, either to enforce some degree of conformity within one's own camp or to subvert the adversary's, has spread throughout the whole world and made the diffusion of political "ways of life" one of the tasks performed by world politics.[17] Consequently, the objectives of states have expanded in such a way that the full realization of the goals of one unit or bloc would often involve the physical or moral death of another actor or camp, and such goals include blueprints for domestic as well as for international order. As for means, they have never been as varied: "total diplomacy" ranges from highly institutionalized military alliances to economic warfare, from propaganda to a host of international organizations; quasi-Doomsday machines and traditional limited wars coexist with revolutionary guerrilla wars. There is one moderating force which makes this revolutionary system an original one: the possibility for one power alone to inflict unacceptable damage on its enemies, however numerous, makes a return to the principle of imbalance unlikely in case of a new multipolar system, but it also makes the actors hesitate far more to resort to violence than the dynamism of a revolutionary system would otherwise allow. Hence the appearance of a highly delicate and uncertain restraint.

Thus, by comparison with the pre-1914 system, the present one is marked both by extraordinary and continuing changes, and by great complexity.[18] Such changes and such complexity have had an enormous

---

[17] Many of the difficulties of the UN operation in the Congo stem from the attempt to distinguish between the domestic and the international aspects of the crisis—an exercise in fiction.

[18] We speak of a "loose bipolar system" in which "bloc actors" tend to become more important than unit actors—but at the same time the rate of obsolescence of strategies and the diffusion of nuclear power challenge such a view. Inversely, we refer to the

impact on international law; the European-made legal order of the past could not be stretched to the dimensions of the new system without major cracks.

Let us look first at the impact of the changes. It has been threefold. In the first place, huge chunks of the traditional body of rules have been destroyed. This destruction has four aspects.

(1) Basic distinctions which translated into the legal order the restraints of the balancing system have lost any meaning or justification in the present one. The distinction between matters of domestic jurisdiction and matters regulated by international law has practically vanished, in a period when the choice of a regime largely determines the international conduct of a state. The distinction between the civilized nations and the others is challenged by the new states' objections to many traditional rules (e.g., in regard to territorial waters or even about diplomatic representation). The distinction between private acts, for which the state is not responsible, and public acts has been destroyed by intervention or subversion by "private" groups manipulated by their governments, or by the growing importance of transactions which a large foreign or international "private" company concludes with a state. The distinction between war and peace has been replaced by what Philip Jessup has called situations of intermediacy: a period of irreconcilable oppositions, ideological clashes, *and* fear of total war could not but engender wars without declaration, armistices without peace, non-belligerency without war, and help for insurgents without recognition of belligerency.

(2) Consequently, many of the traditional rules have been destroyed by massive violations. Numerous provisions on war and neutrality could not outlive the technological and political conditions of the nineteenth century; nor could the law which forbade states to help foreign insurgents or subversives. Similarly, many of the rules which governed territorial jurisdiction have vanished: instead of a fairly clear distinction among a number of separate zones and the sharp definition of the conditions in which state power could be exercised in each of them, there are now blurred, overlapping, and multiplying zones. The size of those on which states claim rights has augmented; the claims them-

---

fragmentation of the old frontier into multiple new sovereignties—but at the same time the necessities of the struggle against colonialism and for development might lead to the gradual emergence of "bloc actors" there. We discuss the atomic age but, as Herz has observed, many interstate relations are still in a pre-atomic phase. We have both a revolutionary system, and a tacit agreement on one rule of the game—the avoidance of total war.

selves have steadily expanded, even over the open seas, and often through unilateral moves. Traditional rules on the treatment of foreign property have been very generally disregarded. Those changes have been the reflection of all the transformations in the international system: the increase in the number of nations has often led the least viable or secure ones to demand the fullest amount of control over the biggest amount of space; the technological revolution has provoked a rush into air space; the decline of the old transnational consensus has affected the freedom of the seas; the modern welfare state, and the totalitarian regimes, have tried to grab resources wherever possible and to remove previously accepted restrictions on territorial sovereignty; the cold war has led to U-2 flights, to weapon tests in the ocean, and has added military overtones to the struggle about the breadth of the territorial seas; the anticolonial revolution has been one of the prime movers in this struggle and in the spread of expropriation; the Arab-Israeli conflict has had repercussions on canals and straits.

(3) Many of the gaps in the body of rules have become opportunities for chaos. The silence of international law on the upper limits of air space may lead to dangerous and conflicting claims. International law has little to say about most of the modern methods of propaganda, subversion, and intervention short of the actual use of force. Nor did it foresee that traditional privileges of domestic jurisdiction, such as the right of a state to grant its nationality, to regulate the conduct of aliens, to treat its own citizens as it sees fit, and to recognize new states or governments, would be used as weapons in the struggle between the states. Here we find what is probably the best example of the different meaning for world order of gaps in stable and revolutionary systems. In the nineteenth century, recognition was deemed a privilege, not a duty, but no arbitrary consequences followed because, on the whole, very simple tests were applied: a double check of whether the state existed or whether the government was in control, and whether it accepted the existing framework of international law and politics. Since the latter was flexible enough, and contained no requirements about regimes or alignments, there were few instances of trouble. Today, the same privilege has become a nightmare, because of the collapse of the old consensus on international legitimacy—so that states use criteria of recognition which are tests of conformity to their own concept of legitimacy—and also because of the appearance of a new dimension of legitimacy: the nature of the regime or the way in which it came to power. This is as true in the case of the anticolonial conflict as it is in

the cold war. Finally, international law has nothing to say about most of the new weapons which have appeared since 1914.

(4) Some of the traditional rules which are still standing have become much more uncertain in their operation because of changes in the international system. Principles dealing with state immunities were established at a time when the state did not engage its "majesty" in trading or manufacturing activities; court reactions to those developments have been conflicting and subject to shifts. The validity of intervention at the request of a foreign government becomes dubious when there is a domestic contest about the legitimacy or legality of this government. Treaties reflect the forces of disintegration which have appeared in the world: the increase in the number of states has led either to the "individualization of rules" through reservations, or to the use of expressions as vague as, say, "genuine link" in the recent Geneva provision dealing with flags of convenience, or to conflicts between obligations accepted by the same nation in agreements which regulate similar matters but bind different groups of states. Domestic reactions against the increasing scope of treaties have brought about difficulties in ratification and moves such as the Bricker offensive. Clashes between new transnational solidarities explain the problem of the colonial clause. The intensity of interstate conflicts has made resort to the *rebus sic stantibus* argument more frequent than ever.

Thus, much of present international law, precisely because it reflects a dead system, is obsolete. But changes in the international system have had a second kind of effect on international law: some of the rules which are supposed to be valid today are premature. These are rules which express attempts at imposing a new scheme of world order which purported to draw the lesson from the ultimate failure of the balance-of-power system, but proved to be thoroughly unfit for the present revolutionary world. There were essentially two types of efforts.

(1) On the one hand, there was an attempt to give to the law of the political framework a far bigger scope than in the past, by curbing states' sovereignty in matters as vital as the settlement of political disputes and the resort to war. The conduct of states would have been subordinated to rules administered by international organization. The success of this effort *presupposed* a stable world which would not be racked by profound ideological splits, in which a basic homogeneity of regimes and beliefs existed, and in which the transnational forces of public opinion and "world parliamentarism" would keep disputes at a reasonably low pitch. The fundamental flaw of the formula was in the ambiguous nature of international organization: it is an "as if"

international community, which leaves the basic character of the world system unchanged, and in which decisions are still made by the states. Consequently, its success depends entirely on the universe outside—i.e., on whether there is a system of basically satisfied, democratic units tied together by a common concept of legitimacy; if not, the organization itself has no power to bring such a world about. If such a happy world does not exist at the start, its indispensable establishment thus depends on the ability of the major powers to bring it to life—an ability which is totally missing. As a result, a new and dangerous gap has come to plague world order: the gap between the Charter provisions and practices on disputes (i.e., the power of the UN organs is limited to frequently ineffective recommendations), and the Charter's sweeping ban on the use of force: a gap which encourages states to devise highly refined techniques of offensive short of force, and drives those which are the victims of such tactics to disregard the ban.[19] The attempt to revert to a "just war" concept has proved to be impossible or absurd in a world of conflicting legitimacies.

(2) The other type of effort was a direct projection, into the international sphere, of the legal relationships which exist between groups or individuals in a constitutional state. The resort to international jurisdiction for the settlement of many disputes, an international protection of human rights, the establishment of a criminal code thanks to which the punishment of warmakers would be the judicial side of a coin whose political side was the outlawry of war—all these measures reflected the utopia of a legal community of mankind, and they have suffered a fate even worse than the fictitious political community. International adjudication can be effective only when international relations are not fundamentally at variance with the conditions which exist within a liberal state: when there is a large zone of private activities uncontrolled by governments, when the objectives of states are not so incompatible as to rule out a joint resort to the judge. The prevalence of the desire to change the law over mere disagreements on interpretation, the opposition in the values of the major ideological camps, have provoked a decline of the role of the World Court and a full-scale revolt against adjudication. Human rights are unlikely to receive adequate international protection at a time when the core of sovereignty is the link between the state and its subjects.

[19] See, for instance, the arguments of D. W. Bowett in *Self-defense in International Law*, New York, 1958, pp. 145ff., and Julius Stone in *Aggression and World Order*, Berkeley, Calif., 1958, ch. 5. Contra, Joseph Kunz, "Sanctions in International Law," *American Journal of International Law*, LIV (April 1960), pp. 324-47.

Out of the dialectic of the obsolete and the premature, contemporary international law has managed to show a third kind of effect of the changes in the international system; there are some pieces of evidence of a "third way" which is neither a return to the old system, nor a realization of the Wilsonian utopia, but the elaboration of rules which correspond to the few elements of stability in the present system. Although Charter provisions are used by all states as instruments for the enhancement of their own interests, procedures and institutions which correspond to the general desire to avoid total war have been developed by the UN. Although the competition of East and West for the allegiance of the "Third World" tends to become constantly more intense, it remains on the whole peaceful; consequently, an international law, and numerous international organs, of technical assistance and economic development have appeared: they correspond to the convergent interests of all three camps in channeling some of those measures through the procedures of an "universal actor." On the ruins of the nineteenth-century law of reciprocity, a few new conventions of delimitation and cooperation have been signed, dealing with the "humanitarian" side of war, or with the continental shelf, or with the joint exploitation of sea resources, or with the Antarctic.

This is not much. Some of those developments (e.g., the continental shelf) reflect a very traditional agreement on increasing, not curtailing, states' powers. The UN apparatus against the extension of conflicts remains an improvised one: contemporary internationalization of trouble spots, designed to avoid direct intervention by one of the superpowers, remains an *ad hoc* practice, despite efforts at turning it into a general rule, and East-West mutual interests in preventing nuclear war have expressed themselves in parallel unilateral measures but not in firm agreements. Only in the area of community—scientific research, health, communications—have the obstacles been few. Nevertheless, such developments suffice to make contemporary international law look like Janus: it has one face which announces chaos, and one which promises order.[20]

Not only does contemporary law thus bear the marks of all the changes in the international system: it reflects also the heterogeneity of the present system—indeed, of every element of this system; hence a permanent contradiction between such heterogeneity and the formal

[20] Similarly, during the period which preceded the peace of Westphalia, every legal development was ambiguous, for it destroyed the previous unity of the Civitas Christiana and the secular authority of the Church, but at the same time brought into shape the modern territorial state through a succession of wars.

homogeneity of a legal system whose members are supposedly equal.

(1) Contemporary law reflects the heterogeneity of the structure of the world. Although the nation-state is the basic unit and the common aspiration of men more than ever before, there is a major disparity between states which meet the traditional criteria of statehood—a population, a territory, a government—and those which are essentially governments still in search of their nation—governments which operate within explosively artificial borders.[21]

(2) Present-day law reflects the asymmetry of domestic regimes: the difficulties met by various attempts at codification, or at regulating international trade, air communications, and raw materials, or at establishing common standards of inspection for arms control have shown how much the attitudes of a welfare state and a free enterprise state and, even more, those of an industrialized and of an underdeveloped country differ in international economic matters, or how radically a democracy's and a totalitarian state's conceptions of secrecy diverge.

(3) Contemporary law reflects the heterogeneity of the system with respect to those forces which cut across the units. Technological unevenness has left its mark: it is from the underprivileged states mainly that pressure has come for a legal regulation of space problems; the opposition of nuclear "haves" and "have-nots" has limited the effectiveness of international cooperation for the peaceful uses of nuclear energy. As for ideological asymmetry, even though Soviet international law appears to differ little in its *rules* from Western law, there are most significant variations in the interpretation of, and the general attitude toward, law which correspond to the differences in the nature of the regimes;[22] in particular, there is a considerable difference in the attitude of each camp toward the use of force within its sphere. Efforts at negotiating various agreements on human rights have shown the incompatibility of the main competing conceptions of world order on crucial issues.

(4) Present-day law reflects numerous contradictions in the relations between the units. In the first place, it shows traces of a basic clash which affects the policy of every state: a clash between the determination to increase its power, security, welfare, and prestige as much as possible by its own means, and the dependence on others for those very purposes. Thus, if we look at the principal source of law—treaties—we see that at the same time as such agreements suffer from the weaknesses

---

[21] See Rupert Emerson, *From Empire to Nation*, Cambridge, Mass., 1960, ch. 6.

[22] For a recent discussion of those points, see the *Proceedings of the American Society of International Law*, 1959, pp. 21-45.

I have mentioned above, their subject-matter has extended to objects never before regulated by world law (i.e., labor, human rights, etc.), and numerous new subjects of law (i.e., international organizations) have been created by agreements. If we look at the military function of the states—the state as fortress—we see that they try to ensure their security both by expanding their sovereignty as far as they can (especially in the air) or by developing their own weapon systems or armies, and also by participating in military alliances, which involve a radical transformation of traditional territorial sovereignty. If we look at the economic function of the states—the state as provider of welfare—we see that they try to develop their own resources and to acquire additional ones wherever they can get them (for instance, under the sea), but also that they have to join with others in order to promote the welfare of their own citizens or to receive indispensable aid.

In the second place, international law reflects the complexity of states' legal situations in the face of the main issues of contemporary world politics. On the one hand, some of the provisions of the Geneva Conventions on the law of the sea, most of the practices of expropriation, and UN stands on the question of self-determination reflect the alignment over one such issue—a coalition of all those states interested in overthrowing the norms of the nineteenth-century system, against the *status quo* states of the West which are the heirs of this system. On the other hand, in the cold war, it is as if the world were composed of layers of states belonging to different ages of politics. On top, the two superpowers enjoy a large amount of independence (except from one another) and extensive advantages within their respective alliances (bases, status-of-forces agreements). Under this layer, there are those allies of the superpowers who are developing their own deterrent; they continue to depend on a superpower for their ultimate protection, but they are capable of bargaining hard before conceding privileges to it. Next we find other allies who tend to be in the position of more or less gilt-edged satellites (depending on the ideological camp to which they belong): hence outbreaks of neutralism and of fear of war. Fourth and last, we find all those states which have joined no military camp and live in a kind of fictitious nineteenth-century world of territorial sovereignty.

In the third place, law reflects the bizarre coexistence of revolutionary relations, exemplified by the dialectic of the obsolete and the premature, with elements of stability introduced by the "mutual dependence" characteristic of the balance of terror, just at the time when the role of the military in decision-making was becoming greater than ever, and weapons began to live a life of their own, almost distinct from events in the political universe.

The outcome of these and other contradictory impulses and situations is, once again, heterogeneity: the development of overlapping regional institutions and rules. They are evidence of partial integration; but they also show the fragmentation of the legal order which has accompanied the extension of the diplomatic field to the whole planet.

The reactions of theorists to those developments reflect both the heterogeneity of the legal order, and the impact of the changes of the international system on this order. On the one hand, there is little in common between totalitarian theories of law and non-totalitarian theories: we have here both conflict and asymmetry. The former are not scholarly discussions of the international system from the viewpoint of world order: they are instruments at the service of a state strategy. They are not normative examinations of the ideal order and of the gaps between the actual and the ideal: they are policy sciences showing how the actual should be used or abused in order to reach the ideal determined by official doctrine. On the other hand, within the non-totalitarian theories, changes in the international system have shattered the fragile rapprochement which had taken place previously between the main tendencies. Both of the nineteenth-century extremes have disappeared. It has become impossible to believe in a dialectic of clashing units with a happy ending, and in the vision of a world which moves inevitably toward law, order, and harmony. Even the middle group—positivism—has suffered severely from the marks that the free wills of states have left on world order. Gone is the common faith in the avoidance of chaos. Dead is the agreement on the indispensable character of the state as the basis of the system: theories today range from those that maintain this claim to those that make anguished pleas for world government. Vanished, also, is the agreement on the differences between international and domestic law: theories today range from those that still stress such differences to those that offer subtle, if unconvincing, demonstrations of the similarities.

It is characteristic of revolutionary systems that doctrines not only multiply but often pose as what they are not. Thus, today's deniers or cynics are either sorrowful (rather than gloating), or else disguised as "policy-oriented" theorists who dissolve rules and principles into a maze of processes, messages, and alternatives. Today's utopians are either straightforward adepts of world government, or outright natural-law revivalists, or natural-law thinkers in pseudo-sociological disguise, or "pure theorists of law" who derive normative order from empirical chaos by what I would call the parthenogenesis of law. In the middle, there are persistent, but troubled, positivists and sociologists of law who—as this author well knows—seem more adept at examining the weaknesses of law than at finding formulas which would conceal them, as positivism used to do, more adept at maintaining that it is absurd to separate the legal order from its political roots than at attempting to close the gap between the aspiration for order and the practices of chaos.

III

Let us now apply our findings about the role of international law in various systems to two of the more important theoretical issues of the discipline of international law: the foundation of obligation, and the meaning of sovereignty.

(a) The basis of obligation is the same in every legal order: the consciousness, which prevails among the subjects of the legal order, of this order's need to realize a common end. Law is not obtained by deduction from a pre-existing natural law or objective law à la Duguit; it is a creation toward an end. Thus, the purpose and the legal order cannot be separated, Kelsen's theory notwithstanding. The solidity or authority of a legal order depends on the nature and substance of the common end—which, finally, depends on the group: if the group shows a high degree of community of purpose, and is organized by central power, the binding force of the legal order will be great—not otherwise.

The feeble consciousness of a common end among multiple units which allow no central power to impose its own vision or to promote theirs, weakens the binding force of international law permanently by comparison with domestic law. But there are variations in the degree to which such a common end exists in international politics, and consequently variations in the binding force of international law. First, we find variations in *level*: as we have seen, there are, in stable periods, three superimposed groups, with different common ends and, consequently, with an international law of varying binding force. The law of community is strongest because it rests on a common positive purpose. The law of reciprocity is relatively strong because it is the law of a limited partnership, whose members' common end is a set of mutual interests. The law of the political framework is weakest, for it is the law of a collection of actors engaged in a struggle, and whose common end is both limited to a narrow sphere—the rules of the game—and subordinated to the fluctuations of the balance of power.

Secondly, the binding force of international law is exposed to variations in *time*: it is not the same in stable and in revolutionary systems. The legal order of the nineteenth-century system was both modest and solid. It was modest, both because of the moderation in the scope and means of international relations and because the freedom of action of the units was curtailed by the operation of the balance rather than by law. It was efficient, because it was able, within these limits, both to serve as a restraint on the states and to consolidate their interdependence. Legal theories reflected both this modesty and confidence in the efficiency of the legal order. Contemporary law, on the contrary, has to serve a system in which the extension of international relations would seem to require a far wider range of common purposes, but in which heterogeneity has reduced this range drastically. Consequently, there is a divorce between the difficulties of practice and the delirium of theory; and practice is both highly ambitious and relatively inefficient. The increase in the scope of law's subject-matter demonstrates such ambition. But on vital issues, "society" is limited to a few identical or convergent interests, which are sometimes even too narrow or too flimsy to provide a firm basis for the development of any law. There is today no strong enough consciousness or representation of a common legal order of mankind.[23]

Finally, such binding force knows variations in *space*. Given the narrow range of common ends and the absence of world-wide central power, regional solidarities, institutions, and legal orders have appeared. They differ, first of all, in their political foundation—i.e., the structure of the group: the Soviet bloc is a "Roman" system in which the common ends are largely imposed by central power, whereas the Atlantic "community" is really a modern version of the limited partnership: the range of common ends is far from all-embracing and cooperation is far from unconditional, but today, owing to technological changes and the revolutionary character of world politics, such ends require a far greater degree of integration than in the past; the organizations of the European "Six" shape a somewhat less narrow or conditional society. These regional orders differ also in their degree of institutionalization,

[23] The statesmen have images of world order which are mutually exclusive, and in which the highest power remains the state; the individual citizens have no way of breaking the statesmen's monopoly: the citizens' efforts at promoting their transnational common ends through law rarely succeed in transcending the borders of the state, which continues to fulfill most of their needs and to be seen as the best protection against outside tempests. Indeed, the development of contemporary law has occurred especially in those areas where individuals raised demands which the state could not satisfy alone: hence the law of international functions and economic integration, whose binding force seems quite strong.

and in the subject-matter which they cover. The binding force of law in these systems depends on all those factors.

(b)   Another problem which should be treated in the light of a theory of the relations between international systems and international law is the problem of sovereignty. Few concepts are as obscure.[24]

Let us start with the classical definition given by the World Court in the Wimbledon case. Sovereignty means that the state "is subject to no other state and has full and exclusive powers within its jurisdiction without prejudice to the limits set by applicable law." Thus, sovereignty is the situation of the state which has no political superior over it, but is nevertheless bound by international law. Three consequences follow. First, the exercise of its sovereignty by a state—for instance, to sign agreements which may restrict its legal freedom of action—does not *exhaust*, and is indeed a demonstration of, its sovereignty. Secondly, the relations between sovereignty and international law are characterized by the principle of domestic jurisdiction: matters not regulated by the former fall within the latter. Thirdly, relations between states are marked by the principle of equality (whatever their size, all states are in the same situation: their only superior is international law), by the duty of non-intervention, and by the right of self-preservation.

The trouble with this set of definitions is that their neatness is an illusion. If we look at the relations between states, we see a broad gamut of situations in between the status of the mythical state-in-isolation which exercises all the privileges of sovereignty without any other limit than that of general international law, and the situation of a member state in a federation. There is in fact a hierarchy of legal statuses according to the amount of sovereignty whose exercise has been given away to, or restricted in favor of, other states or international agencies. The nature and range of this hierarchy vary with each international system. Thus, sovereignty, rather than a reservoir which can be only full or empty, is a divisible nexus of powers of which some may be kept, some limited, some lost. The point at which sovereignty can be assumed to have vanished is a matter of definition. Given such a hierarchy of situations, the equality of states is mythical. If we look next at the relations between states and international law, we find that the definitions are illusory because one of the two terms—international law—is a fuzzy one: the "limit" or "restraint" which such law imposes on states is both ambiguous and shifting. It is ambiguous because of the conditions of elaboration and enforcement of international law, which

[24] For a sharp analysis, see W. J. Rees, "The Theory of Sovereignty Restated," in Peter Laslett, ed., *Philosophy, Politics and Society*, New York, 1956.

are the product of the states. It is shifting because the norms of international law vary from system to system.[25]

Thus, the actual substance of sovereignty depends (1) on the international system and (2), in each system, on the position of a state on the
ladder I have mentioned. In a stable system, such as the nineteenth
century's, sovereignty is a fairly clear nexus of powers with sharp edges:
the world appears as a juxtaposition of well-defined units, whose respective rights are neatly delimited, which allow few exceptions to the
principle of full territorial jurisdiction, and which have few institutional
links among them: cooperation is organized by diplomacy and by the
market. In such a system, the limits of sovereignty are essentially set by
general international law (customs and general treaties); the ladder is
short: the basic distinctions are the double hierarchy I have described
previously. In today's revolutionary system, sovereignty is infinitely
more complex. First, diversity of legal statuses is extreme, owing to the
multiple patterns of military, economic, and political cooperation which
introduce various forms of inequality: hence the predominance of
treaties over customs, and the prevalence of less-than-universal treaties.
Secondly, the sum of powers of which sovereignty is composed as well
as the limitations imposed by law are not only in constant flux: they are
also increasing simultaneously, because of the intensity of international
relations. The same paradox had marked the revolutionary system
before Westphalia. Thus, the edges of sovereignty have become blurred.
Although the basic legal unit remains the state, powers of action in the
world are both widely scattered among states, blocs, and international
organizations, and concentrated among the major industrial centers[26] or
(in matters of life and death for the planet) the full nuclear powers.

After the dust has settled, a new stable system will probably be one in
which a lasting redistribution of many state powers among international
and regional actors will have been accomplished: for despite the very
general aspiration (especially among the new nations) for a return to a

[25] The best combination of change over time and ambiguity is provided by the concept
of domestic jurisdiction. On the one hand, the area regulated by international law has
been drastically expanded in the present system. On the other hand, this increasing
"legalization" of interstate relations could become an effective restraint on states only if
there existed institutions capable of preventing states from extending the plea of domestic jurisdiction to issues where it does not apply—as well as institutions capable of
preventing states from rejecting the plea in those cases where it is still justified. Instead,
we find that states successfully invoke the argument even in areas clearly regulated by
law (cf. the Interhandel dispute), and refuse to listen to it whenever a problem is of
international concern, although it may not be regulated by law (cf. the attitude of the
General Assembly of the UN).
[26] On the impact of such concentration, see François Perroux, La coexistence pacifique,
3 vols., Paris, Presses Universitaires de France, 1958.

world of sovereign states practicing non-intervention, the traditional substance of sovereignty is barely compatible with the political and technological conditions of the present world. However, we are bound to remain in the dust for quite a while: for a decline of military blocs in the missile age would not make the competition of East and West any less fierce, the emergence of new nations does not make their resentment of their former masters, their demands on the well-endowed states, and their own political uncertainties any less dangerous, the spread of nuclear power does not make the international system any less explosive. We are in the midst of a succession of revolutionary systems—not on the verge of a stable one—and the solidity of international law will continue to remain in doubt.

THE CONTRIBUTORS

KLAUS KNORR, Professor of Economics and Director of the Center of International Studies at Princeton University, is chairman of the editorial board of *World Politics*. He contributed to and edited *NATO and American Security* (1959) and, with William J. Baumol, *What Price Economic Growth?* (1961).

SIDNEY VERBA, Assistant Professor of Politics and Research Associate of the Center of International Studies at Princeton, is the author of *Small Groups and Political Behavior: A Study of Leadership* (1961). He is engaged in a comparative study of attitudes toward government and citizenship in Italy, Germany, Mexico, England, and the United States.

MORTON A. KAPLAN is Associate Professor of Political Science and Chairman of the Committee on International Relations at the University of Chicago, as well as Research Associate of the Center of International Studies at Princeton. His latest book is *The Political Foundations of International Law* (1961), of which he and Nicholas de B. Katzenbach are co-authors.

ARTHUR LEE BURNS, Fellow of the Department of International Relations in the Australian National University, Canberra, wrote two monographs issued by the Center of International Studies: *Power Politics and the Growing Nuclear Club* (1959) and *The Rationale of Catalytic War* (1959).

THOMAS C. SCHELLING is Professor of Economics at Harvard University and a faculty member of Harvard's Center for International Affairs. He recently spent a year with The RAND Corporation and serves on the Scientific Advisory Board of the U.S. Air Force. The author of *The Strategy of Conflict* (1960) and *Strategy and Arms Control* (1961), he is currently working in the fields of military strategy, arms control, and theory of bargaining.

RICHARD E. QUANDT, Associate Professor of Economics at Princeton University, is co-author, with James M. Henderson, of *Microeconomic Theory: A Mathematical Approach* (1958) and, with Willard L. Thorp, of *The New Inflation* (1959). He contributed a paper to *What Price Economic Growth?*, edited by William J. Baumol and Klaus Knorr (1961).

J. DAVID SINGER, Associate Research Political Scientist of the Mental Health Research Institute at the University of Michigan, is on the editorial board of the *Journal of Conflict Resolution*. The author of *Financing International Organization: The United Nations Budget Process* (1961), he recently completed a study on *Deterrence, Arms Control and Disarmament: Toward a Synthesis in National Security Policy*.

GEORGE MODELSKI is Senior Fellow in the Department of International Relations at the Australian National University, Canberra. His publications include *The Communist International System* (1960), a monograph issued by the Center of International Studies at Princeton University, where he served as Visiting Research Associate in 1960-1961.

FRED W. RIGGS, Professor of Government at Indiana University and the author of *Ecology of Public Administration* (1961), is at work on a study entitled *Comparative Bureaucracy*. He recently spent two years in Thailand and the Philippines, teaching and engaging in research.

CHARLES A. MCCLELLAND, Professor of History and International Relations at San Francisco State College, is Visiting Fellow of the Institute for Communication Research and Research Associate of the Department of Political Science at Stanford University during 1961-1962. Among his publications are *Nuclear Weapons, Missiles, and Future War* (1960) and *The United Nations: The Continuing Debate* (1960).

STANLEY HOFFMANN, Associate Professor of Government at Harvard University and the editor of *Contemporary Theory in International Relations* (1960), is working on a book entitled *The Politics of Defeat: The Road to Vichy and the Vichy Regime* and on a long essay, *Paradoxes of the French Political Community*, to be included in a volume on postwar France.

DATE DUE

OCT 2 4 '6?			
DEC 1 1 1963	DEPT.		
DEC 3 1964	DEPT.		
DEC 2 9 1967	RESERVED		
Dec 24 RP			
APR 1 1 1974			
DEC 1 8 1974			
MAY 7 1975			
GAYLORD			PRINTED IN U.S.A.